The Haynes Automotive
Anti-lock Brake System Manual

by Alan Ahlstrand
and John H Haynes Member of the Guild of Motoring Writers

The Haynes Automotive Repair Manual for understanding and troubleshooting anti-lock brake systems

ABCDE
FGHIJ
KLMNO
PQRS

AUTOMOTIVE
PARTS &
ACCESSORIES
ASSOCIATION MEMBER

Haynes Publishing Group
Sparkford Nr Yeovil
Somerset BA22 7JJ England

Haynes Publications, Inc.
861 Lawrence Drive
Newbury Park
California 91320 USA

Acknowledgments

We are grateful for the help and cooperation of Chrysler Corporation, Robert Bosch GmbH, and Toyota Motor Company for their assistance with technical information and certain illustrations. Special thanks to Ken Layne for invaluable research assistance.

© Haynes North America, Inc. 2000

With permission from J.H. Haynes & Co. Ltd.

A book in the Haynes Automotive Repair Manual Series

Printed in the U.S.A.

ISBN 1 56392 349 1

Library of Congress Catalog Card Number 00-105491

While every attempt is made to ensure that the information in this manual is correct, no liability can be accepted by the authors or publishers for loss, damage or injury caused by any errors in, or omissions from, the information given.

00-192

Contents

Notes

Chapter 1
Introduction

How to use this manual

This manual is divided into Chapters. Each Chapter is subdivided into sections, some of which consist of consecutively numbered paragraphs (usually referred to as "Steps'" since they're normally part of a procedure). If the material is basically informative in nature, rather than a step-by-step procedure, the paragraphs aren't numbered.

The term **(see illustration)** is used in the text to indicate that a photo or drawing has been included to make the information easier to understand. Also, every attempt is made to position illustrations on the same page as the corresponding text to minimize confusion. The illustrations are referenced by a number preceding the caption. Illustration numbers denote chapter and numerical sequence within the chapter (e.g. 3.4 means Chapter 3, illustration number 4 in order).

The terms "**Note**," "**Caution**" and "**Warning**" are used throughout the book with a specific purpose in mind - to attract the reader's attention. A **Note** simply provides information required to properly complete a procedure or information that will make the procedure easier to understand. A "**Caution**" outlines a special procedure or special steps that must be taken when completing the procedure where the **Caution** is found. Failure to pay attention to a **Caution** can result in damage to the component being repaired or the tools being used. A **Warning** is included where personal injury can result if the instructions aren't followed exactly as described.

Even though extreme care has been taken during the preparation of this manual, neither the publisher nor the author can accept responsibility for any errors in, or omissions from, the information given.

Anti-lock brakes

Anti-lock brake systems are built by a number of different manufacturers, who supply systems to the various auto manufacturers. In a few cases, the auto manufacturers themselves have developed anti-lock brake systems.

Anti-lock brakes, as the name implies, are designed to prevent the wheels from locking up during a stop. This has three safety advantages; it shortens stopping distances, helps stop in a straight line, and allows the vehicle to be steered while it's being stopped. It also prevents the tires from being flat-spotted when rubber is removed from only one spot in the tire.

Stopping distances

In most situations, ABS shortens stopping distances because the tire on a partially locked wheel has greater friction with the road surface than the tire on a completely locked wheel (in engineering terms, it has "negative wheel slip"). The maximum friction occurs at a moderate level of lockup, generally less than 20 percent. Lockup ranges from freely rolling (zero percent) to fully locked (100 percent).

In a hard stop on smooth, dry pavement, a driver with good skill and presence of mind can maintain the wheels at the most efficient degree of lockup by modulating the brake pedal pressure. An average driver, though, is likely to press the brake pedal as hard as possible, locking the wheels completely. And even a skilled driver can't control individual wheels separately, as many ABS systems can. So while a skilled driver can match or beat the performance of ABS on smooth, dry pavement, under less-than-ideal conditions ABS will produce shorter stopping distances than non-ABS brakes because it keeps the tires near their point of maximum friction. **Note:** *Because ABS allows some wheel lock-up to occur, some tire noise and patchy rubber marks may occur during an ABS stop.*

In two situations, loose gravel or fluffy snow, a fully locked wheel will produce a shorter stopping distance than a partially locked one. These materials form a wedge in front of a locked wheel, slowing the vehicle. This is why some vehicles are equipped with an override switch that allows the driver to shut off the ABS.

Straight-line stops

If the vehicle is on a road with uneven traction (patchy snow or ice, for example), the vehicle will tend to yaw or spin when the brakes are applied. This is because the wheels on the slippery surface will tend to lock sooner than the wheels on the high-traction surface. Because the locked wheels have less traction than the unlocked wheels, the vehicle will tend to spin toward the locked wheels. Multi-channel ABS systems control the wheels separately, so they lock more evenly.

Steering control

The tires on fully locked front wheels will continue in a straight line if the driver tries to steer the vehicle. ABS, by preventing full lockup, allows the driver to steer the vehicle during a hard stop. This means that even if there's no chance to stop in time to avoid a collision, it may still be possible to steer around an obstacle rather than hitting it.

ABS precautions

The most important precaution to take with ABS is to realize that it won't make a vehicle accident-proof. Overconfidence or inattention can still get you into a situation that no amount of braking power or steering control can get you out of. ABS does provide shorter, straighter stops on slippery surfaces, but it will still take longer to stop than it would on a smooth, dry road.

Don't pump the brake pedal with your foot when using ABS brakes. The control module will assume that you've let off the brakes and will not activate the system.

It's important to keep the main braking system in good working order by performing regular inspections and maintenance. Worn linings, low brake fluid and air in the hydraulic system are just as dangerous with an ABS brake system as with a conventional system.

Diagnosis and repair should be done immediately if the ABS warning light (usually amber colored) comes on when it isn't supposed to (it's supposed to come on briefly when the engine is started, and also during an ABS stop). ABS systems are designed to shut down if a failure occurs, allowing the brakes to work like a conventional brake system. For this reason, you might not notice any loss of braking performance during normal driving, where you don't stop hard enough to activate the ABS. However, the ABS won't work if you need it, so the problem should be fixed right away. If the red brake warning light comes on (except for a few early systems), there is a problem in the main brake hydraulic system.

ABS terminology

Several different terms apply to the hydraulic systems used with anti-lock brakes. There are open and closed systems, integrated and non-integrated systems, circuits, and channels. Each term has a specific meaning that applies to all manufacturers' systems.

Open vs. closed systems

Refer to illustrations 1.1, 1.2 and 1.3

An open anti-lock brake system is one in which the brake fluid released from the brakes during an ABS stop isn't returned to the brake during the ABS stop; instead, the fluid is stored in an accumulator during the ABS stop, then returned to the master cylinder reservoir afterwards **(see illustration)**. This type is used in simple rear-wheel-only

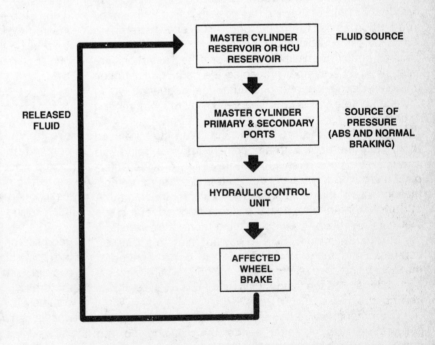

1.1 Brake fluid flow in an open anti-lock brake system

ABS designs. A disadvantage of the open system is that the brake pedal will drop during a long ABS stop as fluid flows from the brake lines. Some open systems have a pump that restores fluid to the master cylinder to keep the pedal from sinking, but the pump is not involved in the actual anti-lock function.

A closed system has some means, generally an electrically-powered pump, to restore hydraulic pressure that's bled off during an ABS stop **(see illustrations)**. The pump supplies fluid to an accumulator, where it's stored under pressure until it's needed to increase brake line pressure. In some cases, pump pressure is applied to the brakes during the ABS stop, with the amount and timing of pressure application controlled by a solenoid valve.

Integrated vs. non-integrated systems

An integrated system gets its name from the fact that the major hydraulic components - the brake booster and the hydraulic modulator - are integrated into a unit with the master cylinder. Other components, such as the accumulator and hydraulic modulator, may also be part of the assembly. Many of these systems have no vacuum booster. In such systems, the ABS pump provides brake boost as well as the pressure necessary for anti-lock brake operation. The pump forces fluid into one or more accumulators, where it is stored at very high pressures, typically 2000 to 3000 psi, until it is needed. On systems without a vacuum booster, the booster is a valve, controlled by the driver's foot on the brake pedal, that regulates the amount of boost applied.

Several early systems - Bendix 9 and 10, Bosch 3 and Teves II - were integrated. This approach fell out of favor because of the cost and complexity of the hydraulic assembly, high-powered pump and high-pressure accumulator(s).

Non-integrated systems, also known as "add-on" ABS, are installed in conventional brake systems between the master cylinder and the wheel brakes. A vacuum booster is used. The master cylinder is very much like, or in some cases identical to, the master cylinder used with non-anti-lock brakes. The hydraulic modulator is installed near the master cylinder. The brake fluid lines from the master cylinder connect to the hydraulic modulator. Brake lines run from the hydraulic modulator to each of the wheel brakes. During normal braking, it's as if the hydraulic modulator weren't there - hydraulic pressure from the master cylinder flows uninterrupted through the modulator to the brakes. During an ABS stop, the hydraulic modulator rapidly changes the hydraulic pressure at

1.2 Brake fluid flow in a closed anti-lock brake system with a hydraulic booster

1.3 Brake fluid flow in a closed anti-lock brake system with a vacuum booster

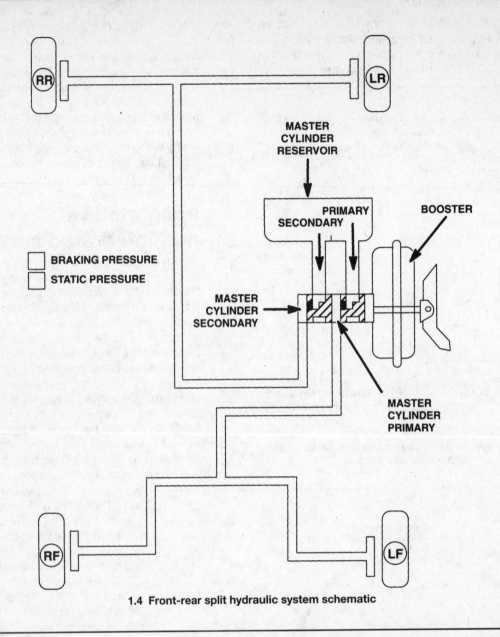

MASTER CYLINDER RESERVOIR

PRIMARY
SECONDARY

BOOSTER

☐ BRAKING PRESSURE
☐ STATIC PRESSURE

MASTER CYLINDER SECONDARY

MASTER CYLINDER PRIMARY

1.4 Front-rear split hydraulic system schematic

the wheel brakes, holding it steady, reducing it, or letting it increase. Fluid pressure is reduced by allowing some of the high-pressure fluid to return to its source (under low pressure). This low-pressure fluid in an ABS system is commonly referred to as "decayed" fluid.

Non-integrated ABS is simple, reliable and inexpensive. For these reasons, most modern ABS designs are non-integrated.

Hydraulic circuits

Even though the words are similar, "circuit" and "channel" have specific and different meanings. Hydraulic circuits are part of the main braking system. The brakes at two of

the vehicle's wheels are on one hydraulic circuit and the other two brakes are on the other hydraulic circuit. This is a safety mechanism meant to ensure that a sudden loss of brake pressure in one hydraulic circuit (due to a cracked brake hose, for example) will not leave the vehicle completely without brakes. Two of the four wheel brakes will still function, although stopping distances will be increased. All modern vehicles have two hydraulic circuits, whether or not they are equipped with ABS.

Hydraulic circuits are called "primary" and "secondary". The primary circuit is normally operated by the master cylinder piston closest to the rear of the master cylinder, and thus in direct contact with the booster pushrod. The secondary circuit is operated by the master

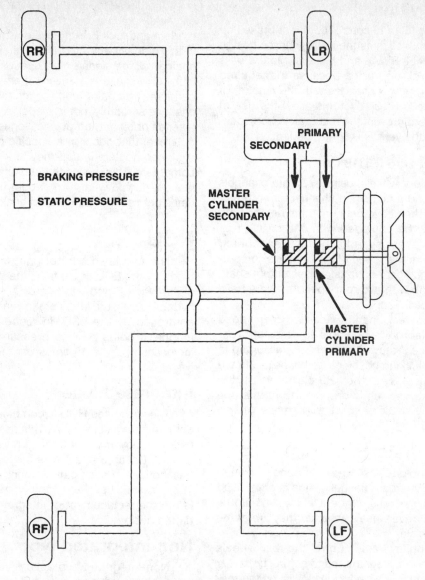

1.5 Diagonal split hydraulic system schematic

cylinder piston closest to the front of the master cylinder. In the case of front-rear split circuits, the primary circuit operates both front brakes and the secondary circuit operates both rear brakes. In the case of diagonally split circuits, the primary operates one front brake and the diagonally opposite rear brake, while the secondary operates the remaining front brake and rear brake.

Front-rear split circuits

Refer to illustration 1.4

This design is common in vehicles with fairly even front-rear weight distribution. Both front brakes are in the primary circuit and both rear brakes are in the secondary circuit **(see illustration)**.

Diagonal split circuits

Refer to illustration 1.5

This design is common in front-heavy vehicles such as mini-vans, where most of the braking is done by the front wheels. If one of the circuits fails, the vehicle will still have 50 percent of its braking power **(see illustration)**.

ABS channels

Channels are part of the anti-lock braking system. The word refers to the hydraulic control system that the ABS uses to alter the pressure to the brakes at each wheel. Each channel has a separate set of hydraulic control valves, which the ABS opens and closes to reduce and increase hydraulic pressure.

One-channel systems

A single channel is used to control both rear brakes on rear-wheel-only systems, such as the Kelsey-Hayes design that Dodge and Ford call RWAL and General Motors calls RABS. It's useful in pick-up trucks, because the required amount of rear braking power changes with the amount of weight in the truck bed. These systems allow the use of powerful rear brakes, but prevent the rear brakes from locking prematurely when the vehicle is lightly loaded.

Three-channel systems

These control all four wheels, using separate channels for each front wheel and a combined channel for both rear wheels. Even though they have only one channel for both rear wheels, they may be equipped with one or two rear speed sensors. Single rear speed sensors are mounted where they can measure the speed of the transmission output shaft, differential ring gear or transfer case output shaft. Three-channel systems with two rear speed sensors have one speed sensor at each rear wheel.

Systems with one rear channel and two rear speed sensors use the "select low" principle to calculate rear wheel speed. The slowest-moving rear wheel is assumed to be the one closest to locking up, since both wheels should be moving at the same speed. The ABS electronic control unit is programmed to use the information from this one wheel to control the hydraulic pressure to both rear wheels simultaneously.

Four-channel systems

These systems include a separate channel for each front and rear wheel. The four-channel design is often used with traction control systems, since it allows individual braking control of the drive wheels, whether they are at the front or rear of the vehicle.

Some four-channel systems control the rear wheels individually, but others are programmed to control both rear channels (and thus both rear wheels) identically, on the theory that uneven locking of the rear wheels can produce unstable handling.

ABS components

Electronic Control Unit (ECU)

The electronic control unit is the computer that operates the anti-lock brake system. It is referred to by several different names, which vary according to the ABS manufacturer and vehicle manufacturer. Chrysler Corporation originally used the term Electronic Control unit (ECU), but uses Controller, Anti-lock Brake (CAB) in all current systems. Ford uses ECU in many systems, and "control module" in others. General Motors uses the term Electronic Brake Control Module (EBCM) for all of its systems.

All of these terms apply to the same device. A few very early anti-lock brake systems used analog computers. In all modern anti-lock braking systems (and all systems covered in this manual), the ECU is a digital computer that receives analog voltage signals from speed sensors at the wheels or in the driveline, then converts them into digital signals that it can use. An analog voltage signal is infinitely variable (it changes smoothly, not in steps). A digital signal consists of a series of on and off pulses ("ones" and "zeroes", in computerese) that occur in a specific order. The advantage of digital computers is that they are much faster than analog computers. This means that a digital ECU can receive information, decide what to do about it, then do it, many more times per second than the old analog ECUs could.

HCU

The hydraulic control unit carries out the decisions made by the ECU. It contains the devices (solenoids, modulator valves and modulator pistons) that change the hydraulic pressure in the brake lines. The HCU is electrically controlled by the ECU. In response to the ECU's commands, it holds braking pressure steady, reduces it, or increases it, up to 15 times per second depending on the system.

Integrated type

The integrated HCU is combined with the master cylinder into a single assembly. This design, which also provides hydraulic power assist for the brakes, was used in Bendix 9 and 10, Bosch 3 and Teves II systems, and more detailed descriptions of each can be found in the relevant chapters. These assemblies were complicated and expensive, which led to the replacement of integrated systems by non-integrated designs.

Non-integrated type

Non-integrated hydraulic units are separate from the master cylinder, and mounted in the brake lines between the master cylinder and the wheel brakes. Non-integrated systems are also known as "add-on" systems, since they can be easily added to a conventional braking system on the assembly line. Non-integrated designs are used on most current systems.

In most non-integrated designs, the HCU is mounted separately from the ECU, but in some they are combined into a single unit.

Pump

Refer to illustrations 1.6 and 1.7

Pumps supply the hydraulic pressure for ABS operation (except in most rear-wheel-only systems, where the only source of hydraulic pressure is the driver's foot on the pedal). In integrated systems which don't have a vacuum brake booster, they supply hydraulic pressure for brake boost as well as for ABS operation.

Pumps use electric motors for power, and convert the rotary motion of the motor into back-and-forth motion that operates one or two pistons. Single-piston pumps use an eccentric bearing on the end of the shaft **(see illustration)**. The oscillating motion of the bearing pushes against a piston, which in turn pumps brake fluid.

Dual-piston pumps use a similar approach, but one motor operates two pistons **(see illustration)**. Generally, dual-piston pumps have one piston for each hydraulic circuit.

Master cylinder

Refer to illustrations 1.8, 1.9 and 1.10

Master cylinders used with ABS are generally the same as for non-ABS brakes, but there are two significant differences.

Master cylinders used with some integrated systems have a boost piston and valve in addition to

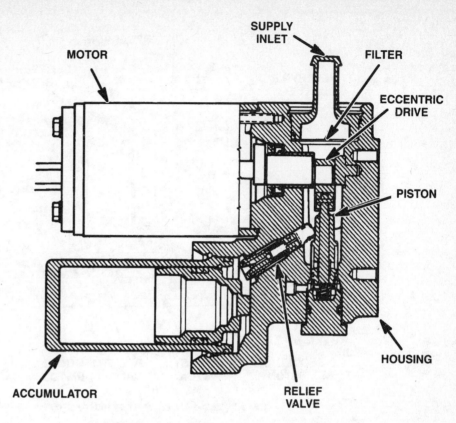

1.6 Single piston ABS pump - cross-sectional view

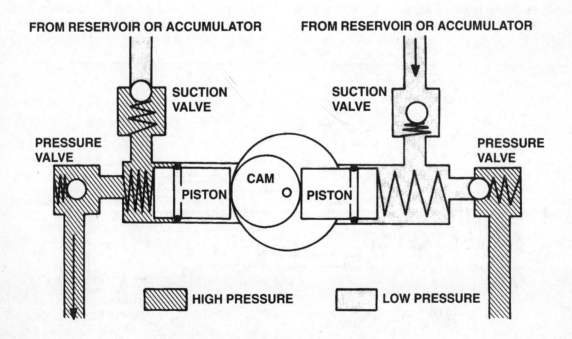

1.7 Dual piston ABS pump - cross-sectional view

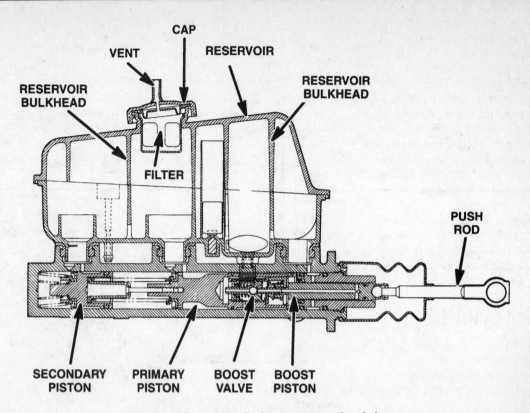

1.8 Integrated ABS master cylinder - cross-sectional view

the primary and secondary pistons that operate the main braking system **(see illustration)**. The boost piston is operated directly by the brake pedal. It opens the boost valve, which allows hydraulic pressure stored in the accumulator to move the primary piston, which in turn moves the secondary piston.

The master cylinders used with some non-integrated systems have central valves in the pistons **(see illustration)**. Central valves are used in place of the compensating ports in a standard master cylinder **(see illustration)**. This is because rapid back-and-forth movement of the master cylinder pistons during ABS operation would cause rapid

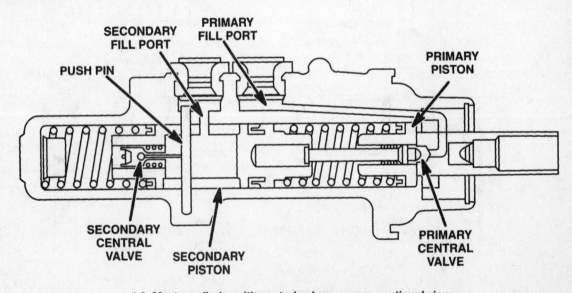

1.9 Master cylinder with central valves - cross-sectional view

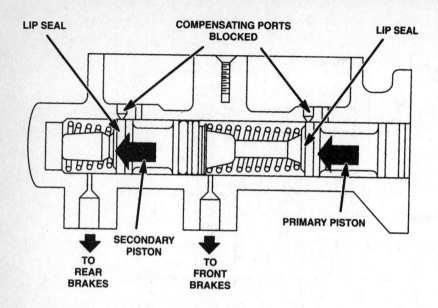

LIP SEAL

COMPENSATING PORTS BLOCKED

LIP SEAL

PRIMARY PISTON

SECONDARY PISTON

TO REAR BRAKES

TO FRONT BRAKES

1.10 Master cylinder with compensating ports - cross-sectional view

Three-position solenoids

Refer to illustration 1.11

Three-position solenoids used in Bosch systems have an at-rest position, when no current is applied to the solenoid; an intermediate position, when about 2 amps of current are applied; and a fully extended position, when about 5 amps of current are applied. In the at-rest position (no current applied), they allow pressure to build during normal braking or ABS operation. In the intermediate position (2 amps applied), they hold pressure steady. In the fully extended position (5 amps applied), they release pressure. More details about their operation during an ABS stop can be found in Chapter 4. This Section deals with the construction and internal functioning of the solenoid.

Bosch 3-position solenoids are adapted to different vehicles by the addition of restrictors in the inlet and outlet valves **(see illustration)**. The solenoid is precisely machined, and for this reason requires inlet and outlet filters to protect it from contaminants in the brake fluid. The solenoid winding is coated with a synthetic material, also to protect it from contamination.

wear of the piston cups as they rubbed across the compensating port openings. With central valves, brake fluid flows from the reservoir through passages to the central valves, then into the master cylinder bore, while the brake pedal is released. This eliminates the need for compensating ports. When the pedal is applied, the central valves close, so that brake fluid in the bores is used for brake operation instead of flowing back to the reservoir. Releasing the pedal opens the central valves and allows the brake fluid to return to the reservoir.

Solenoids

Solenoids - or more precisely, solenoid-controlled valves - regulate the increase and decrease of hydraulic pressure in the brake lines during ABS operation. There are two basic designs: the three-position solenoid used in Bosch 2 and Bosch 3 systems, and the two-position solenoid used in Bosch 5 and most other systems.

Solenoids rely on electromagnetism for their operation. An iron core, wrapped in a coil of wire, forms the magnet. The core is not normally magnetic, but when current flows through the coil of wire, it becomes magnetic. The suddenly-magnetic core attracts the valve inside the solenoid, pulling it into a new position (some valves are normally open and are pulled closed; others are normally closed and are pulled open). This happens very rapidly during an ABS stop, up to 15 times per second depending on the system. The valve either stops the flow of brake fluid, or opens to let it through. **Note:** *One widely used ABS design, Delphi Chassis ABS VI, uses screw-driven pistons in place of solenoids. This design is described in detail in Chapter 5.*

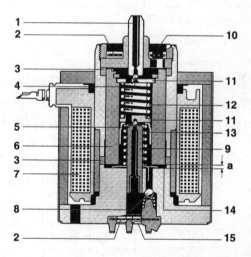

1.11 Bosch 3-position solenoid - cross-sectional view

1	Return line fitting	9	Valve body
2	Filter	10	Outlet to wheel brake
3	Non-magnetic bearing ring	11	Carrier plate
4	Outlet valve	12	Auxiliary spring
5	Inlet valve	13	Main spring
6	Armature	14	Recess step
7	Winding	15	Inlet from master cylinder
8	Check valve	a)	Air gap

Due to its extremely rapid response time, the solenoid must be carefully manufactured magnetically as well as mechanically. The armature moves in bearing rings made of non-magnetic material. This material not only provides a bearing surface, it diverts the magnetic field surrounding the wire coil into the armature and then across the gap. A recess step is machined into the solenoid at the end of the armature's travel to accommodate the end face of the armature.

Because it must seal against very high hydraulic pressures (up to 3000 psi), the sealed openings are kept small. The seals consist of carrier plates with steel pellets soldered to them. The pellets seat against precisely machined, hardened seats.

Because the stroke of the armature is very short (about 0.010-inch), the solenoid must be carefully assembled.

The solenoid has a check valve in a passage parallel to the input passage. This allows quick reduction of pressure when the brake is released, by opening a large-diameter passage between the master cylinder and the wheel brake. It also prevents the brake from being stuck in the applied position if the solenoid should fail in the applied position due to a frozen armature or a broken spring.

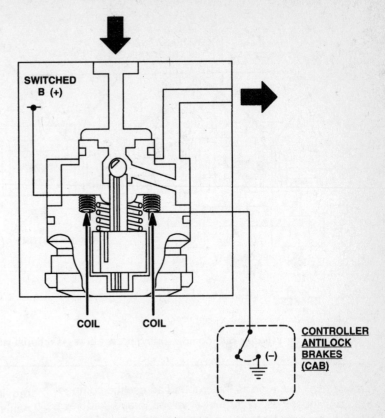

1.12 A two-position solenoid like this one receives battery voltage and is grounded by the ECU

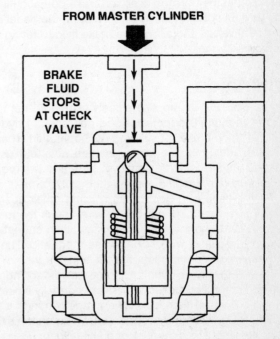

1.13 This normally open solenoid allows brake fluid to flow past the check valve when it's energized

1.14 Applying voltage to the solenoid causes the check valve to close, blocking the flow of brake fluid

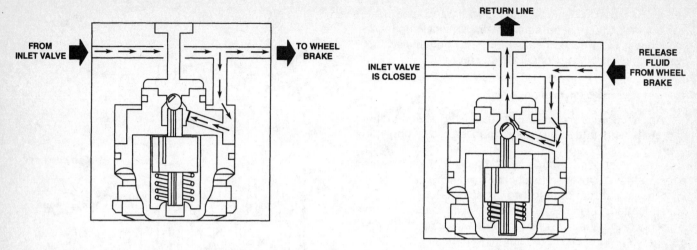

1.15 This normally closed solenoid holds brake line pressure when it's not energized . . .

1.16 . . . and opens to release pressure when it is energized

Two-position solenoids

Refer to illustrations 1.12 through 1.17

This simpler design replaced three-position solenoids in Bosch systems, and is widely used by other ABS manufacturers. This type of solenoid is either open, allowing the passage of brake fluid through it, or closed, preventing the passage of brake fluid **(see illustration)**. Some solenoids are normally closed, meaning that they are closed when no current is applied and open when current is applied **(see illustrations)**. Others are normally open, meaning that they are open when no current is applied and closed when current is applied **(see illustrations)**.

In some systems, voltage is supplied constantly to the solenoid, with the ground circuit being switched on and off by the ECU to control solenoid opening and closing. In others, the ground circuit is always complete, and battery voltage is switched on and off to control the opening and closing of the solenoid.

Because solenoids have only two positions, most systems require more than one of them in each hydraulic channel **(see illustration)**. A normally open solenoid allows brake fluid flow during normal braking, but closes to isolate the wheel brake from the master cylinder during an ABS stop. A normally closed solenoid in the same channel opens during an ABS stop to allow the release of pressure

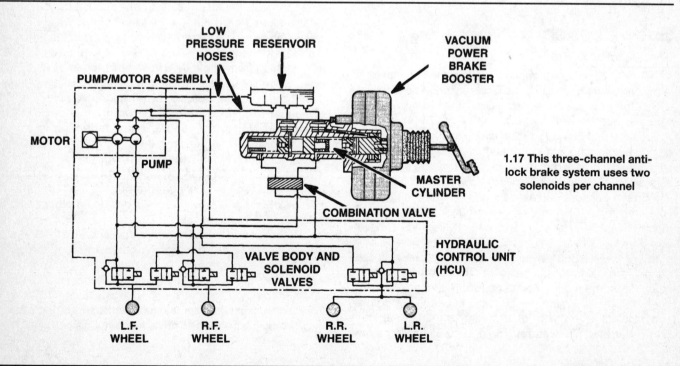

1.17 This three-channel anti-lock brake system uses two solenoids per channel

at the wheel brake. Some systems need only two solenoids per channel. Others need a third solenoid, which opens to allow pressure to build once the ECU has determined that the affected wheel is no longer locking up.

Accumulators

An accumulator does just that - it accumulates hydraulic fluid under pressure, then stores it until it's needed for ABS operation (in integrated systems, the stored, pressurized fluid is also used for power brake boost, but that's a separate function from ABS).

Accumulators come in two types: gas-charged and spring-loaded. Gas-charged types are divided internally by a flexible diaphragm. On one side of the diaphragm is nitrogen gas, compressed to a fairly high pressure (typically, 1000 psi). On the other side of the diaphragm is brake fluid. The ABS pump forces fluid into the accumulator, compressing the nitrogen even further, to about 2000 to 3000 psi depending on the system. The brake fluid remains in the accumulator until it's needed for the pressure increase cycle in ABS operation. Then a valve opens and the highly compressed nitrogen gas pushes the brake fluid out into the lines. After pressure drops to a certain point, a low-pressure switch turns the pump on and it starts to pump fluid back into the accumulator.

Spring-loaded accumulators work in a similar way to gas-charged types, but they operate at much lower pressures (from 450 psi to as little as 50 psi). Instead of a diaphragm with nitrogen gas on one side, they contain a spring and a piston. The pump forces fluid into the accumulator against the piston, which compresses the spring. When needed, the accumulator releases the pressurized fluid into the brake lines.

Speed sensors

Refer to illustration 1.18

The main source of information that the ECU relies on in making its decisions is the speed sensors. These fall into two categories: wheel speed sensors and vehicle speed sensors. Both rely on the same principles of physics and are constructed in a very similar way. The main difference is in mounting methods and location, since wheel speed sensors detect the speed of the wheels and vehicle speed sensors detect the speed of a driveline component.

Speed sensors consist of a permanently magnetized core with a coil of wire wrapped around it. The sensor is mounted in a fixed position. The coil of wire ends in a two-wire harness, which runs to the ECU. This harness is often made of "twisted pair" wiring, similar to that used in telephone cords, and for the same reason - the twisting helps keep electromagnetic interference from affecting the sensor's output. The magnetic core is shaped like a pointer, and it points at the teeth of a rotating armature that looks like a gear **(see illustration)**. The armature is called a tone

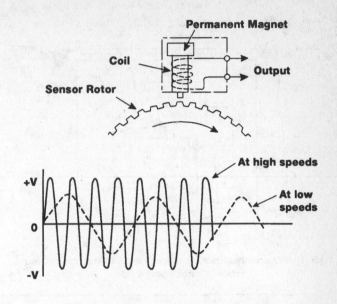

1.18 Here's how a speed sensor works

ring, tone wheel, or gear pulser by different ABS and vehicle manufacturers. It's mounted on a rotating component. In the case of wheel speed sensors, this is a component that rotates with the wheel, usually a hub or CV joint at the front and a hub or axleshaft at the rear. In the case of vehicle speed sensors, it's a component that rotates at the speed of the rear wheels, usually the output shaft of the transmission or transfer case or the differential ring gear.

The magnetic field created by the sensor's permanent magnet overlaps the teeth of the sensor wheel. As the teeth rotate through the magnetic field, they cause the magnetic field to alternately strengthen and decrease, which in turn causes an electrical current to be produced in the wire coil around the magnet. This is a low-voltage alternating current, ranging from about 0.65 volts at 5 mph to as high as 9 volts. Since the voltage varies with the speed of the wheels, this is an accurate indication to the ECU of how fast the wheels are moving. The ECU is programmed to detect changes in wheel speed. A gradual reduction in wheel speed indicates that the vehicle is slowing down normally. An abrupt reduction in wheel speed indicates that a wheel is locked up, or about to be locked up. This is especially true if one wheel is slowing more quickly than the others. The ECU uses this information to decide whether to activate the ABS.

Wheel speed sensors are relatively delicate, and are often mounted where they are vulnerable to road dirt, corrosion, and damage from flying debris. The sensor rings can also be affected by built-up dirt or damaged by debris. Another common form of sensor damage is demagnetizing from being hammered on during replacement of the sensor or a nearby suspension or driveline component.

Other ECU input devices

Lateral acceleration switch

This is a switch used in some Corvettes and Toyota models that detects when the vehicle is being subjected to high g-force from a turn. Since this loads the tires at the outside of the turn and lightens the loads on the inside tires, the ABS needs to adjust its strategy for the situation. The lateral acceleration switch signals to the ECU when g-force exceeds 0.6g.

Lateral acceleration sensor

This device serves the same purpose as the lateral acceleration switch, but the sensor provides a variable voltage signal, rather than the simple on-off signal provided by the switch. These sensors are used on some Corvettes and Toyota models, and are described in detail in the various system chapters.

Deceleration switch

This type of switch, in varying designs, is used in numerous 4WD and all-wheel drive models. It provides the ECU with information that it uses to compare the rate of vehicle deceleration with the rate of wheel deceleration. For example, hard brake application on a surface such as ice will produce very little vehicle deceleration and very rapid wheel deceleration, or locking. In this situation, the ECU needs to control the duty cycles (on and off times) of the HCU solenoids in a different pattern than it would on a smooth, dry surface.

Brake light switch

The brake light switch is used in most systems to tell the ECU that the brakes have actually been applied. On some early GM systems, rough terrain could cause the wheel sensors to send a false deceleration signal, initiating anti-lock braking when the brakes weren't applied. The brake light switch prevents this because ABS won't activate unless the brakes are applied.

Brake fluid level switch

Some systems won't activate ABS unless they receive a signal that there is sufficient brake fluid in the system. The fluid level switch, generally mounted in the reservoir cap, will signal the ECU if fluid level drops too low. This may also cause one or both warning lamps to illuminate.

How ABS works

The traditional way to stop a vehicle on a slippery surface is to "pump" the pedal with your foot - that is, apply and release the pedal in short stages to prevent the wheels from locking up. Anti-lock brake systems do the same thing, but they do it much more quickly and precisely than a driver can. Anti-lock brake systems can apply and release the brakes up to 15 times per second. Not only that, but each "pump" is precisely timed in response to electrical signals from the vehicle's speed sensors, and the system can tell exactly when to stop pumping and let the driver apply the brakes in the normal way.

When you operate the brake pedal, you vary the hydraulic pressure in the brake lines. Holding the pedal steady holds the hydraulic pressure steady, pressing the pedal increases pressure, and releasing the pedal reduces pressure.

The ABS hydraulic modulator also holds, releases and increases brake line pressure. The exact ways it does this vary widely from system to system, and are described in detail in the individual system chapters.

The brake line pressure that the ABS works with is provided initially by the driver's foot on the pedal. In integrated systems, the pressure is increased by the hydraulic boost, but this is part of the main braking system, not ABS. Additional pressure in most systems is provided by a pump. In some systems, pump pressure is used directly to affect ABS operation; in others, pressurized fluid is stored in an accumulator and released when ABS operation demands it.

The ECU receives signals from the speed sensors that tell it how fast the wheels are decelerating. If this happens too quickly at one of the sensors (the sensor voltage drops too rapidly), the ECU assumes that the affected wheel is about to lock up. The ECU then activates the hydraulic modulator, maintaining brake line pressure at a level that will achieve the most efficient degree of wheel lock-up.

Traction control

Traction control has a similar function to anti-lock brakes, but it prevents wheel slip on acceleration rather than deceleration. The same wheel speed sensors used for the anti-lock brake system indicate to the ECU when the drive wheels are spinning due to acceleration (positive wheel slip). Depending on system design, the traction control system may then apply the brake at the slipping wheel(s), reduce engine power or both. Power reduction is accomplished by retarding ignition timing, physically limiting the movement of the throttle, switching off some of the fuel injectors, or in some cases a combination of these.

Traction control systems normally work only up to a specified speed (typically 35 mph). At higher speeds, reduction of engine power could cause a loss of vehicle control.

Some traction control systems (Corvettes with Bosch ABS/ASR, for example) have a yaw control function. A lateral acceleration sensor tells the ECU when the side slip of the wheels has reached a predetermined point, and engine power is reduced to compensate.

Traction control systems generally can be switched off by the driver.

Notes

Chapter 2
Troubleshooting

Inspection

A number of ABS problems can be found with visual inspections and simple tests.

Follow the ABS wiring harnesses to each connector. Check carefully for damage to the wires. Disconnect each connector and check for corrosion or damaged terminals. Reconnect the connectors and make sure they're securely attached.

Check the hydraulic lines from the master cylinder all the way to each wheel brake. Look for fluid leaks, and for bent or cracked metal lines. Make sure the lines are securely attached to their components.

Check the system relays. Make sure they're securely installed and that none of their terminals are bent or corroded.

Check each component for visible damage.

Wheel speed sensors

The wheel speed sensors are often in vulnerable locations and can be affected by road dirt, corrosion, physical damage, or a build-up of metal particles on the sensor's magnetic tip. If you've recently repaired or replaced components near the sensor, the sensor may have been demagnetized from impact or its harness may have been damaged.

Clean the sensor tip and make sure nothing is stuck to it. The tip is magnetic and will attract metal. Anything on the sensor, especially metal, will interfere with the voltage output of the sensor and cause it to produce inaccurate readings. On externally mounted sensors, metal can come from severely worn pads or shoes. On internally mounted sensors (in the transmission, transfer case, differential or integral with the wheel hub and bearing assembly), metal can come from normal wear of the unit the sensor is mounted in.

Slowly rotate the armature and check its teeth. On externally mounted sensors, you can do this by rotating the wheel, although you may have to remove a brake drum for access. On internally mounted sensors, you may have to remove the sensor and look into its mounting hole to see the armature. Make sure there's nothing stuck in the gaps between the teeth, and make sure none of the teeth are damaged or missing.

Check the air gap between the sensor and its armature, using a non-magnetic (brass or plastic) feeler gauge. This generally ranges from 0.015 to 0.050-inch. If it's well outside this range, the sensor will give inaccurate readings to the ECU (computer).

Some early models have adjustable sensor air gaps; the procedure is described in the system chapters. Most have a fixed air gap, so if the air gap is outside the specified range, check for problems that would allow the armature to rotate unevenly, such as worn wheel bearings. Check the sensor to make sure it's securely attached, and check the component it's mounted on for bending.

Follow the wiring harness from the sensor to the connector. Check for damage (even partly worn insulation can cause inaccurate sensor readings) and missing harness clips. Make sure the harness is routed in such a way that it's safe from damage. Disconnect the connector and examine it closely for bent or missing pins and corrosion.

Brake light switch

The brake light switch lets the ECU know that the driver has actually applied the brakes, so it won't initiate anti-lock braking at the wrong time. If the switch is out of adjustment or has failed completely, the ABS will not work in most cases, and the ECU will set a trouble code and illuminate the amber warning lamp.

Main brake system

If you suspect an ABS problem, don't forget to check the main brake system as well. Some brake problems, such as a low fluid level, will also affect ABS operation. If a coating of metal particles on a sensor tip came from a brake shoe that wore down to the metal, it's clearly time for brake system repairs. If you've just done repairs that included machining the discs with an on-vehicle brake lathe, particles from the disc may have become stuck to the sensor tip.

ABS diagnosis

Modern anti-lock brake systems include a self-diagnosis function, which provides diagnostic information. Actually getting the information ranges from very easy to nearly impossible.

Interpreting the warning lamp

Problems with an anti-lock brake system are usually - but not always - indicated by the amber ABS warning lamp in the instrument panel. The light should come on briefly when the vehicle is started, then go out, only coming on during an ABS stop. If it comes on and stays on, there's a problem with the ABS. If it doesn't come on at all, check the bulb and the lamp circuit.

In some systems, the light may flash or glow steadily to indicate different kinds of problems. A flashing light may indicate a problem that needs attention, but isn't serious enough to disable the ABS. A steadily glowing light normally indicates that the ABS has been disabled due to a problem (although the vehicle's main braking system will still work). If the red brake warning lamp glows, there's usually a problem in the main braking system (some early systems, such as Bendix 9, could illuminate the red lamp for an ABS problem). If both the red and amber warning lamps glow, there may be separate problems in the main braking system and the ABS, or there may be a main system problem that affects ABS, such as a loss of brake fluid.

Warning: *An illuminated red lamp should always be taken as an indication that the vehicle is unsafe to drive.*

Reading codes

Some early systems required a special-purpose ABS tester to read diagnostic information. The testers were provided by the ABS manufacturer only to new car dealers. No equivalent tool was available from the major tool suppliers.

Some later systems display codes by flashing the ABS warning lamp in special sequences. These sequences represent numbers, which in turn stand for specific problems (for example, a Code 2 might indicate a problem with the left front wheel speed sensor). Information on obtaining and reading flash codes is included in the specific system chapters.

Many modern anti-lock brake systems require a scan tool to read trouble codes. Aftermarket scan tools are available from auto parts stores, as well as from the major tool suppliers who sell to professional mechanics. Aftermarket

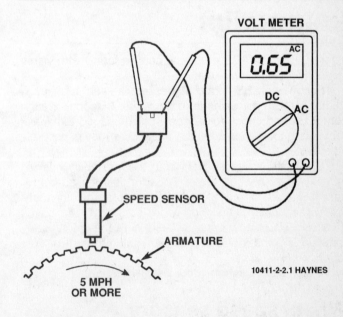

VOLT METER

0.65

AC

DC

AC

SPEED SENSOR

ARMATURE

5 MPH
OR MORE

10411-2-2.1 HAYNES

2.1 Checking speed sensor output with an AC voltmeter

scan tools were originally very expensive, and some still are. However, their prices have been dropping while their capabilities increase. A scan tool that might not make economic sense today could be a realistic purchase six months from now. If you're considering a scan tool, shop around. If you can, wait for a while and shop around again later.

Wheel speed sensor test

Refer to illustration 2.1

If the problem seems to be a defective wheel speed sensor, you can check its output with an AC voltmeter. Note that the voltmeter must be able to measure small amounts of voltage on the alternating current (AC) scale, not direct current (DC).

Follow the wiring harness from the speed sensor to its connector. Disconnect the connector, then connect the AC voltmeter to the speed sensor side of the connector (not the side that runs to the ECU) **(see illustration)**.

Jack up the end of the vehicle with the wheel you're checking, then support it securely on jackstands.

Spin the affected wheel at 5 mph or more (turning it by hand will work, and is safe). Have an assistant read the voltmeter. It should be at least 0.65 volt, and it should increase as wheel speed increases. Wheel speed sensors can produce up to 9 volts AC. If the sensor doesn't indicate at least 0.65 volt, it's probably defective. Inspect it as described at the beginning of this Chapter.

Notes

Chapter 3
Bendix systems

Bendix ABX-4

Refer to illustrations 3.1, 3.2 and 3.3

This is a non-integrated, four-channel system used on the 1995 through 1997 Chrysler Cirrus and Sebring, Dodge Stratus and Dodge and Plymouth Neon. It can be identified by its master cylinder, which has only two outlet lines (non-ABS models have four), and its hydraulic unit **(see illustrations)**.

The main brake system is conventional, with a master cylinder and vacuum brake booster. The two outlet lines for the master cylinder are for the primary and secondary brake circuits; they connect the master cylinder to the hydraulic modulator. Internally, the master cylinder has center valves so the ABS can pull brake fluid from the master cylinder without damaging the piston seals.

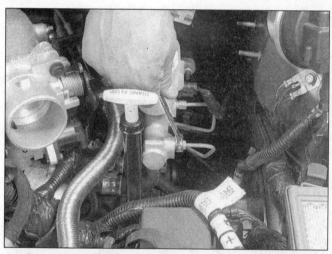

3.1 The Bendix ABX-4 master cylinder has only two fluid lines (non-ABS models have four)

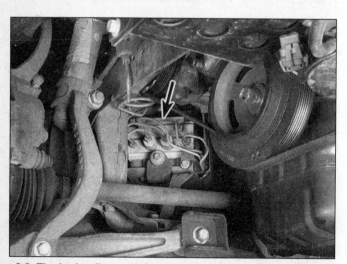

3.2 The hydraulic control unit on the Chrysler Cirrus, Dodge Stratus and Plymouth Breeze is mounted below the power steering pump

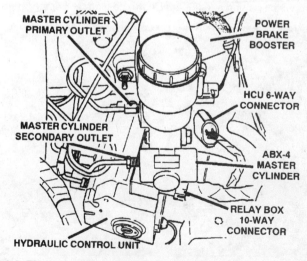

3.3 The hydraulic control unit on Neon models is mounted below the master cylinder

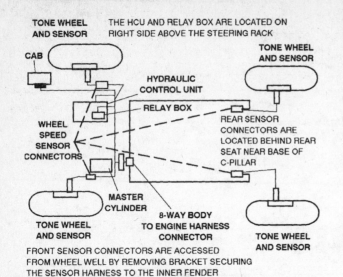

3.4 Bendix ABX-4 component locations
(Cirrus, Stratus, Sebring)

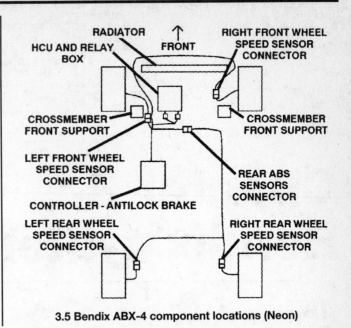

3.5 Bendix ABX-4 component locations (Neon)

3.6 The Controller, Anti-lock Brake on Cirrus, Stratus and Sebring models is located on the right radiator support; on Neons, it's behind a kick panel in the passenger compartment

System components

Refer to illustrations 3.4, 3.5, 3.6, 3.7 and 3.8

The system consists of the master cylinder, hydraulic modulator, relay box, four wheel speed sensors and the electronic control unit - which Chrysler calls the Controller, Anti-lock Brake (CAB) **(see illustrations)**. The hydraulic modulator contains four solenoids, which combine the pressure build and decay functions into one. It also contains shuttle orifice valves, one for each circuit, and a pump with one piston for each circuit. The proportioning valves for the rear brakes are mounted directly to the hydraulic modulator **(see illustration)**. The CAB on early models can

3.7 The proportioning valves for the rear brakes are threaded into the hydraulic control unit (arrows)

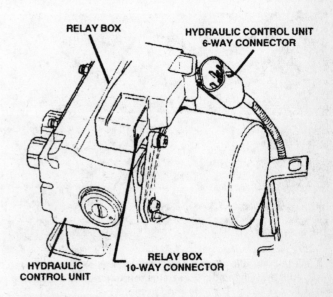

3.8 The relay box is mounted on the hydraulic control unit

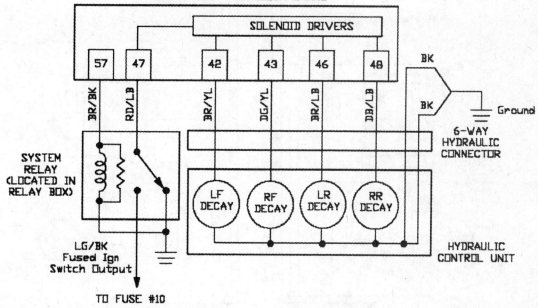

42 – LF DECAY SOLENOID CONTROL
43 – RF DECAY SOLENOID CONTROL
46 – LR DECAY SOLENOID CONTROL
47 – ABS SYSTEM RELAY OUTPUT
48 – RR DECAY SOLENOID CONTROL
57 – ABS SYSTEM RELAY CONTROL

3.9 System relay and solenoid circuit (Bendix ABX-4)

store 16 trouble codes; later versions can store 38 codes.

The relay box is mounted on top of the hydraulic unit **(see illustration)**. The relay box has a ten-pin connector and the hydraulic modulator has a six-pin connector. The CAB has a 60-pin connector.

System operation

Refer to illustrations 3.9, 3.10, 3.11 and 3.12

Although the system has four channels, the rear channels are controlled together as one to prevent loss of vehicle stability that might occur from uneven locking of the rear wheels.

The system relay draws current from the ignition switch through a fuse **(see illustration)**. The CAB draws current from the system relay through pin 57. The CAB checks the system relay during startup to make sure it isn't working when it isn't supposed to. The CAB also checks the system voltage to make sure it is least the minimum nine volts required for system operation.

The four wheel speed sensors supply voltage signals to the CAB. When one of the signal voltages drops too rapidly, indicating a wheel about to lock up, the CAB initiates ABS braking.

During ABS braking, the CAB controls the four decay solenoids through its solenoid driver circuits. The solenoids can release pressure at a wheel about to lock **(see illustration)**. The released hydraulic fluid is stored in a pair of

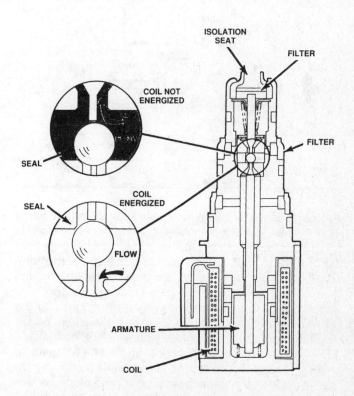

3.10 The decay solenoids open to release hydraulic pressure at each wheel brake

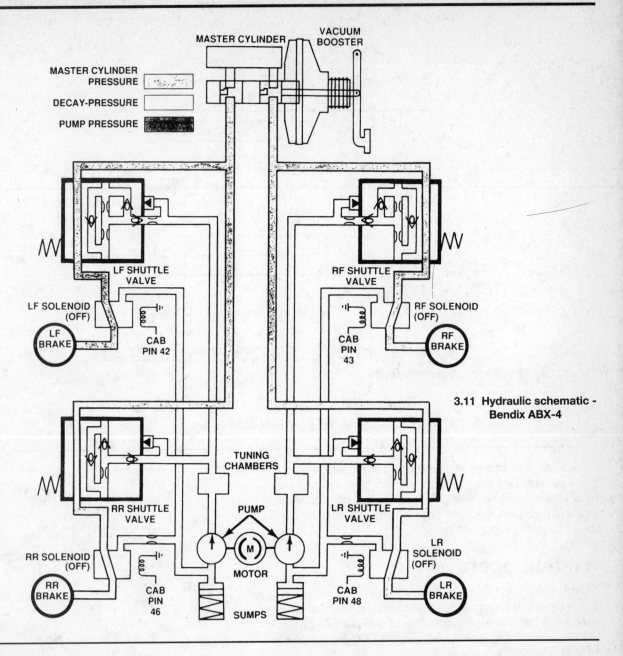

MASTER CYLINDER PRESSURE

DECAY-PRESSURE

PUMP PRESSURE

MASTER CYLINDER

VACUUM BOOSTER

LF SHUTTLE VALVE

RF SHUTTLE VALVE

LF SOLENOID (OFF)

LF BRAKE

CAB PIN 42

CAB PIN 43

RF SOLENOID (OFF)

RF BRAKE

3.11 Hydraulic schematic - Bendix ABX-4

RR SHUTTLE VALVE

TUNING CHAMBERS

LR SHUTTLE VALVE

PUMP

MOTOR

RR SOLENOID (OFF)

RR BRAKE

CAB PIN 46

SUMPS

CAB PIN 48

LR SOLENOID (OFF)

LR BRAKE

sumps at about 50 psi. When pressure buildup is required at the wheel, the pump supplies it, using the fluid stored in the sumps **(see illustration)**. The pump draws current from its own relay, mounted in the relay box **(see illustration)**. The CAB controls the relay, and thus the pump, through terminal 16. A shuttle orifice valve in each hydraulic circuit restricts hydraulic pressure between the pump and the solenoids, which prevents the pressure buildup from occurring too suddenly. This provides smoother ABS operation.

The CAB performs a series of diagnostic tests at startup, during normal braking and during ABS braking. At startup, it tests the warning lamp circuit and diode, as well as the system relay and its ground circuit. While the engine is running, it tests the pump motor every three seconds

(every 200 milliseconds during ABS braking). It tests the pump motor relay circuit during drive-off and continuously when the pump is running (or should be running). If pump relay voltage, monitored by the CAB at pin 20, is below seven volts for 200 ms during pump operation or 100 ms during the drive-off test, the CAB stores a trouble code. It also stores a code if pump relay voltage is above six volts for three seconds when the pump is supposed to be off.

The CAB monitors the system voltage at pins 47 and 57 continuously after drive-off, or after three minutes if the vehicle is started and allowed to idle without being driven. If system voltage is less than nine volts when the system relay is energized, the CAB shuts off the ABS and sets a code.

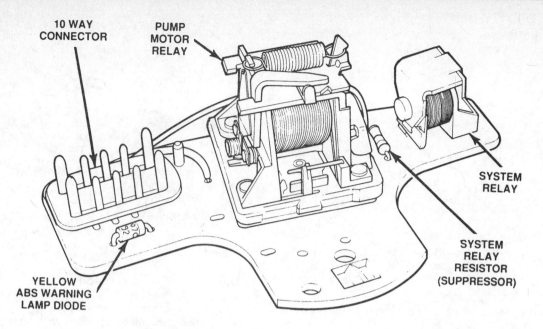

3.12 Relays - Bendix ABX-4 (cover removed)

10 WAY CONNECTOR

PUMP MOTOR RELAY

SYSTEM RELAY

SYSTEM RELAY RESISTOR (SUPPRESSOR)

YELLOW ABS WARNING LAMP DIODE

The CAB times the operation of the decay solenoids during ABS braking. If any two solenoids stay on for more than 4.5 seconds, the CAB sets a code and illuminates the ABS warning lamp until vehicle speed drops to 3 mph. It disables the front-wheel ABS, allowing rear ABS operation.

The CAB monitors the wheel speed sensor signals during vehicle operation, and looks for different signs of trouble. At any time while ABS is not engaged, the CAB checks the wheel speed sensor signals for consistency every 5 milliseconds. If six or more changes in a signal occur at an unrealistically fast rate, the CAB sets a code. It also checks for a missing signal. This check starts when the vehicle reaches 8 mph, or when the two fastest-moving wheels reach 15 mph. If the signal from any one wheel disappears for more than 2.5 seconds, the CAB sets a code. If the signal from both rear wheels disappears for more than 20 seconds, the CAB will also set a code. The longer time for the combined rear wheel signals is to allow for the fact that the vehicle might be stuck in mud or snow and the drive (front) wheels are spinning without moving the vehicle.

The CAB also performs a static check of wheel speed sensor continuity after the other start-up tests have been performed and before the vehicle reaches 5 mph. Above that speed, it checks dynamic wheel speed sensor continuity every 5 milliseconds. In either case, if continuity is missing for more than 35 milliseconds, the CAB sets a code.

The CAB checks the solenoid circuits for shorts or opens. A reference voltage is obtained from the system relay output voltage and the solenoid channel voltage is compared to this. Test frequency ranges from once a minute for a short-circuit test when ABS is not in operation to every 620 milliseconds when ABS is engaged.

System service

Master cylinder and brake booster seal

There's a seal between the master cylinder and booster that prevents vacuum leaks. The seal must be replaced with a new one whenever the master cylinder is separated from the booster.

Wheel speed sensors

Refer to illustrations 3.13, 3.14 and 3.15

Sensor replacement is a bolt-in operation **(see illustration)**. The tone wheels are integral with the outer CV joint at

3.13 The ABS front wheel sensors are bolted to the knuckles and the tone rings are integral with the outer CV joints

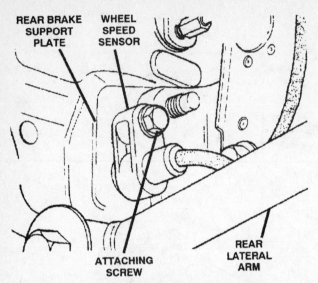

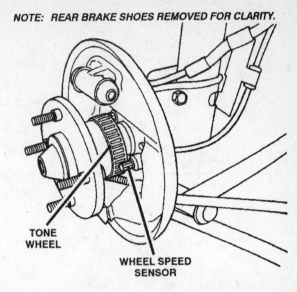

NOTE: REAR BRAKE SHOES REMOVED FOR CLARITY.

3.14 The rear wheel speed sensors are bolted to the brake backing plates . . .

3.15 . . . and protrude through the backing plate next to the tone ring, which is integral with the hub

the front and with the wheel hub at the rear **(see illustrations)**.

Brake bleeding

Warning 1: *Wear eye protection when bleeding the brake system. If the fluid comes in contact with your eyes, immediately rinse them with water and seek medical attention.*

Warning 2: *Never use old brake fluid. It contains moisture which can boil, rendering the brake system inoperative.*

Warning 3: *If, after bleeding the system you do not have a firm brake pedal, or if the ABS light on the instrument panel does not go off, or if you have any doubts whatsoever about the effectiveness of the brake system, have it towed to a dealer service department or other repair shop equipped with the necessary tools for bleeding the hydraulic modulator.*

Caution: *Brake fluid will damage paint. Cover all painted surfaces and be careful not to spill fluid during this procedure.*

Bleeding of the main brake system is conventional. Bleeding the hydraulic modulator requires a DRB III scan tool or equivalent. Follow the tool manufacturer's instructions.

Bendix 6 and Bendix III (LC-4)

Refer to illustration 3.16

Bendix 6 is used on 1991 through 1993 Chrysler LeBaron, Dodge Daytona and Spirit, Plymouth Acclaim and Laser, and Eagle Talon and Premier. Bendix LC-4 is Chrysler's designation for the Bendix III system, a more compact version of Bendix 6. Bendix LC-4 is used on 1994 and later Chrysler LeBaron, Dodge Spirit and Shadow, Plymouth Acclaim and Sundance, as well as 1994 and later Chrysler Corporation minivans.

Both are non-integrated systems that operate all four wheels and have four wheel speed sensors. Bendix 6 has three channels, while Bendix LC-4 has four.

The main brake system is conventional, with a master cylinder and vacuum brake booster. The two outlet lines for the master cylinder are for the primary and secondary brake circuits; they connect the master cylinder to the hydraulic modulator.

The Bendix 6 system can be identified by its modulator, which includes four bleed valves on the top **(see illustration)**. The LC4 modulator is similar, but has a bleed valve on each side as well as four on the top.

System components

Refer to illustrations 3.17, 3.18, 3.19 and 3.20

The system includes the master cylinder, hydraulic modulator, three relays, four wheel speed sensors, and the electronic control unit - which Chrysler calls the Controller, Anti-lock Brake (CAB) **(see illustrations)**.

The Bendix 6 hydraulic modulator contains six solenoids; two are isolation solenoids, and the remaining four are build/decay solenoids. The build/decay solenoids combine the pressure buildup and release functions into one unit. The modulator also contains two shuttle orifice valves, one for each circuit, a pump with one piston for each circuit, a sump for each circuit and an accumulator for

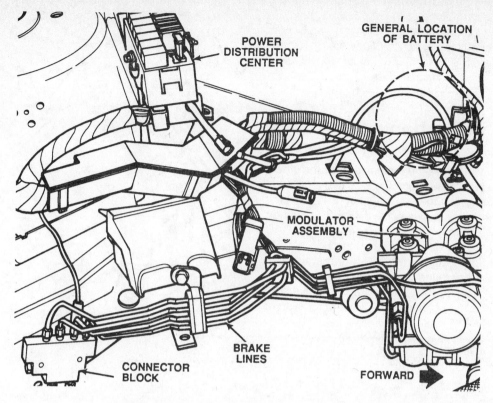

3.16 Bendix 6 modulator (Bendix LC4 similar)

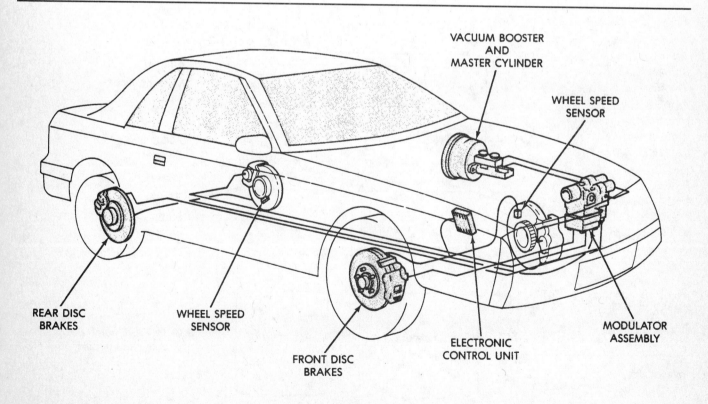

3.17 Bendix 6 component locations

each circuit **(see illustration)**. The accumulators are spring-loaded piston types.

The Bendix LC4 modulator is similar to the Bendix 6 design, but contains only build/decay solenoids, not isolation solenoids. Since each of the four wheel brakes has its own hydraulic channel, there's no need to isolate the front and rear brakes from each other.

System operation

Refer to illustrations 3.21, 3.22 and 3.23

The system receives input signals from the wheel speed sensors and brake light switch, as well as voltage from the ignition switch through a fuse or fusible link.

The system relay draws current from the ignition switch through a fuse **(see illustration)**. The CAB draws current from the system relay through pin 57. The CAB checks the system relay during startup to make sure it isn't working when it isn't supposed to. The CAB also checks the system voltage to make sure it is at least the minimum nine volts required for system operation.

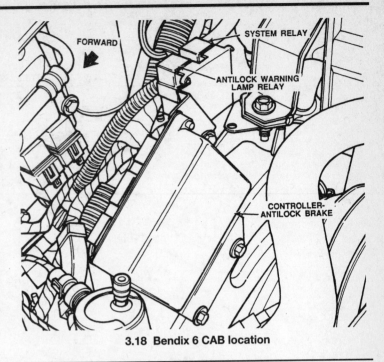

3.18 Bendix 6 CAB location

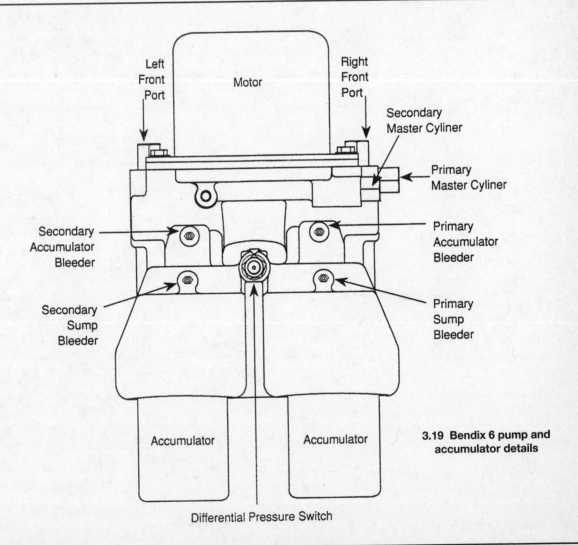

3.19 Bendix 6 pump and accumulator details

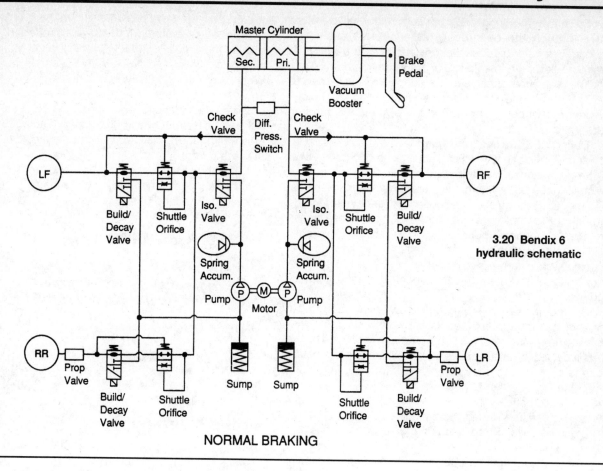

3.20 Bendix 6
hydraulic schematic

NORMAL BRAKING

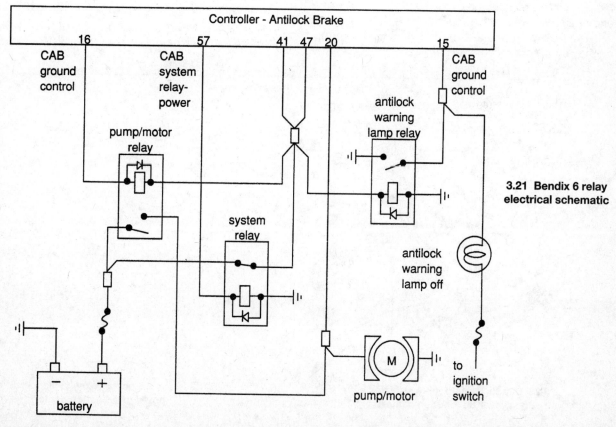

3.21 Bendix 6 relay
electrical schematic

During normal (non-ABS) braking, hydraulic pressure flows through the build/decay solenoids to the wheel brakes. The solenoids are spring-loaded in the released position, allowing a free flow of hydraulic pressure.

The four wheel speed sensors supply voltage signals to the CAB. When one of the signal voltages drops too rapidly, indicating a wheel is about to lock up, the CAB initiates ABS braking.

During ABS braking in the Bendix 6 system, the isolation solenoids close whenever ABS braking occurs at either of the front wheels, isolating the brakes from the master cylinder. In the LC4 system, there are no isolation solenoids.

The CAB controls the four build/decay solenoids through its solenoid driver circuits. The solenoids release pressure at a wheel about to lock. The released hydraulic fluid is stored in a pair of sumps, then pumped into a pair of accumulators where it is stored at about 50 psi. When pressure buildup is required at the wheel, the accumulators supply it.

The pump draws current from its own relay, mounted in the engine compartment (see illustrations). The CAB controls the relay, and thus the pump, through terminal 16. The CAB provides ground to the relay coil, which has a constant voltage supply. The relay coil closes the relay, supplying current to the pump motor.

A shuttle orifice valve in each hydraulic circuit restricts hydraulic pressure during the build cycle, which prevents the pressure buildup from occurring too suddenly. This provides smoother ABS operation.

The CAB disengages ABS when vehicle speed drops to 3 mph. For this reason, there may some wheel lockup at the end of an ABS stop. This is normal.

The CAB performs self-diagnostic tests on startup and during vehicle operation. When the ignition key is turned to the On position, the CAB checks continuity of the electrical components, including the wheel speed sensors and relays. The amber anti-lock warning lamp stays on during this check, which takes one to two seconds.

When the vehicle is driven off, the ABS checks to make sure there is output from the wheel speed sensors, and operates the solenoids and pump to make sure they work. If the vehicle is not driven off, but left running for three minutes after startup, the CAB skips the solenoid test but operates the pump.

During vehicle operation, the CAB tests the solenoids every 15 seconds when ABS is not engaged. This increases to every 1/2 second during an ABS stop.

System service

Diagnosis

Diagnosis requires a DRB II, DRB III or equivalent scan tool. Refer to the tool manufacturer's instructions.

Wheel speed sensors

Refer to illustration 3.24

Sensor replacement is a bolt-in operation (see illustration). The tone wheels are integral with the outer CV joint at the front and with the wheel hub at the rear.

Brake bleeding

Warning 1: *Wear eye protection when bleeding the brake system. If the fluid comes in contact with your eyes, immediately rinse them with water and seek medical attention.*

Warning 2: *Never use old brake fluid. It contains moisture which can boil, rendering the brake system inoperative.*

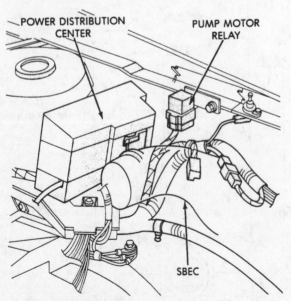

3.22 Bendix 6 pump relay (vehicles with power distribution center)

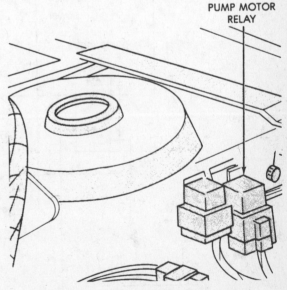

3.23 Bendix 6 pump relay (vehicles without power distribution center)

Warning 3: *If, after bleeding the system you do not have a firm brake pedal, or if the ABS light on the instrument panel does not go off, or if you have any doubts whatsoever about the effectiveness of the brake system, have it towed to a dealer service department or other repair shop equipped with the necessary tools for bleeding the hydraulic modulator.*

Caution: *Brake fluid will damage paint. Cover all painted surfaces and be careful not to spill fluid during this procedure.*

Bleeding of the main brake system is conventional. Bleeding the hydraulic modulator requires a scan tool. Follow the tool manufacturer's instructions.

Bendix 9

Refer to illustration 3.25

Bendix 9, used in the 1989 through 1991 Jeep Cherokee, is an integrated anti-lock brake system that combines the master cylinder and hydraulic boost unit into one assembly. The unit provides power brake assist as well as the boost needed for ABS operation.

The system uses three channels, one for each front wheel and one for both rear wheels. There are four wheel speed sensors, one at each wheel. The rear wheels are controlled together, using the select low principle.

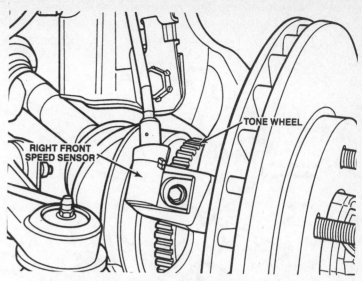

3.24 Right front wheel speed sensor (Bendix 6 shown)

The main brake system in vehicles equipped with Bendix 9 is conventional, with the exception of the hydraulic brake booster. All models use front disc brakes and rear drum brakes.

The Bendix 9 system in Jeeps can be identified by the combined master cylinder/brake booster in the left rear corner of the engine compartment **(see illustration)**.

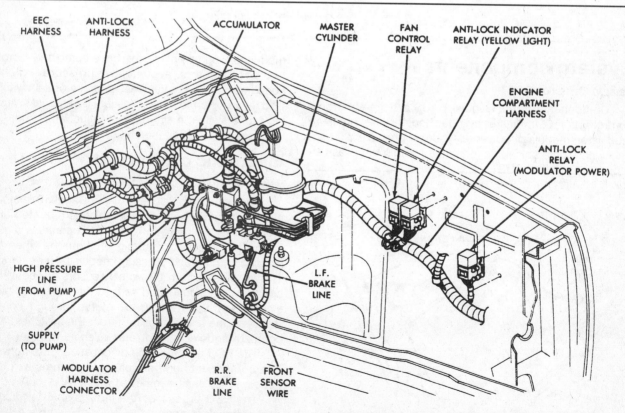

3.25 Hydraulic unit location (Bendix 9)

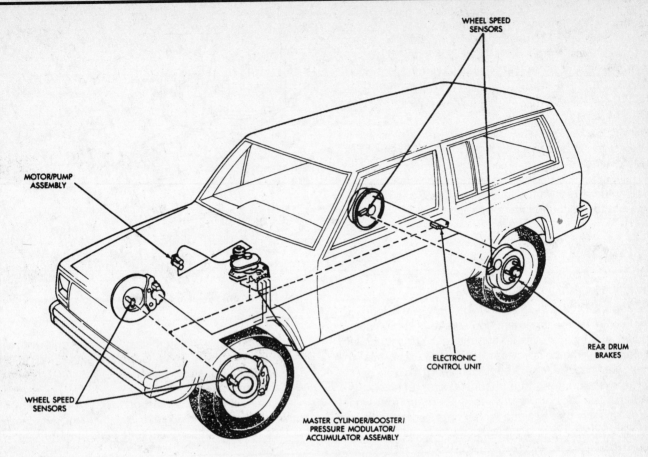

WHEEL SPEED SENSORS

MOTOR/PUMP ASSEMBLY

ELECTRONIC CONTROL UNIT

REAR DRUM BRAKES

WHEEL SPEED SENSORS

MASTER CYLINDER/BOOSTER/ PRESSURE MODULATOR/ ACCUMULATOR ASSEMBLY

3.26 Bendix 9 component location

System components

Refer to illustration 3.26

Components of the Bendix 9 ABS are the electronic control unit (ECU), master cylinder/booster unit, pressure modulator, modulator power relay, boost pressure differential switch, nine solenoids (contained within the pressure modulator), pump and motor, three pump and motor relays, two accumulators, accumulator pressure switch, wheel speed sensors and tone wheels, brake pedal switch, brake fluid level switch, booster pressure differential switch, parking brake switch, main brake warning lamp (red) and ABS warning lamp (amber) **(see illustration)**.

Electronic control unit

Refer to illustrations 3.27 and 3.28

The central component of the Bendix 9 system is the electronic control unit (ECU), which is mounted under the rear seat **(see illustration)**. The ECU contains a microprocessor that receives input signals from the wheel sensors, switches, pump and pressure modulator **(see illustration)**. The AC signals from the wheel sensors are converted into square wave signals and sent to the microprocessor. The signals from the switches are routed through input buffers to isolate the microprocessor from the switches. A voltage comparator detects modulator solenoid voltage.

The ECU also receives diagnostic inputs from the system components and stores any problems as diagnostic codes, which can be retrieved with a scan tool.

The ECU processes the input signals and then uses output signals to control the relays, the amber ABS warning

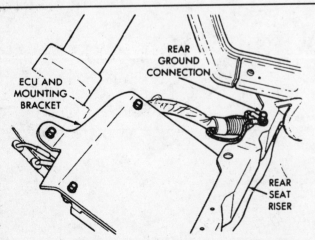

ECU AND MOUNTING BRACKET

REAR GROUND CONNECTION

REAR SEAT RISER

3.27 The Bendix 9 electronic control unit is under the rear seat

Inputs

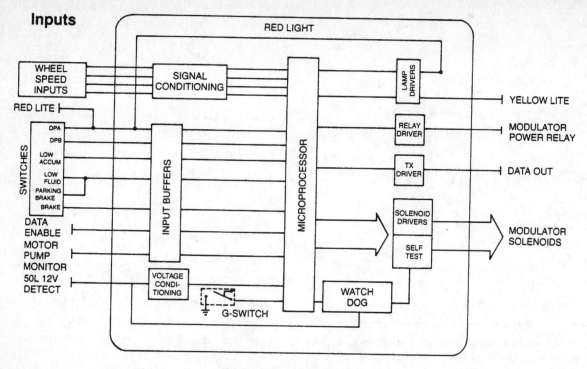

3.28 Bendix 9 ECU schematic

lamp and the solenoids in the pressure modulator. It also uses its "watchdog" (self-test) circuit to check for faults. The watchdog circuit will shut the ABS off if it monitors solenoid voltage less than 6 volts; if two of the decay solenoids are energized for longer than 1 to 2 seconds; or if a build solenoid and decay solenoid in the same hydraulic channel are energized simultaneously.

The ECU contains a g-switch. This is a mercury switch that indicates the rate of vehicle deceleration to the microprocessor.

Master cylinder and booster

Refer to illustration 3.29

The master cylinder and hydraulic booster consists of a single one-piece aluminum casting that contains the pistons and boost valve **(see illustration)**. A one-piece plastic reservoir, mounted on top of the aluminum body, is divided into three chambers, one for each brake circuit and one for the hydraulic boost and ABS.

The boost valve is controlled by the driver through the

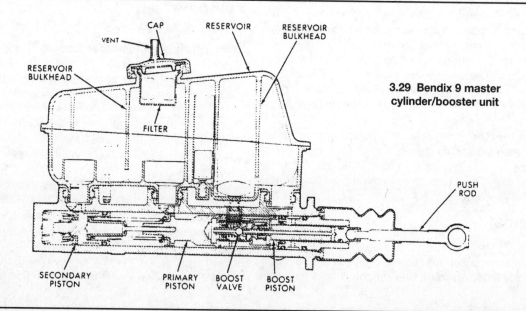

3.29 Bendix 9 master cylinder/booster unit

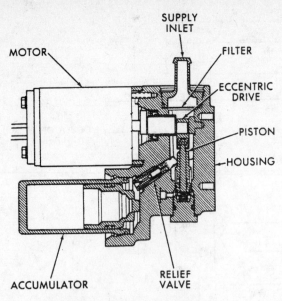

3.30 Bendix 9 pump and motor

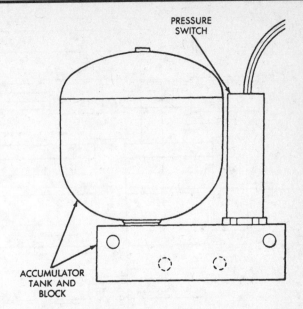

3.31 Bendix 9 accumulator and low pressure switch

brake pedal, opening to allow brake boost or ABS operation only when needed. The necessary high hydraulic pressure is supplied by the pump, which is located on the passenger side of the engine compartment.

A fluid level switch in the reservoir indicates to the ECU if the brake fluid level is low, causing the ECU to illuminate the red warning light.

Hydraulic pressure modulator

The hydraulic pressure modulator is mounted on the master cylinder **(see illustration 3.25)**. The modulator contains nine solenoids, three for each hydraulic channel. One of the solenoids in each channel is an isolation valve, one is an inlet valve and one is an outlet valve.

Boost pump

Refer to illustration 3.30

The pump supplies hydraulic boost for normal braking, as well as the pressure needed for ABS operation **(see illustration)**. It's mounted on the passenger side of the engine compartment. A pressure switch closes when accumulator pressure drops below 1700 psi, which energizes the pump relay, turning on the pump motor. An eccentric drive on the end of the motor shaft operates the pump piston.

The motor runs until pressure reaches approximately 2000 psi, when the switch opens. A relief valve opens if the pump pressure reaches approximately 3000 psi. A thermal fuse shuts off the pump if its operating temperature exceeds 385-degrees F.

Accumulators

Refer to illustration 3.31

There are two accumulators, one inside the booster/master cylinder unit and one mounted next to it **(see**

illustration 3.25). Both reservoirs supply hydraulic pressure for brake boost, as well as for ABS operation. They also act as a reserve source of brake boost in case the pump fails.

Both accumulators are pre-charged with nitrogen gas, and both store brake fluid at a pressure of approximately 1700 to 2000 psi. The smaller accumulator, located inside the booster/master cylinder unit, is a piston type pre-charged to 450 psi. The larger accumulator is a diaphragm type pre-charged to 1000 psi.

A low pressure switch, which is normally grounded to the vehicle body, opens when accumulator pressure drops below 1050 psi **(see illustration)**. This causes the ECU to illuminate the amber warning lamp, then after 20 seconds, the red warning lamp.

Wheel speed sensors and tone wheels

Refer to illustrations 3.32, 3.33 and 3.34

The front wheel speed sensors are attached to the steering knuckles **(see illustration)**. The rear sensors are bolted to the brake backing plate **(see illustration)**. The front and rear tone wheels are mounted at the outboard ends of the axleshafts. The front and rear wheel speed sensors are different; the front sensors have three-tooth pickups and their tone wheels have 117 teeth. The rear sensors have a two-tooth pickup and their tone wheels have 51 teeth.

The sensor air gaps can be checked with a feeler gauge. **Caution:** *Use a non-magnetic (brass) feeler gauge.* The sensor gaps are adjustable. New sensors have a built-in spacer on the sensor face that sets the gap correctly when the sensor is pushed against the tone wheel **(see illustration)**. The rotating tone wheel then peels the spacer material off while the vehicle is in motion, leaving the gap.

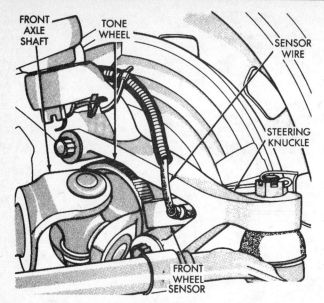

3.32 Front wheel speed sensor (Bendix 9)

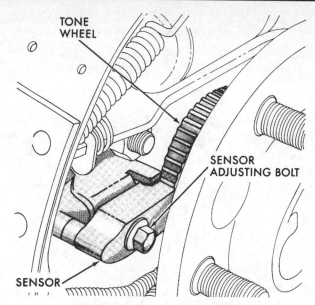

3.33 Rear wheel speed sensor (Bendix 9)

Boost pressure differential switch

Refer to illustration 3.35

This switch is screwed into the pressure modulator **(see illustration)**. The normally-open switch measures the difference between the master cylinder primary system pressure and hydraulic boost pressure. If it detects an incorrect pressure, it closes, grounding through the vehicle body. This causes the ECU to illuminate the red and amber warning lamps.

Brake light switch

Besides operating the brake lights, this switch, mounted to the brake pedal, sends the ECU a signal to indicate that the pedal has been pressed. Anti-lock braking will not happen unless this signal is received.

Parking brake switch

This switch grounds the low fluid circuit when the parking brake is applied, illuminating the red warning lamp. If the vehicle is driven with the parking brake on, the ECU will read this as a low fluid condition, illuminate the amber warning lamp and store a low fluid fault code in memory.

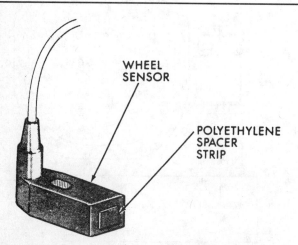

3.34 Replacement wheel speed sensors come with a polyethylene spacer strip attached

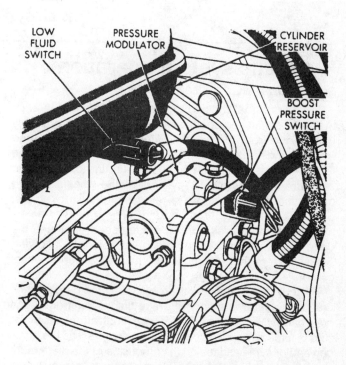

3.35 Bendix 9 fluid level switch and boost pressure differential switch locations

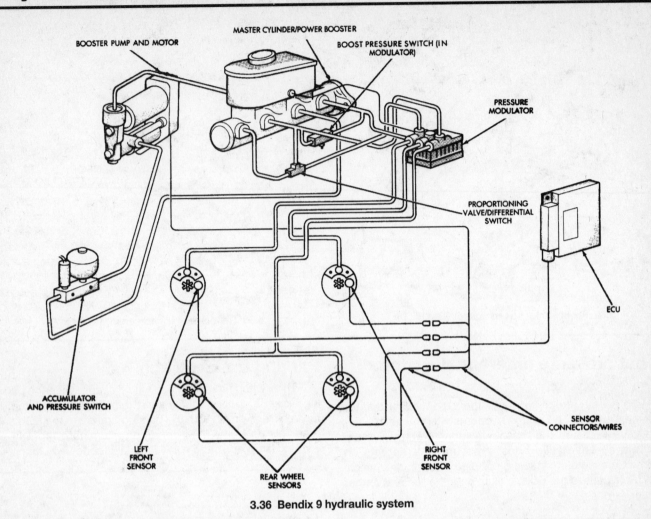

BOOSTER PUMP AND MOTOR

MASTER CYLINDER/POWER BOOSTER

BOOST PRESSURE SWITCH (IN MODULATOR)

PRESSURE MODULATOR

PROPORTIONING VALVE/DIFFERENTIAL SWITCH

ECU

ACCUMULATOR AND PRESSURE SWITCH

SENSOR CONNECTORS/WIRES

LEFT FRONT SENSOR

RIGHT FRONT SENSOR

REAR WHEEL SENSORS

3.36 Bendix 9 hydraulic system

Hydraulic system operation

Refer to illustrations 3.36, 3.37 and 3.38

Under normal braking, the isolation solenoid in each hydraulic channel is open, allowing pedal pressure to flow unimpeded from the master cylinder to the calipers and wheel cylinders **(see illustration)**. During ABS braking, the ECU closes the isolation solenoids, cutting off hydraulic pressure from the master cylinder to the wheels. It then opens the decay solenoid to release hydraulic pressure, preventing the wheel from locking. When the ECU determines that more brake pressure is needed, it closes the decay solenoid and opens the build solenoid, allowing pressure from the accumulators into the caliper or wheel cylinder.

Accumulator pressure is produced by the pump. When the accumulator is empty of brake fluid, the nitrogen gas pre-charge fills the accumulator **(see illustration)**. As brake fluid is forced into the accumulator, it compresses the nitrogen and occupies space on the other side of the diaphragm or piston **(see illustration)**. This pressure is then available for use during brake boost or ABS operation.

At the end of the ABS stop, the ECU holds the build

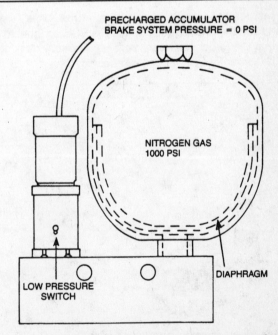

PRECHARGED ACCUMULATOR
BRAKE SYSTEM PRESSURE = 0 PSI

NITROGEN GAS
1000 PSI

DIAPHRAGM

LOW PRESSURE SWITCH

3.37 Brake hydraulic pressure entering the accumulator compresses the gas . . .

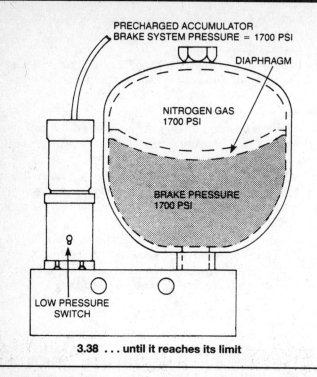

PRECHARGED ACCUMULATOR
BRAKE SYSTEM PRESSURE = 1700 PSI

DIAPHRAGM

NITROGEN GAS
1700 PSI

BRAKE PRESSURE
1700 PSI

LOW PRESSURE
SWITCH

3.38 . . . until it reaches its limit

and isolation valves open briefly to allow the pump to rebuild pressure at the brakes. This prevents the pedal from dropping excessively. Pedal drop may occur after a long stop on a low-friction surface because the ECU shuts off

the isolation valves and restores normal braking. If master cylinder pressure is greater than boost pressure at this point, the pedal will drop.

Electrical system operation

Refer to illustration 3.39

Electronic control unit (ECU)

The ECU receives power for its internal operation from the ignition switch through the ABS IGN and ABS BAT fuses in the fuse block **(see illustration)**.

When the ignition switch is turned to the Start position, power from the switch illuminates the red and amber warning lights. The lights will stay on until the key is released to the Run position. Two seconds after the key is released to the Run position, battery voltage from the ignition switch powers up the ECU. The ECU then operates the solenoids, using the modulator power relay, to check their operation. This causes the brake pedal to pulsate, which will be felt by the driver if the pedal is applied during the check. A clicking sound may also be heard from the solenoids. Battery voltage from the modulator power relay is sent to the yellow light relay, which closes and turns off the light.

The ECU needs two inputs to start ABS operation: the signals from the wheel sensors, indicating partial lockup and the signal from the brake light switch, indicating that the brake pedal has been applied. Until these signals are received, the ABS system is dormant and the main brake

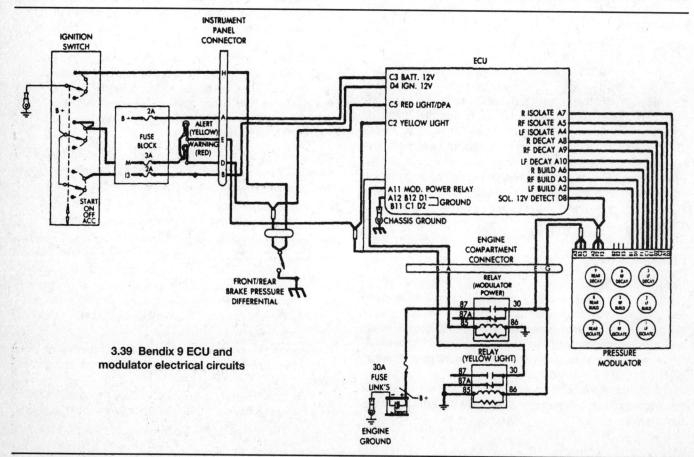

3.39 Bendix 9 ECU and modulator electrical circuits

system functions normally. The ECU does not engage ABS until the vehicle reaches 12 to 15 mph, and disengages it when vehicle speed drops to about 3 mph.

The ECU obtains a reference signal from the wheel speed sensor at the fastest moving wheel. If the wheel sensor signal from one of the wheels drops significantly below this, indicating impending lockup, The ECU starts ABS braking.

Once ABS operation starts, the ECU controls the solenoids and the pump as described in *Hydraulic system operation* above.

Wheel sensors

The wheel sensors send the ECU a variable AC voltage signal as described in Chapter 1.

Solenoids

There are three solenoids per hydraulic channel, one isolation, one decay and one build. During ABS braking, the normally-open isolation solenoids close, cutting off master cylinder pressure from the affected brake. The normally closed decay solenoid opens, releasing hydraulic pressure at the brake. Once sufficient pressure release has occurred and the wheel can be braked again, the decay solenoid closes and the normally-closed build solenoid opens to admit pressure from the accumulators.

Brake light switch

The brake light switch tells the ECU that the brake has been applied.

G-switch

This switch, sometimes called an acceleration switch, is used in Jeeps to let the ECU know how quickly the vehicle is decelerating, which indicates to the ECU how high the coefficient of friction of the road surface is. Ideally, the ECU should be able to vary the duty cycles (open vs. closed time) of the solenoids according to the coefficient of friction. The signals from the wheel speed sensor tell the ECU that ABS braking is necessary, but they don't provide information about the friction of the road surface. The g-switch does.

System service

Diagnosis

Refer to illustration 3.40

Diagnosis requires a Chrysler DRB II or equivalent scan tool. Refer to the scan tool manufacturer's instructions for diagnostic procedures. However, system faults will illuminate the red and yellow warning lights in distinct patterns, which are of some help in determining faults **(see illustration)**.

A number of driving conditions can cause a display of the warning lights when there is actually no ABS problem, as follows:

a) *Long stop on a slick surface (ice or water): The yellow warning light comes on and stays on until the key is turned off and back on.*

b) *Wheelspin due to acceleration: This may cause a wheel speed fault. The yellow warning light comes on and stays on until the key is turned off and back on.*

c) *Sharp deceleration without using the brakes: This may occur in off-road driving, as on a steep hill or in low range. It will cause a brake fault (red light comes on during deceleration).*

d) *Borderline low brake fluid: May cause a flashing red light, and possibly a flashing yellow light, if the vehicle is driven on a bumpy surface or braked hard on a smooth surface.*

e) *Driving above 2-4 mph with the parking brake on: This will cause the red light, yellow light or both to flash. It will occur if the parking brake is accidentally left on or if the parking brake lever is pulled while driving.*

System pressure relief

Due to the high pressure in this system, the system pressure must be relieved before disconnecting any hydraulic lines. Make sure the ignition key is in the Off position, then press the brake pedal firmly as far as it will go 25 to 40 times.

Brake fluid fill procedure

Because the system's two accumulators act as fluid reservoirs, both of them must be filled to get an accurate fluid level. Fill the reservoir on the master cylinder/booster unit to the full line with DOT 3 brake fluid. Start the engine and have an assistant listen for the sound of the booster pump. Pump the brake pedal until the pump starts to run, then stop pumping the pedal and wait for the pump to shut off. Check the fluid again, adding as necessary.

System bleeding

Warning 1: *Wear eye protection when bleeding the brake system. If the fluid comes in contact with your eyes, immediately rinse them with water and seek medical attention.*

Warning 2: *Never use old brake fluid. It contains moisture which can boil, rendering the brake system inoperative.*

Warning 3: *If, after bleeding the system you do not have a firm brake pedal, or if the ABS light on the instrument panel does not go off, or if you have any doubts whatsoever about the effectiveness of the brake system, have it towed to a dealer service department or other repair shop equipped with the necessary tools for bleeding the hydraulic modulator.*

Caution: *Brake fluid will damage paint. Cover all painted surfaces and be careful not to spill fluid during this procedure.*

This procedure is conventional, but the accumulators must be kept full. To do this, periodically switch the ignition

	INDICATOR LIGHT DISPLAY		
CONDITION	INITIAL. DISPLAY (ign in ON pos)	START UP DISPLAY (ign in START pos)	ENG. RUN. DISPLAY (ign in RUN pos)
Normal	Yellow On For 2 Sec	Yellow & Red	No lights
Low Fluid or Parking Brake	Red	Yellow & Red	Yellow & Red Above 2.5 MPH
Low Accumulator	Yellow & Red After 20 sec	Yellow & Red	Yellow & Red
Front to Rear Pressure Differential	Red	Yellow & Red	Yellow & Red Above 3 MPH
Low Boost Pressure	Yellow & Red	Yellow & Red	Yellow & Red
Sensor Faults	Yellow On For 2 Sec	Yellow & Red	Yellow Above 15 MPH
Excess Decay	Yellow On For 2 Sec	Yellow & Red	Yellow
Solenoid Faults	Yellow	Yellow & Red	Yellow
Pump Fault	Yellow On For 2 Sec	Yellow & Red	Red
Low Voltage	Yellow	Yellow & Red	Yellow
Brake Switch	Yellow On For 2 Sec	Yellow & Red	Red During Stop Only
Relay	Yellow	Yellow & Red	Yellow
ECU Self-test	Yellow	Yellow & Red	Yellow

3.40 Lamp sequence - Bendix 9

key to the On position (don't start the engine) during the bleeding procedure. This runs the pump. When the pump shuts off, turn off the key and continue bleeding.

Start by bleeding the master cylinder/boost unit and its internal accumulator. Bleed this unit by loosening the brake line fittings on the side of the modulator one at a time while an assistant holds the brake pedal down with steady pressure. Then bleed the wheel brake lines, starting at the fitting farthest from the master cylinder and working to the closest fitting (right rear, left rear, right front, left front).

Wheel sensor adjustment

Refer to illustration 3.41

Measure the wheel sensor gap with a non-magnetic (brass or plastic) feeler gauge **(see illustration)**. It should be 0.013 to 0.019 inch for front sensors and 0.030 to 0.036 inch for rear sensors. Loosen the wheel sensor adjusting bolt and reposition the sensor as needed.

Component replacement

The following components can be replaced separately:
a) *Master cylinder/booster unit*
b) *External modulator*

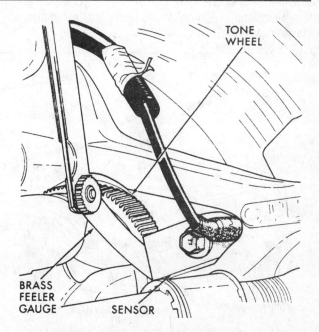

3.41 **Measure wheel speed sensor air gap with a non-magnetic (brass or plastic) feeler gauge**

c) *Pump and motor assembly*

d) *Master cylinder reservoir cap and filter (but not the reservoir)*

e) *Electronic control unit*

f) *Wheel sensors and tone wheels*

Be sure to depressurize the hydraulic system as described above before undoing any lines.

Bendix 10

Refer to illustration 3.42

Bendix 10 is used in some 1990 through 1993 Chrysler cars, including the New Yorker, Imperial and Park Avenue, and the 1991 and later Dodge Monaco ES. It's also used in 1991 through 1993 Chrysler Corporation minivans, as well as the 1991 and 1992 Eagle Premier.

The system is very similar to Bendix 9, but uses four isolation solenoids instead of three to reduce excessive pedal pulsation during anti-lock braking. This gives it a total of ten solenoids, hence the name Bendix 10.

The system uses three channels, one for each front wheel and one for both rear wheels. There are four wheel speed sensors, one at each wheel. The rear wheels are controlled together, using the select low principle.

The main brake system in vehicles equipped with Bendix 10 is conventional, with the exception of the hydraulic brake booster. The main brake hydraulic system is split diagonally, with one front brake and the diagonally opposite rear brake on each circuit.

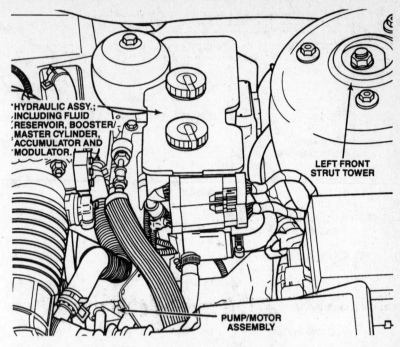

HYDRAULIC ASSY.; INCLUDING FLUID RESERVOIR, BOOSTER, MASTER CYLINDER, ACCUMULATOR AND MODULATOR.

LEFT FRONT STRUT TOWER

PUMP/MOTOR ASSEMBLY

3.42 Bendix 10 hydraulic assembly and pump

The Bendix 10 system can be identified by the combined master cylinder/brake booster in the left rear corner of the engine compartment **(see illustration)**.

System components

Refer to illustration 3.43

Components of the Bendix 10 ABS are the electronic control unit, which Chrysler refers to as the Controller, Anti-lock Brake (CAB), hydraulic assembly (which includes the

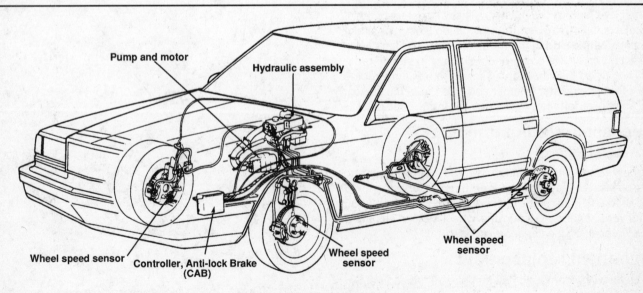

Pump and motor

Hydraulic assembly

Wheel speed sensor

Controller, Anti-lock Brake (CAB)

Wheel speed sensor

Wheel speed sensor

3.43 Bendix 10 component locations

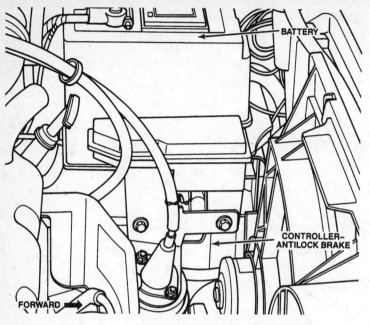

3.44 Bendix 10 Controller, Anti-lock Brake (CAB)

pump and motor, four wheel speed sensors and tone wheels, two proportioning valves for the rear brakes, boost pressure transducer, primary pressure transducer, differential pressure switch, three relays (for the pump, solenoids and warning lamp, main brake warning lamp (red) and ABS warning lamp (amber). The major components are located in the engine compartment (see illustration).

Controller, Anti-lock Brake (CAB)

Refer to illustrations 3.44 and 3.45

The central component of the Bendix 10 system is the electronic control unit, which Chrysler calls the Controller, Anti-lock Brake (CAB). It's mounted under the battery tray in the engine compartment (see illustration). The ECU contains a microprocessor that receives input signals from the wheel sensors, switches and transducers (see illustration). The ECU also receives diagnostic inputs from the system components and stores any problems as diagnostic codes, which can be retrieved with a scan tool through the diagnostic connector. Fault codes are stored in non-volatile memory. They can be cleared with a scan tool or by turning the ignition on and off 50 times.

The ECU processes the input signals and then uses output signals to control the relays, the amber and red warning lamps and the solenoids in the pressure modulator.

master cylinder, booster unit, pressure modulator and brake fluid level switch), ten solenoids (contained within the hydraulic unit), two accumulators (one external and one within the pump assembly), accumulator pressure switch,

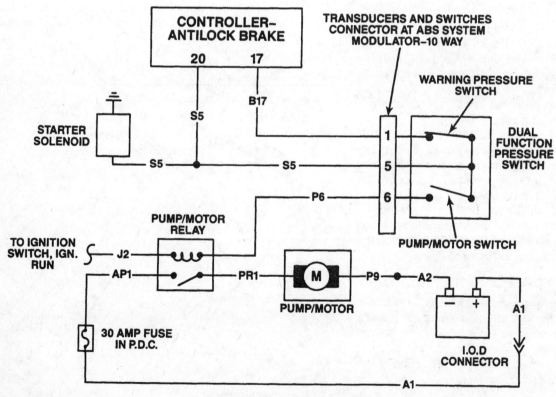

3.45 Bendix 10 ABS switch circuits

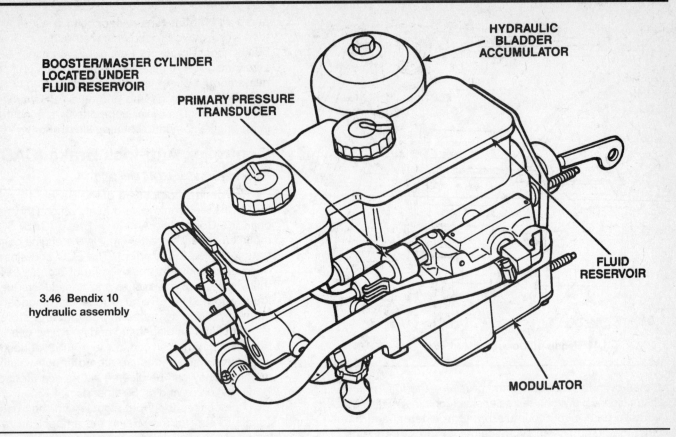

BOOSTER/MASTER CYLINDER
LOCATED UNDER
FLUID RESERVOIR

PRIMARY PRESSURE
TRANSDUCER

HYDRAULIC
BLADDER
ACCUMULATOR

FLUID
RESERVOIR

MODULATOR

3.46 Bendix 10
hydraulic assembly

Hydraulic assembly and pump

Refer to illustrations 3.46 and 3.47

The hydraulic assembly consists of a single one-piece aluminum casting that contains the master cylinder pistons and boost valve **(see illustration)**. A one-piece plastic reservoir is mounted on top of the aluminum body. The primary pressure transducer and bladder accumulator are mounted alongside the assembly and the modulator is mounted beneath it.

The boost valve is controlled by the driver through the brake pedal, opening to allow brake boost or ABS operation only when needed. The necessary high hydraulic pressure is supplied by the pump, which is located just forward of the hydraulic unit **(see illustration)**.

A fluid level switch in the reservoir indicates to the CAB if the brake fluid level is low, causing the CAB to illuminate the red warning light.

Hydraulic pressure modulator

The hydraulic pressure modulator is mounted under the master cylinder **(see illustration 3.46)**. The modulator contains ten solenoids. There is an isolation solenoid for each of the four wheels, plus an inlet valve and an outlet valve for each of the three ABS hydraulic channels.

Pump and motor

The pump supplies hydraulic boost for normal braking, as well as the pressure needed for ABS operation **(see illustration 3.47)**. It's mounted on the passenger side of the engine compartment. A pressure switch (one of two switches in the dual-function pressure switch) closes when

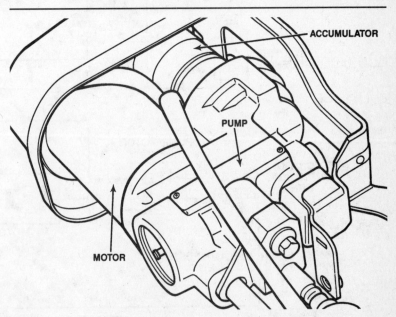

ACCUMULATOR

PUMP

MOTOR

3.47 Bendix 10 accumulator and pump

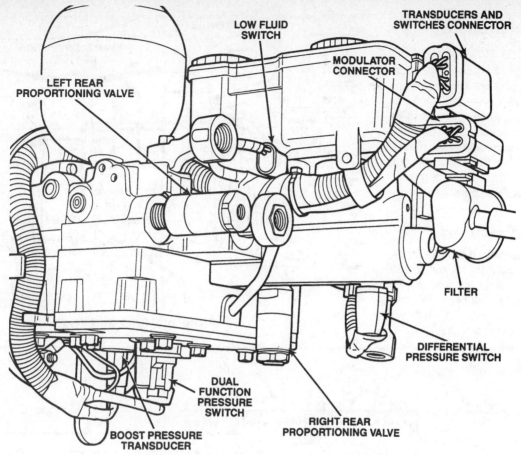

LEFT REAR PROPORTIONING VALVE

LOW FLUID SWITCH

TRANSDUCERS AND SWITCHES CONNECTOR

MODULATOR CONNECTOR

FILTER

DIFFERENTIAL PRESSURE SWITCH

DUAL FUNCTION PRESSURE SWITCH

BOOST PRESSURE TRANSDUCER

RIGHT REAR PROPORTIONING VALVE

3.48 Bendix 10 hydraulic assembly - bottom view

accumulator pressure drops below 1600 psi. This grounds the pump relay, turning on the pump motor. An eccentric drive on the end of the motor shaft operates the pump piston.

The motor runs until pressure reaches approximately 2000 psi, when the switch opens and the motor shuts off.

Accumulators

There are two accumulators, one inside the pump housing and one mounted next to the master cylinder reservoir (see illustrations 3.47 and 3.46). Both accumulators supply hydraulic pressure for brake boost, as well as for ABS operation. They also act as a reserve source of brake boost in case the pump fails.

Both accumulators are pre-charged with nitrogen gas, and both store brake fluid at a pressure of approximately 1700 to 2000 psi. The smaller accumulator, located inside the pump housing, is a piston type pre-charged to 460 psi. The larger accumulator is a diaphragm type pre-charged to 1000 psi.

A warning pressure switch, which is part of the dual function pressure switch, is normally closed, grounding pin 17 of the CAB. The switch opens when accumulator pressure drops below 1000 psi. When the CAB senses the resulting voltage at pin 17, it shuts off the ABS and lights both the red

and amber warning lamps. If the low-pressure condition continues for two minutes, the CAB stores a fault code.

Wheel speed sensors and tone wheels

The front wheel speed sensors are attached to the steering knuckles and look like those used with Bendix 6 (see illustration 3.24). The rear sensors are bolted to the brake backing plate. The front and rear tone wheels are mounted at the outboard ends of the axleshafts. The sensor gaps are not adjustable.

Pressure transducers

Refer to illustration 3.48

There are two pressure transducers. The primary pressure transducer, which measures pressure in the master cylinder primary circuit, is mounted on the left side of the master cylinder (see illustration 3.46). The boost pressure transducer, which measures boost servo pressure, is mounted to the underside of the modulator (see illustration). Both transducers produce variable voltage signals, ranging from 0.25 volts to 5 volts, in response to hydraulic pressure changes. If these signals differ excessively, the CAB shuts off the ABS.

Differential pressure switch

This switch compares hydraulic pressure in the primary and secondary circuits and shuts off the ABS or lights the brake warning lamp, depending on model, if it exceeds 300 psi. It's mounted to the underside of the master cylinder body **(see illustration 3.48)**. Both pressure transducers and the differential pressure switch share a connector.

Brake light switch

Besides operating the brake lights, this switch, mounted to the brake pedal, sends the CAB a signal to indicate that the pedal has been pressed. Anti-lock braking will not happen unless this signal is received.

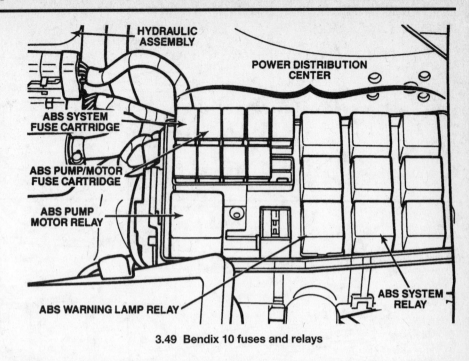

3.49 Bendix 10 fuses and relays

3.50 Bendix 10 hydraulic schematic

Fluid level switch

This switch grounds the low fluid circuit when the fluid level is low, illuminating the red warning lamp. If the vehicle is being driven above 3 mph when this occurs, the CAB will illuminate the amber warning lamp and deactivate the ABS. If the vehicle is not moving, the ABS warning light will not illuminate.

Relays and fuses

Refer to illustration 3.49

The relays and fuses are mounted in the power distribution center near the hydraulic assembly **(see illustration)**.

Hydraulic system operation

Refer to illustration 3.50

Under normal braking, the isolation solenoid in each hydraulic channel is open, allowing pedal pressure to flow unimpeded from the master cylinder to the calipers and wheel cylinders **(see illustration)**. The build and decay solenoids are closed. During ABS braking, the ECU closes the isolation solenoids, cutting off hydraulic pressure from the master cylinder to the wheels. It then opens the decay solenoid to release hydraulic pressure, preventing the wheel from locking. When the ECU determines that more brake pressure is needed, it closes the decay solenoid and opens the build solenoid, allowing pressure from the accumulators into the caliper or wheel cylinder.

The accumulators work in the same way as the Bendix 9 system described earlier in this Chapter.

A check valve between the two accumulators prevents the external accumulator from releasing any stored fluid in case a brake line is loosened without depressurizing the system (this doesn't prevent the internal accumulator from releasing its fluid, however).

Three check valves in the booster servo circuit open if the driver releases the pedal while the ABS is in the hold cycle. This allows high pressure in the wheel brakes to return to the booster servo, so the brakes aren't unintentionally applied by the ABS.

Electrical system operation

Electronic control unit (ECU)

The CAB receives power for its internal operation from the ignition switch through the system relay when it is on the Run or On position. The CAB grounds the system relay coil through pin 57, closing the relay so it can supply battery power to pins 47 and 50 (solenoid operation). As this happens, the system relay also closes the anti-lock warning lamp relay, causing the lamp to go out.

The CAB performs an electrical self-test immediately after startup. The anti-lock warning lamp will come for one to two seconds, then go out if the system is working normally.

When the vehicle reaches a speed of about 3 mph, it operates the solenoids to test them. If the driver is pressing the brake at this time, the CAB will skip the test.

The CAB obtains a reference signal from the wheel speed sensor at the fastest moving wheel. If the wheel sensor signal from one of the wheels drops significantly below this, indicating impending lockup, The ECU starts ABS braking.

Once ABS operation starts, the CAB controls the solenoids and the pump as described in *Hydraulic system operation* above.

Wheel sensors

The wheel sensors send the ECU a variable AC voltage signal as described in Chapter 1.

Solenoids

Each of the three hydraulic channels (left front, right front and both rear brakes) has one build solenoid and one decay solenoid. Each wheel brake has an isolation solenoid, for a total of four. During ABS braking, the normally-open isolation solenoids close, cutting off master cylinder pressure from the affected brake. The normally closed decay solenoid opens, releasing hydraulic pressure at the brake. Once sufficient pressure release has occurred and the wheel can be braked again, the decay solenoid closes and the normally closed build solenoid opens to admit pressure from the accumulators.

Brake light switch

The brake light switch tells the ECU that the brake has been applied.

System service

Diagnosis

Diagnosis requires a Chrysler DRB II or equivalent scan tool. The DRB II displays errors in words, such as "wheel speed sensor." Refer to the scan tool manufacturer's instructions for diagnostic procedures. The diagnostic connector is blue, with six pins, and is located below the dash to the left of the steering column.

System pressure relief

Due to the high pressure in this system, the system pressure must be relieved before disconnecting any hydraulic lines. Make sure the ignition key is in the Off position, then press the brake pedal firmly as far as it will go 25 to 40 times.

Brake fluid fill procedure

Because the system's accumulator acts as a fluid reservoir, it must be discharged to get an accurate fluid level. Depressurize the system as described above, then fill the fluid reservoir in the normal way.

System bleeding

Warning 1: *Wear eye protection when bleeding the brake system. If the fluid comes in contact with your eyes, immediately rinse them with water and seek medical attention.*

Warning 2: *Never use old brake fluid. It contains moisture which can boil, rendering the brake system inoperative.*

Warning 3: *If, after bleeding the system you do not have a firm brake pedal, or if the ABS light on the instrument panel does not go off, or if you have any doubts whatsoever about the effectiveness of the brake system, have it towed to a dealer service department or other repair shop equipped with the necessary tools for bleeding the hydraulic modulator.*

Caution: *Brake fluid will damage paint. Cover all painted surfaces and be careful not to spill fluid during this procedure.*

This procedure is conventional, but the accumulators must be kept full. To do this, periodically switch the ignition key to the On position (don't start the engine) during the bleeding procedure. This runs the pump. When the pump shuts off, turn off the key and continue bleeding.

Start by bleeding the master cylinder/boost unit and its internal accumulator. Bleed this unit by loosening the brake line fittings on the side of the modulator one at a time while an assistant holds the brake pedal down with steady pressure. Then bleed the wheel brake lines, starting at the fitting farthest from the master cylinder and working to the closest fitting (right rear, left rear, right front, left front).

Wheel sensors

The wheel sensors can be replaced separately, but the tone wheels can't. The front tone wheels are part of the outboard CV joints; the rear tone wheels are part of the hubs. The wheel sensors are not adjustable.

Bendix Mecatronic II

The Bendix Mecatronic II system was introduced on the 1995 Ford Contour and Mercury Mystique. Traction control is optional.

The system is a non-integrated four-channel type. It uses a conventional main brake system, together with a hydraulic unit installed between the master cylinder and the four wheel brakes. The hydraulic unit consists of a hydraulic actuator, an ABS brake pressure pump, an electronic module with built-in relay box, and two pressure-control relief valves. Braking at each of the four wheels is controlled by separate solenoids in the hydraulic actuator. If wheel lock-up is detected at a wheel when the vehicle speed is above 3 mph, the valve opens, releasing pressure to the affected brake, until the wheel regains a rotational speed corresponding to the speed of the vehicle. The cycle can be repeated many times a second. In the event of a fault in the ABS system, the conventional brake system is not affected.

The traction control system uses the basic ABS system, with an additional pump and valves installed in the hydraulic modulator. If wheelspin due to acceleration is detected at one of the drive wheels at a speed below 30 mph, one of the valves opens, allowing the pump to pressurize the affected brake and slow the spinning wheel. This has the effect of transferring torque to the wheel with the most traction. At the same time, the throttle plate is closed slightly, to reduce the torque from the engine. At speeds above 30 mph, the TCS operates by throttle plate adjustment only, to prevent instability that might occur if only one drive wheel brake were applied.

System service

Precautions

While working on a Mecatronic system, do not test any part of the system with a 12-volt test light, and be careful not to let any of the wires in the system short to anything.

Diagnosis

Diagnosis requires a scan tool; refer to the tool manufacturer's instructions. The diagnostic connector is located on the left front suspension tower.

Note: *Don't spin a wheel by hand with the ignition switch On; this may set a false trouble code for the speed sensor on the wheel that you spun.*

Bleeding

Warning 1: *Wear eye protection when bleeding the brake system. If the fluid comes in contact with your eyes, immediately rinse them with water and seek medical attention.*

Warning 2: *Never use old brake fluid. It contains moisture which can boil, rendering the brake system inoperative.*

Warning 3: *If, after bleeding the system you do not have a firm brake pedal, or if the ABS light on the instrument panel does not go off, or if you have any doubts whatsoever about the effectiveness of the brake system, have it towed to a dealer service department or other repair shop equipped with the necessary tools for bleeding the hydraulic modulator.*

Caution: *Brake fluid will damage paint. Cover all painted surfaces and be careful not to spill fluid during this procedure.*

Bleeding is conventional, with no special ABS steps required. The hydraulic system is split diagonally (one front brake and the diagonally opposite rear brake on the same circuit). Bleed one hydraulic circuit at a time.

Wheel speed sensors

The sensors can be replaced separately. The sensor gaps are not adjustable.

Caution: *Be sure the ignition switch is in the Off position before disconnecting the wheel speed sensor's electrical connector.*

Chapter 4
Bosch systems

Bosch 2

Bosch 2S ABS is a non-integrated system first used in Europe in 1978, and in North America (by BMW and Mercedes) beginning in 1985. It has been used by a number of auto manufacturers, including Audi, BMW, Chrysler, Ford, General Motors, Isuzu, Nissan, Porsche, Subaru, Suzuki and Toyota. The Bosch 2 system comes in several variations, in three-channel and four-channel versions. These include Bosch 2S, 2E, 2U and 2S Micro.

Vehicles whose main brake system is separated into front and rear hydraulic circuits use the three-channel version, with one hydraulic channel at each front wheel and a single channel for both rear wheels. Each front wheel has its own wheel speed sensor. On some models, there's a separate speed sensor for each rear wheel. On others, a single speed sensor in the differential monitors both rear wheels.

Vehicles whose main brake system has diagonally separated hydraulic circuits (that is, one front brake and the diagonally opposite rear brake on each circuit) use a four-channel ABS.

System components

Refer to illustrations 4.1 and 4.2

Components of the Bosch 2S ABS are the control unit, hydraulic modulator, solenoids, pump and accumulator (contained within the hydraulic modulator), wheel speed sensors and tone wheels, solenoid relay, pump relay, brake light switch and ABS warning lamp **(see illustration)**. Bosch 2 systems can be identified by the hydraulic modulator **(see illustration)**.

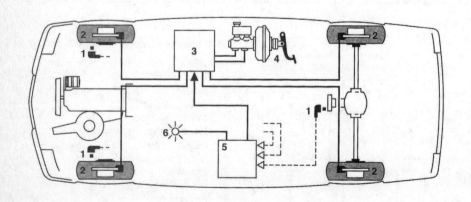

4.1 Bosch 2S ABS component locations

1	Wheel speed sensors	4	Master cylinder/power booster
2	Wheel brakes	5	Electronic control unit
3	Hydraulic modulator	6	ABS warning lamp

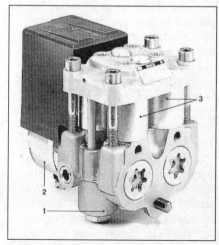

4.2 Bosch 2S hydraulic modulator

1. Accumulator
2. Return pump
3. Solenoids

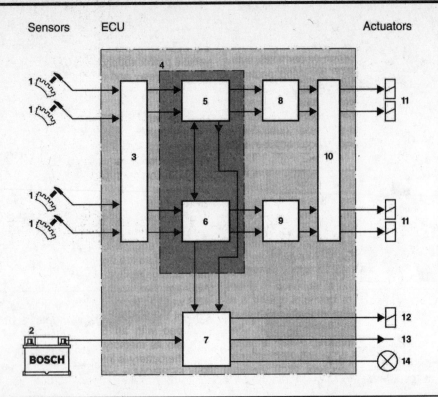

Sensors   ECU   Actuators

4.3 Bosch 2S electronic control unit schematic

1   Wheel speed sensors
2   Battery
3   Input circuit
4   Digital controller
5   LSI circuit no. 1
6   LSI circuit no. 2
7   Voltage stabilizer/fault memory
8   Output circuit no. 1
9   Output circuit no. 2
10 Output drivers
11 Solenoids
12 Safety relay
13 Stabilized battery voltage
14 ABS warning lamp

Electronic control unit

Refer to illustrations 4.3 and 4.4

The central component of the Bosch 2 system is the control unit, which is mounted in various locations, depending on model. The control unit contains an input circuit, two identical digital LSI circuits, a combination voltage stabilizer/trouble code memory, two output circuits and a solenoid driver. Each of the LSI circuits receives input signals from two of the four wheel sensors **(see illustration)**. Separating the signals into two circuits allows faster processing.

The wheel sensors enter the input circuit, where they are converted into analog square-wave signals and amplified. The square-wave signals are sent to the digital controller, where they are converted into digital signals (10-bit "words"). In the process, interference from rough roads and suspension movement is filtered out. The converted signals enter the arithmetic unit, where they are analyzed and converted into the operating signals that control the solenoids **(see illustration)**.

The ECU's monitoring circuits, one in each LSI circuit, check all of the ABS electrical components for proper operation. The monitoring circuit checks for such things as illogical signal combinations and signal durations. When a monitoring circuit detects an error, it switches off the ABS, sets a diagnostic code and illuminates the ABS warning lamp.

The ECU's output circuits use power transistors as switches to control the ABS solenoids through the solenoid driver, which produces signals with enough current to operate the solenoids.

The voltage stabilizer/fault memory keeps the ABS voltage within specific limits, and shuts the system off if it drops too low. It also stores diagnostic trouble codes and controls the ABS warning lamp.

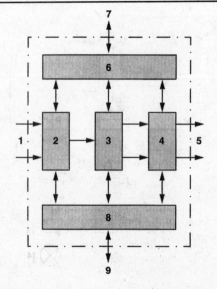

4.4 Electronic control unit LSI circuit

1   Wheel speed sensor inputs (from input circuit)
2   Input stage (frequency control loop)
3   Arithmetic unit
4   Controller logic
5   Valve control command to the output circuit
6   Data transmission
7   Interface
8   Monitoring circuit
9   Error signal

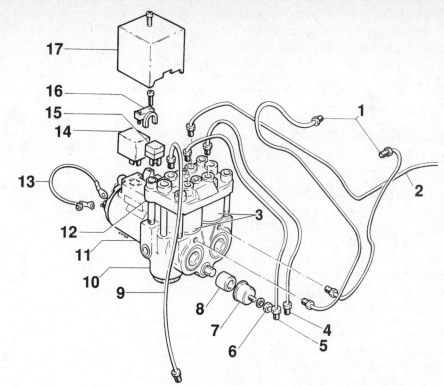

4.5 Bosch 2S hydraulic modulator as installed in an Audi 5000

1. Brake lines to master cylinder
2. Right front brake line
3. Solenoids
4. Left rear brake line
5. Right rear brake line
6. Self-locking nut
7. Retainer
8. Rubber mount
9. Left front brake line
10. Accumulator
11. Return pump
12. Hydraulic modulator
13. Ground lead
14. Solenoid relay
15. Return pump relay
16. Wiring retainer
17. Relay cover

Hydraulic modulator

Refer to illustrations 4.5 and 4.6

The hydraulic modulator is mounted near the master cylinder and connected to it by hydraulic lines **(see illustrations)**. It contains the solenoids (one for each hydraulic channel), two accumulators (one for each hydraulic circuit) and pump.

The accumulators collect brake fluid that is released from the hydraulic circuits during the release phase of ABS operation. On vehicles with a front-rear split between the hydraulic circuits, there is an accumulator for the front circuit and one for the rear. On vehicles with a diagonal split between the circuits, there is an accumulator for the left front right/rear circuit and another for the right front/left rear circuit.

The pump collects fluid from the accumulators and returns it to the master cylinder.

The solenoids are three-position types, which move to the hold position or the release position as commanded by the ECU. There are either three or four solenoids, one for each hydraulic channel.

Wheel speed sensors

Refer to illustrations 4.7 and 4.8

Bosch 2 wheel speed sensors are available in two basic types, called DS2 and DS3 **(see illustration)**. Shapes and mounting fittings vary according to the vehicle they're

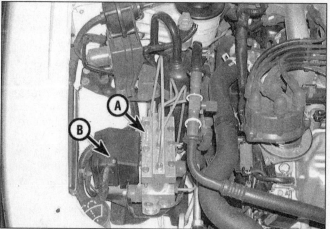

4.6 Bosch 2U hydraulic modulator (A) as installed in the Nissan Quest/Mercury Villager and relays (B)

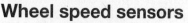

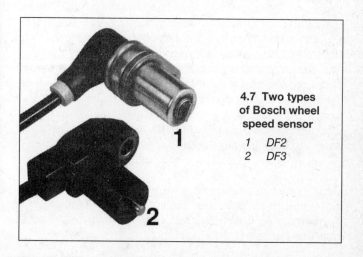

4.7 Two types of Bosch wheel speed sensor

1. DF2
2. DF3

installed in. The pole pin comes in chisel, rhombus and round shapes, and may be mounted so the signal pickup from the tone wheel is axial (outside the outer circumference of the tone wheel) or radial (alongside the outer circumference of the tone wheel) **(see illustration)**.

The wheel sensors send the CAB a variable AC voltage signal as described in Chapter 1.

Brake light switch

The brake light switch tells the CAB that the brake has been applied.

Deceleration switch

This switch, sometimes called a g-switch, is used in some Toyota installations to let the ECU know how quickly the vehicle is decelerating, which indicates to the ECU how high the coefficient of friction of the road surface is. Ideally, the ECU should be able to vary the duty cycles (open vs. closed time) of the solenoids according to the coefficient of friction. The signals from the wheel speed sensor tell the ECU that ABS braking is necessary, but they don't provide information about the friction of the road surface. The deceleration switch does.

The switch consists of two mercury switches, contained in a single housing. One of the mercury switches closes during acceleration and the other during deceleration. This change in inputs to the ECU signals it to adjust the duty cycle of the ABS solenoids.

Lateral acceleration switch

This switch is used in 1986 through 1989 Corvettes. It's similar to the deceleration switch, but the two mercury switches within the switch housing are mounted sideways. On a hard right turn (exceeding 0.6 g), one of the normally closed switches opens; the other switch opens in a left turn exceeding 0.6 g. Either of these signals tells the ECU to adjust its ABS strategy for the driving conditions.

Lateral accelerometer

This sensor is used in Corvette models equipped with ABS/ASR. It contains a micromachined silicon beam with a weight on the end. Positioned on the beam is a permanent magnet, which is located directly above a Hall-effect sensor. On a hard turn in either direction, the beam deflects under the g-force, which moves the magnet away from the Hall sensor, changing its electrical capacitance. The sensor receives a 5-volt reference signal from the ECU, then returns it to a ground terminal at the ECU. The sensor also sends a signal current to the ECU. This signal current is changed as the magnet on the flexible beam moves away from and back toward the Hall sensor.

A defective lateral accelerometer can produce minor brake pedal pulsations during normal driving. However, more common causes of this problem, such as warped brake discs, should be checked before blaming the accelerometer. If it is replaced, keep in mind that it's delicate and can be ruined if you drop it.

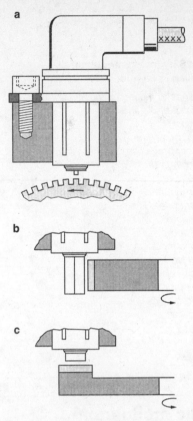

4.8 Bosch wheel speed sensor designs

a)   *Chisel-type pole pin with radial installation and radial signal pick-up*
b)   *Rhombus-type pole pin with axial installation and radial signal pick-up*
c)   *Round pole pin with radial installation and axial pick-up*

System operation

Refer to illustration 4.9

On startup and again when the ignition is turned off, the ECU performs a self-test to check the system for faults. To check the monitoring circuit, it simulates faults and checks its response.

During ABS braking, the ECU controls hydraulic pressure at the brakes by cycling the solenoids in the HCU four to 10 times per second, depending on the conditions. The cycles occur in three stages: pressure hold, pressure reduction and pressure build.

Hold cycle

Under normal braking, the solenoid in each hydraulic channel is open, allowing pedal pressure to flow unimpeded from the master cylinder to the calipers and wheel cylinders **(see illustration)**.

When a wheel begins to lock, the impending lockup is detected by the ECU. The ECU then applies a holding current (50 percent of full current) to the solenoid, which closes the inlet valve in the wheels' hydraulic channel, cutting off

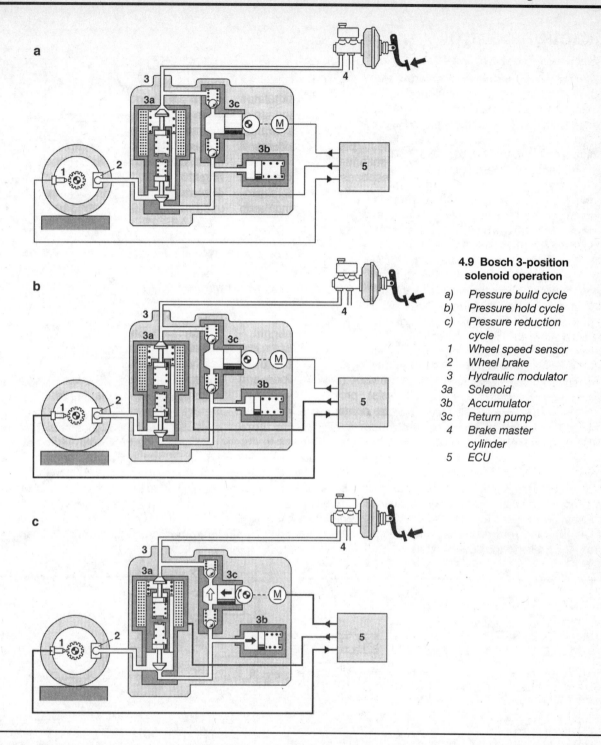

4.9 Bosch 3-position solenoid operation

a) Pressure build cycle
b) Pressure hold cycle
c) Pressure reduction cycle
1 Wheel speed sensor
2 Wheel brake
3 Hydraulic modulator
3a Solenoid
3b Accumulator
3c Return pump
4 Brake master cylinder
5 ECU

pedal pressure to the wheel. The outlet passage in the solenoid remains closed. As a result, hydraulic pressure at the wheel remains steady, neither increasing nor decreasing. This is called the hold or isolation cycle.

Reduction cycle

If the lockup condition continues, the ECU applies full current to the solenoid. This opens the outlet passage, releasing hydraulic pressure to the accumulator or back to

the master cylinder reservoir. Since the inlet passage is still closed, hydraulic pressure at the wheel is reduced.

Build cycle

Once the lockup condition ceases and the wheel starts to turn at a rate the CAB considers acceptable, the ECU returns the solenoid to its open position. The pump returns fluid from the accumulator to the master cylinder, restoring brake pedal height that was lost during the reduction cycle.

Traction control

Refer to illustrations 4.10 and 4.11

The 1986 and later Corvette and some Cadillac models equipped with Bosch 2 ABS also use traction control, which Bosch calls Acceleration Slip Regulation (ASR). The combined ABS and traction control system is called ABS/ASR. In its simplest form, ASR controls the throttle valve opening through the engine management system, and uses an expanded version of the ABS to apply the brake at one or both drive wheels. This system is called ASR2-DKB **(see illustration)**. The "2" means the system is used with Bosch 2 ABS. The "DK" stands for the German word *Drosselklappe* (throttle valve) and the "B" stands for *Bremsen* (brakes).

If a drive wheel begins to spin due to acceleration, the signal voltage from the wheel speed sensor will increase relative to the other sensors. The ECU monitors the wheel sensor signals and activates the traction control system when this occurs.

During the time ASR is not in use, a charging pump fills the accumulator with fluid **(see illustration)**. When a spinning drive wheel is detected, the ECU switches the pilot valve into ABS mode, allowing the pre-charged accumulators to feed hydraulic pressure to the brake at the spinning wheel. Braking at the wheel is controlled by the ABS solenoid, using the same three cycles (hold, release and pressure) as it uses for ABS. While ASR is in operation, the ECU runs the return pump, which returns fluid released from the brake to the accumulator.

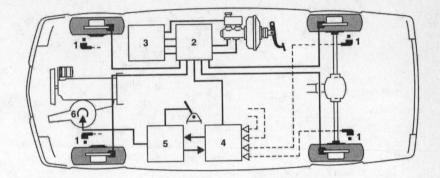

4.10 Bosch ASR2-DKB anti-lock brake system with traction control

1. *Wheel speed sensor*
2. *ABS hydraulic modulator*
3. *Traction control hydraulic modulator*
4. *ABS/ASR electronic control unit*
5. *Engine management system electronic control unit*
6. *Throttle valve*

A more sophisticated version of ASR retards ignition timing, cuts off ignition pulses (spark) and shuts off fuel injectors to reduce engine power. It starts by retarding the timing, and if this isn't enough, shuts off spark at the plugs. To prevent unburned fuel mixture from passing into the catalytic converter, the system shuts off fuel injectors in synchronization with the spark shutoff. Shutting off spark provides a quicker response than cutting off the fuel pulses alone would do. When traction control is no longer needed, spark and fuel are restored. Ignition timing is gradually returned from retard setting to normal setting for a smooth transition.

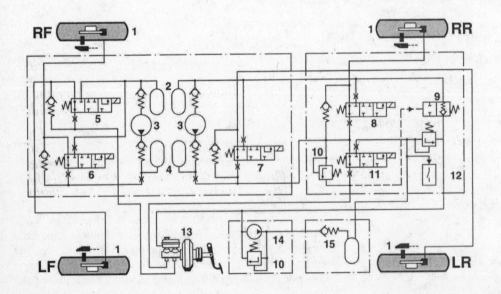

4.11 Bosch ABS/ASR hydraulic system schematic

1. *Drive wheels*
2. *Accumulator*
3. *Return pump*
4. *Damper*
5. *Solenoid*
6. *Solenoid*
7. *Solenoid*
8. *Solenoid*
9. *Load valve*
10. *Pressure limiting valve*
11. *ASR pilot valve*
12. *Pressure switch*
13. *Brake master cylinder*
14. *Charging pump*
15. *Accumulator*
RF. *Right front*
LF. *Left front*
RR. *Right rear*
LR. *Left rear*

System service

Diagnosis

1   Diagnostic code retrieval in Bosch 2 systems varies according to vehicle manufacturer. On early models, a dedicated ABS scanner, available only to dealers, is required to retrieve diagnostic information. If you're using a scan tool on later models (2S, 2U), follow the tool manufacturer's instructions to retrieve codes. In some vehicles, codes can be retrieved by flashing the ABS warning light. There are many different methods of doing this; they vary not only by manufacturer, but from model to model within each manufacturer's vehicle line. Some typical examples follow.

Ford

2   The Bosch 2U system, used in the 1993 and 1994 Mercury Villager and 1994 and 1995 Mustang, allows code retrieval using the flash method.

3   Drive the vehicle above 20 mph for at least one minute. Stop the vehicle and turn the engine off.

Mercury Villager

Refer to illustrations 4.12, 4.13 and 4.14

4   If you're working on a Villager, ground terminal L on the data link connector (DLC) **(see illustration)**. With terminal L grounded, turn the ignition key to On (but don't start the engine). After 3.2 seconds, the ABS warning light will begin by flashing a code 12. The code is determined by counting the number of ON and OFF flashes **(see illustration)**. The sequence always begins with a 3.2 second off period, followed by a flash, then a 1.2 second off period, then two flashes. This "code 12" (the start code, not a trouble code)

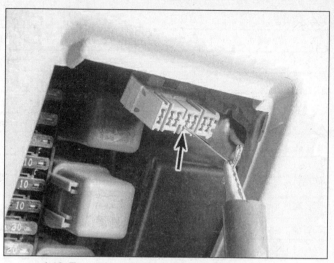

4.12 To retrieve ABS trouble codes on a Nissan Quest/Mercury Villager, ground the L terminal (arrow) on the data link connector

is followed by another 3.2 second off period, then the trouble codes are displayed, in the order in which they were stored, starting with the latest stored code. All codes are two-digit codes, so the first flash(es) indicate the tens place, followed by a longer delay, followed by the single-digit flash(es). For example, a sequence of four flashes, then a pulse, followed by a sequence of five flashes, would indicate a code 45. Count the number of flashes of the ABS light, then refer to the accompanying table **(see illustration on next page)**.

5   To clear the trouble codes after repairing the problem, unground terminal L (with the ignition still On). Ground terminal L three more times within 10 seconds, with each grounding period lasting at least one second. The ABS warning light should now go out.

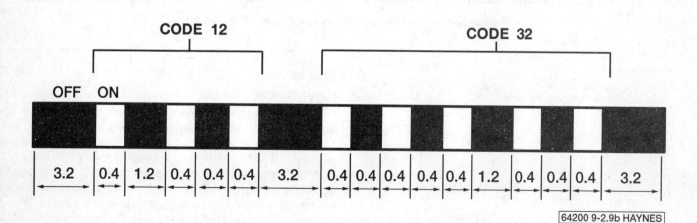

CODE 12   **CODE 32**

OFF ON

| 3.2 | 0.4 | 1.2 | 0.4 | 0.4 | 0.4 | 3.2 | 0.4 | 0.4 | 0.4 | 0.4 | 0.4 | 1.2 | 0.4 | 0.4 | 0.4 | 3.2 |

64200 9-2.9b HAYNES

4.13 The LED on the ABS control unit indicates trouble codes with patterns of flashes. For example, three 0.4-second flashes, followed by a 1.2-second interval, followed by two more 0.4-second flashes indicates a code 32, which means there's a short in the right rear sensor circuit.

Code	Malfunctioning part
12	Start code
18	Sensor rotor
21	Front right sensor (open circuit)
22	Front right sensor (short circuit)
25	Front left sensor (open circuit)
26	Front left sensor (short circuit)
31	Rear right sensor (open circuit)
32	Rear right sensor (short circuit)
35	Rear left sensor (open circuit)
36	Rear left sensor (short circuit)
41	Front right actuator solenoid valve
45	Front left actuator solenoid valve
55	Rear actuator solenoid valve
61	Actuator motor or motor relay
63	Solenoid valve relay circuit
71	Control module

Symptom	Malfunctioning part or circuit
ABS warning light stays on when ignition switch is turned on	Control module power supply circuit ABS warning light bulb circuit Control module or control module connector Solenoid valve relay stuck Power supply for solenoid valve relay coil Blown fuse (10A ELECTRON IGN, 15A STOP LAMP 10A METER, 20A ANTI SKID, 30A ANTI SKID)
ABS warning light stays on during self-diagnosis	Control module
ABS warning light does not come on when ignition switch is turned on	Fuse, warning light bulb or warning light circuit Control module
ABS warning light does not come on during self-diagnosis	Control module

4.14 Trouble codes - Nissan Quest/Mercury Villager with Bosch 2U ABS

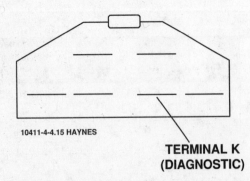

10411-4-4.15 HAYNES

TERMINAL K (DIAGNOSTIC)

4.15 ABS diagnostic connector – Ford Mustang with Bosch 2U

Mustang

Refer to illustrations 4.15 and 4.16

6 If you're working on a Mustang, ground terminal K of the diagnostic connector **(see illustration)**. With terminal K grounded, turn the ignition key to On (but don't start the engine). The ABS warning light will flash a code 12 if there are no trouble codes stored. If there are trouble codes stored, the ABS warning light will skip the Code 12 and go directly to the trouble codes. The code is determined by counting the number of ON and OFF flashes **(see illustration 4.13)**. All codes are two-digit codes, so the first flash(es) indicates the tens place, followed by a longer delay, followed by the single-digit flash(es). For example, a sequence of four flashes,

Code	Malfunctioning part or circuit
12	System OK – no codes stored
19	Control module
22	Right front solenoid
24	Left front solenoid
26	Rear solenoid
31	Right front wheel speed sensor continuity
32	Right rear wheel speed sensor continuity
33	Left front wheel speed sensor continuity
34	Left rear wheel speed sensor continuity
41	Right front wheel speed sensor
42	Right rear wheel speed sensor
43	Left front wheel speed sensor
44	Left rear wheel speed sensor
61	Pump motor or relay
63	Voltage supply interruption
69	Vehicle battery voltage below 10 volts
78	Incorrect wheel speed sensor frequency

4.16 Trouble codes – 1994 and 1995 Mustang with Bosch 2U

then a pulse, followed by a sequence of four flashes, would indicate a code 44. Count the number of flashes of the ABS light, then refer to the accompanying table (see illustration). The codes will flash once. To repeat them if necessary, turn the key to Off, then back to On.

7 To clear the trouble codes after repairing the problem, switch the ignition to Off and unground terminal K. Switch

4.17 A typical Assembly Line Communications Link (ALCL) or Assembly Line Data Link (ALDL) connector – connect the ABS diagnostic terminal to the ground terminal to access ABS codes

the ignition to On, then Off. Start the engine and drive the vehicle above 15 mph to clear the codes.

General Motors (except Corvette with ABS/ASR)

Refer to illustrations 4.17 and 4.18

8 Some, but not all, codes can be retrieved from GM vehicles equipped with Bosch 2S or 2U by flashing the ABS warning light, but GM recommends using a scan tool. Most codes can be cleared with a grounding sequence at the ALDL connector or by turning the ignition on and off 50 to 100 times, but some codes can only be cleared with a scan tool.

9 To retrieve codes using the flash method, locate the ALDL connector (it's somewhere under the dash, generally below the instrument panel, located so you can get at it without too much trouble).

10 Connect terminals A and H of the connector to each other with a jumper wire (see illustration).

11 Turn the ignition key to On, but don't start the engine. The ABS warning light will flash, first a code 12 (the start code), then any trouble codes that can be retrieved with the

Code	Malfunctioning part or circuit
12	Initialization code
21	Right front wheel sensor open/short to body ground or short to power
22	Left front wheel sensor toothed wheel frequency error
25	Left front wheel sensor open/short to body ground or short to power
26	Left front wheel sensor toothed wheel frequency error
31	Right rear wheel sensor (four-sensor systems)
32	Right rear wheel sensor toothed wheel frequency error (four-sensor systems)
35	Left rear wheel sensor (four-sensor systems) or rear sensor (three-sensor systems) open/short to body ground or short to power
36	Left rear wheel sensor (four-sensor systems) or rear sensor (three-sensor systems) toothed wheel frequency error
41	Right front solenoid fault*
45	Left front solenoid fault*
55	Rear solenoid fault*
61	Pump motor or relay fault*
63	Solenoid valve fault*
71	EMCB fault
72	Serial data link fault
75	Lateral accelerometer short to power or ground or open (Corvette only)
76	Lateral accelerometer signal fault (Corvette only)
*These codes will not blink the ABS lamp. A scanner is required to read them.	

4.18 Trouble codes – 1991 through 1993 General Motors front wheel drive vehicles with Bosch 2S "flash" method (see illustration). The system can store as many as three trouble codes. It will flash the Code 12, then each stored trouble code three times. Then it will repeat the sequence, starting with Code 12.

12 To clear the codes once the problems have been repaired, flash the codes until you reach Code 12, then remove the jumper wire from ALDL terminal H (but leave it connected to terminal A). Turn the ignition to Off, then to On (but don't start the engine). When the codes start flashing, connect the jumper wire to terminal H, leave it connected for at least one second, then disconnect it. Do this three times in ten seconds, connecting the jumper wire for at least one second each time. After the third time, wait at least 15 seconds, then turn the ignition to Off. Connect the jumper wire to pin H again, then turn the ignition to On. The ABS lamp should now flash Code 12, but no trouble codes. If it still flashes trouble codes, either the code clearing procedure wasn't done correctly, or the problem that caused the code to set in the first place still exists.

General Motors (1992 through 1995 Corvette with ABS/ASR)

Refer to illustration 4.19

13 The Bosch 2U ABS/ASR system is used on 1992 through 1994 Corvettes, as well as 1995 Corvettes with the LT5 engine (1995 LT1 models use Bosch 5.0). General Motors recommends using a scan tool to read trouble codes on these models, but trouble code numbers can also be read by causing the Central Control Module to display them, using the digital speedometer. Note that if the ABS lamp is off when the codes are displayed, none of them is current. If the lamp is on, at least one of them is current. The EBCM can store as many as three codes at a time.

14 With the ignition Off, connect pins A and G in the ALDL connector to each other, using a short jumper wire (see illustration 4.17).

15 Turn the key to ON (but don't start the engine) and note the speedometer. In the lower left corner, it displays a small number (1, 4 or 9), while at the same time the miles-per-hour digits display trouble code numbers. The number 1 in the lower left corner indicates that the codes being displayed are for the Central Control Module. The number 4 indicates that the codes being displayed are for the engine control module. The number 9 in the lower left corner indicates that the codes being displayed are for the anti-lock brake system. The system will automatically display any codes for 1, 4 and 9 in order, unless you tell it to skip ahead. You can do this by pressing the TRIP ODO button on the instrument panel. When the lower left corner displays 9.0, it means the ABS diagnosis system is ready. Press the TRIP/ODO button again so the lower left corner displays 9.1, and the speedometer will display ABS trouble codes. To identify the codes, refer to the accompanying table (see illustration).

16 Once you've read the codes, turn the key to Off and disconnect the jumper wire from the ALDL connector G terminal.

17 One way to clear ABS codes is to turn the key to On, then Off, 100 times. A faster way is as follows: Reconnect the jumper wire between the ALDL connector A and G terminals, then turn the key to On (but don't start the engine). Press the TRIP ODO button while watching the display in the lower left corner of the speedometer. When it reaches 9.7, release the TRIP ODO button and press the ENG MET button until the 9.7 is replaced by a blank. The codes should now be cleared. To confirm this, try to read codes as described in Step 15.

Code	Malfunctioning part or circuit
12	Initialization code
23	Right front wheel speed sensor continuity
25	Left front wheel speed sensor
27	Left front wheel speed sensor continuity
28	Wheel speed sensor frequency
31	Right rear wheel speed sensor
33	Right rear wheel speed sensor continuity
35	Left rear wheel speed sensor
37	Left rear wheel speed sensor continuity
41	Right front solenoid
44	Pilot valve solenoid
45	Left front solenoid
51	Right rear solenoid
55	Left rear solenoid
57	Cruise control output monitor
58	EBCM internal adjuster
61	Pump motor or relay
62	Tachometer pulses
63	Solenoid relay circuit
64	Throttle position signal
65	Throttle aduster assembly
66	Throttle adjuster assembly control
71	EBCM internal failure
72	Serial data link
73	Spark retard monitor
74	Low system voltage
75	Lateral accelerometer circuit
76	Lateral accelerometer signal beyond specifications
83	Low brake fluid

4.19 Trouble codes – 1992 through 1994 Corvette and 1995 Corvette LT5 with ABS/ASR

Bleeding

Warning 1: *Wear eye protection when bleeding the brake system. If the fluid comes in contact with your eyes, immediately rinse them with water and seek medical attention.*

Warning 2: *Never use old brake fluid. It contains moisture which can boil, rendering the brake system inoperative.*

Warning 3: *If, after bleeding the system you do not have a firm brake pedal, or if the ABS light on the instrument panel does not go off, or if you have any doubts whatsoever about the effectiveness of the brake system, have it towed to a dealer service department or other repair shop equipped with the necessary tools for bleeding the hydraulic modulator.*

Caution: *Brake fluid will damage paint. Cover all painted surfaces and be careful not to spill fluid during this procedure.*

Bleeding Bosch 2S systems is the same as for the equivalent model without ABS. If you're working on a 1986 through 1989 Corvette, jack up the rear end of the vehicle so the bleed valves on the rear calipers are in the 12 o'clock position. This prevents air from being trapped in the calipers.

Bleeding of the Bosch ABS/ASR system in the 1992 through 1994 Corvette (and 1995 Corvette with LT5 engine) is conventional, but bleed the prime pipe at the modulator valve first, followed by the right rear, left rear, right front and left front calipers.

Bleeding of other Bosch 2 systems varies by manufacturer; consult a vehicle-specific service manual for the correct bleeding sequence and any special conditions that apply.

Wheel speed sensors

The wheel speed sensors on most GM models are bolt-in replacements. However, some, such as 1997 and later Corvette front sensors, are integrated with the wheel hub and can't be replaced separately. The sensor gap is non-adjustable on all GM models.

ECU and hydraulic modulator

The electronic control unit and the hydraulic modulator can be replaced separately from each other. However, neither of these units can be disassembled for replacement of internal parts. The solenoid power relay and pump motor relay are part of the ECU and can't be replaced separately. The pump, motor, accumulators and solenoids are part of the HCU and can't be replaced separately.

Bosch 3

Refer to illustration 4.20

Bosch 3 (also called Bosch III) is used in several 1988 through 1990 Chrysler Corporation sedans and in the 1987 through 1992 Cadillac Allante. It's an integrated anti-lock brake system that combines the master cylinder and hydraulic boost unit into one assembly. The unit provides power brake assist as well as the boost needed for ABS operation. The version used in the 1990 through 1992 Aliante includes traction control.

The system uses four channels, one for each wheel. There are four wheel speed sensors, one at each wheel. The two rear channels are controlled simultaneously to prevent a loss of vehicle stability.

The main brake system in vehicles equipped with Bosch 3 is conventional, with the exception of the hydraulic brake booster. All models use disc brakes at all four wheels.

The Bosch 3 system can be identified by the combined master cylinder/brake booster in the left rear corner of the engine compartment **(see illustration)**.

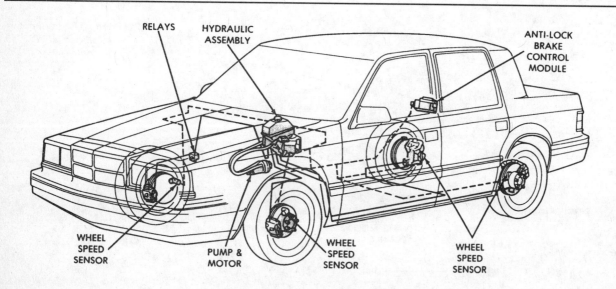

4.20 Bosch 3 ABS components (Chrysler installation shown)

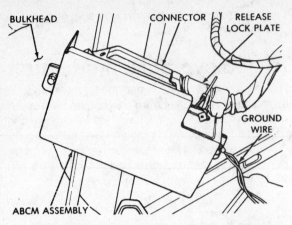

4.21 Bosch 3 ECU – Chrysler installation shown

System components

Components of the Bosch 3 ABS are the electronic control unit (ECU), master cylinder/booster unit, valve block, four solenoids (contained within the valve block), replenishing valve, pump and motor, accumulator, pressure monitoring module, control pressure switch, sensor block,

valve relay (contained within the sensor block), reed block, two boost piston travel switches (contained within the reed block), wheel speed sensors and tone wheels, brake pedal switch, brake fluid level switch, parking brake switch, main brake warning lamp (red) and ABS warning lamp (amber) **(see illustration 4.20)**.

Electronic control unit

Refer to illustration 4.21

The central component of the Bosch 3 system is the electronic control unit (ECU), which Chrysler calls an anti-lock brake control module (ABCM) and General Motors calls an electronic brake control module. The Chrysler version is mounted in the trunk, between the seat bulkhead and its trim panel **(see illustration)**. In Allante installations, it's mounted behind the instrument panel to the left of the steering column. The ECU contains a microprocessor that receives input signals from the wheel sensors, switches, warning pressure line, valve relay feedback line and replenishing valve feedback line. The ECU also receives diagnostic inputs from the system components and stores problems as diagnostic codes, which can be retrieved by flashing the brake warning lamp.

The ECU processes the input signals and then uses

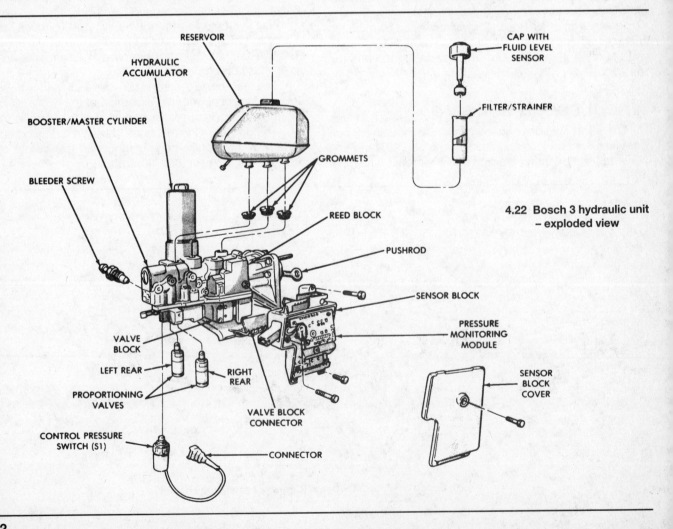

4.22 Bosch 3 hydraulic unit – exploded view

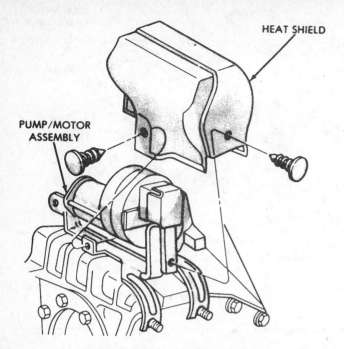

4.23 Bosch 3 pump and motor

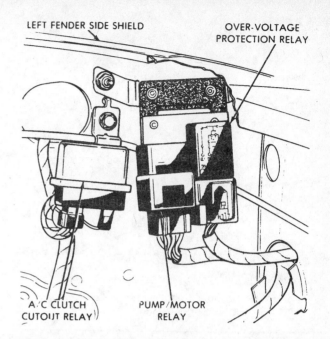

4.24 Pump relay and over-voltage protection relay (Chrysler installation shown)

output signals to control the relays, the red brake warning lamp (and amber ABS lamp on Chryslers) and the solenoids in the valve block.

Master cylinder and booster

Refer to illustration 4.22

The master cylinder and hydraulic booster, which is part of the hydraulic assembly, consists of an aluminum casting that contains the pistons and boost valve **(see illustration)**. A one-piece plastic reservoir, mounted on top of the aluminum body, contains brake fluid for the primary and secondary brake circuits as well as the booster. A fluid level sensor is built into the reservoir cap.

The boost valve is controlled by the driver through the brake pedal, opening to allow brake boost or ABS operation only when needed. The necessary high hydraulic pressure is supplied by the pump, which is located on the transaxle bracket, on the left side of the engine compartment, in Chrysler and GM installations.

The fluid level sensor in the reservoir cap indicates to the ECU if the brake fluid level is low, causing the ECU to illuminate the red warning light.

Valve block

The valve block is mounted on the master cylinder **(see illustration 4.22)**. The valve block contains four solenoids, one for each hydraulic channel. It also contains a replenishing valve and control pressure switch S1.

Solenoids

The solenoids are the three-position type, similar to those used in Bosch 2 systems. They are operated in two

stages, first by applying about 2 amps current, then by applying about 5 amps.

Replenishing valve

The replenishing valve routes brake fluid from the booster servo circuit to the master cylinder during hard normal braking and during anti-lock braking. This maintains pedal height.

Boost pump and relay

Refer to illustrations 4.23 and 4.24

The pump supplies hydraulic boost for normal braking, as well as the pressure needed for ABS operation **(see illustration)**. It's mounted on the left side of the engine compartment on the transaxle bracket.

The motor runs until pressure in the accumulator reaches approximately 2100 to 2600 psi. The ECU controls the pump relay, which is mounted on the left inner wheel well just forward of the battery in Chrysler installations **(see illustration)**. In Allantes, the relay is mounted behind the coolant reservoir on the passenger side inner fender. The relay in turn controls the pump.

Accumulator

The accumulator is part of the booster/master cylinder unit **(see illustration 4.22)**. It supplies hydraulic pressure for brake boost, as well as for ABS operation. It also acts as a reserve source of brake boost in case the pump fails.

The accumulator is a sliding piston design, precharged with nitrogen gas to approximately 800 psi. It stores brake fluid at a pressure of approximately 2100 to 2600 psi.

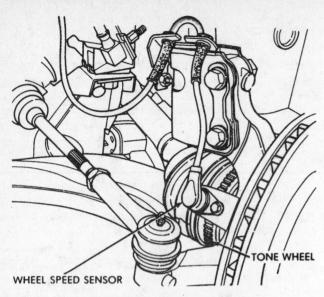

4.25 Bosch 3 front wheel speed sensor (Chrysler installation shown)

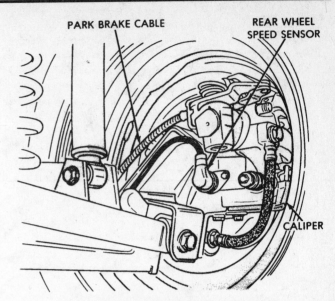

4.26 Bosch 3 rear wheel speed sensor (Chrysler installation shown)

Sensor block

The sensor block is part of the booster/master cylinder unit **(see illustration 4.22)**. It contains control pressure switch S1, valve (solenoid) relay, pressure monitoring module, two-pin reed block connector, 12-pin valve block connector, and 15-pin sensor block connector.

Control pressure switch S1

This switch, along with the brake light switch and boost piston travel switches S2a and S2b, indicates to the ECU that proper brake application has occurred. This normally-closed switch opens when booster servo pressure reaches about 400 psi as the brakes are applied by the driver.

Pressure monitoring module

This module is mounted on the sensor block **(see illustration 4.22)**. It controls accumulator pressure by grounding the pump relay, thus turning the pump on, when it senses low pressure in the accumulator. The two pressure switches in the module should give the same pressure signal; if they don't, the ECU shuts off the system and switches on the red brake warning light. In Chryslers, it also switches on the amber ABS light.

Solenoid relay

This relay is used by the ECU to control the operation of the four wheel solenoids. In its normal (non-anti-lock) position, the relay grounds the solenoid circuits, as well as the relay feedback line. During ABS braking, the relay switches voltage to the solenoids and the replenishing valve.

Over-voltage protection relay

This relay controls voltage to the ABS components. In Chrysler installations, it's mounted next to the pump relay on the left side of the engine compartment **(see illustration 4.24)**. In Allantes, it's attached to the steering column bracket under the instrument panel. The relay protects the sensor block and ECU circuits from voltage spikes.

Reed block

The reed block is part of the booster/master cylinder unit **(see illustration 4.22)**. It contains the boost piston travel switches, S2a and S2b.

Wheel speed sensors and tone wheels

Refer to illustrations 4.25 and 4.26

The front wheel speed sensors are attached to the steering knuckles **(see illustration)**. The rear sensors are bolted to the caliper bracket **(see illustration)**. The front tone wheels are mounted on the outboard CV joints. The rear tone wheels are mounted on the rear hubs.

Brake light switch

Besides operating the brake lights, this switch, mounted to the brake pedal, sends the ECU a signal to indicate that the pedal has been pressed. Anti-lock braking will not happen unless this signal is received.

Hydraulic system operation

Operation of the four solenoids is basically the same as those used in Bosch 2 systems, described earlier in this chapter. Under normal braking, the solenoid in each hydraulic channel is open, allowing pedal pressure to flow unimpeded from the master cylinder to the calipers. During

ABS braking, the ECU moves the solenoids to the hold position, cutting off hydraulic pressure from the master cylinder to the wheels. If a decrease in hydraulic pressure is needed, it then moves the solenoid to the release position, preventing the wheel from locking. When the ECU determines that more brake pressure is needed, it allows pressure from the accumulator into the caliper.

The replenishing valve opens during an ABS stop or hard non-ABS braking, allowing pressurized brake fluid into the master cylinder. This keeps the pedal from sinking due to brake fluid flow in the wheel circuits.

Accumulator pressure is produced by the pump. When the accumulator is empty of brake fluid, the nitrogen gas pre-charge fills the accumulator. As brake fluid is forced into the accumulator by the pump, it compresses the nitrogen and occupies space on the other side of the piston. This pressure is then available for use during brake boost or ABS operation.

Pump operation is controlled by the pump relay, which in turn is controlled by the pressure monitoring module. When the switches in the module indicate a predetermined low pressure level, they ground the pump relay coil, which closes the relay and supplies voltage to the pump motor.

Electrical system operation

At startup, the ECU illuminates the red brake warning lamp (and the amber lamp on Chrysler installations) for one or more seconds (the amber ABS lamp in Chrysler installations may illuminate for as long as 30 seconds). As the vehicle reaches approximately 3 to 4 mph, the ECU operates the solenoids and the replenishing valve briefly to test their function. This can be heard as a series of clicking sounds, and if the brake pedal is pressed during this test, the driver will feel pulsations in the pedal.

The ECU receives power for its internal operation from the over-voltage protection relay. This relay receives power through a 20-amp fusible link (Chrysler) or 20-amp brake fuse (Allante). In the event of a voltage spike, the fuse or fusible link will blow, protecting the ECU and sensor block circuits.

The ECU receives input signals (varying AC voltage) from the four wheel speed sensors. It uses these signals to detect impending wheel lockup.

The ECU also receives input from the control pressure switch S1, boost piston travel switches S2a and S2b, and the brake light switch. The switches operate in a normal sequence: first the brake light switch closes indicating that the pedal has started to move. Then switch S2a opens, indicating that the boost piston has started to move. Further pedal movement causes booster servo pressure to increase; as it reaches 400 psi, control pressure switch S1 opens. As the pistons reach the end of their travel, switch S2b opens. The opening of switch S2b activates the replenishing valve, which causes brake fluid to be routed from the booster servo to the master cylinder circuits. This will be felt as a sudden push in the brake pedal.

The switches must operate in the correct order to let the ECU know the system is working properly. It's okay if switch S2a opens at the same time as or slightly before the brake light switch closes, since changes in the brake light switch adjustment may affect the timing of its opening and closing. However, other changes in the sequence will cause the ECU to disable the system and set a code. Some faults in the main brake system can cause switch S2b to open prematurely, even though there is not a problem with the ABS. These include air in the hydraulic system, excessively soft brake pad material, and pumping the brake pedal to position new pads while the key is in the On position.

The brake fluid level sensor lets the ECU know that there's enough fluid in the system for normal and ABS brake operation. If fluid drops too low, the sensor illuminates the red brake warning lamp and disables the ABS.

The ECU monitors accumulator pressure, solenoid relay position and replenishing valve position. Accumulator pressure is monitored through the warning pressure line, which runs from the sensor block to the ECU. The position of the solenoid relay is monitored through the solenoid relay feedback line. If the relay is not in the position the ECU has commanded it to be in, the ECU shuts off the ABS and sets a code. Replenishing valve position is monitored through the replenishing valve feedback line. As with the solenoid relay, the ECU will shut off the ABS and set a code if the replenishing valve is not in the position the ECU has commanded.

The ECU supplies power to the solenoids and the replenishing valve through the valve relay. Power to the solenoids is supplied at all times; the ECU changes the positions of the solenoids by controlling the ground circuit. The replenishing valve operation is controlled by the ECU through a separate switch.

Once ABS operation starts, the ECU controls the solenoids and the pump as described in *Hydraulic system operation* above.

Traction control

Traction control is included with Bosch 3 on 1990 through 1992 Allante models. When the ECU detects wheelspin due to acceleration at a front wheel, it starts by applying the brake at the affected wheel, using the ABS solenoid. Pressure is modulated in the same hold, release and build cycles as are used for ABS.

If applying the brake doesn't eliminate the wheelspin after three seconds, the ECU will start by shutting off the fuel injector at one cylinder. If this still isn't enough, it will continue to shut off fuel injectors until a total of four have been shutoff. When traction has been restored, the ECU will switch the injectors back at a rate of one per second until all are working.

Traction control operation is indicated by the operation of a TRACTION ACTIVE lamp on the instrument panel.

Code	Malfunctioning part or circuit
1	Left front solenoid
2	Right front solenoid
3	Left rear solenoid
4	Left rear solenoid
5	Left front wheel speed sensor
6	Right front wheel speed sensor
7	Right rear wheel speed sensor
8	Left rear wheel speed sensor
9	Left front/right rear wheel speed sensor
10	Right front/left rear wheel speed sensor
11	Replenishing valve
12	Valve relay
13	Excessive displacement or circuit failure
14	Piston travel switches
15	Brake light switch
16	ECU

4.27 Trouble codes – Chrysler models with Bosch 3 (1987 through 1989 Cadillac Allante similar)

Code	Malfunctioning part or circuit
12	Start code or no codes stored
21	Right front wheel speed sensor
25	Left front wheel speed sensor
31	Right rear wheel speed sensor
35	Left rear wheel speed sensor
41	Right front solenoid
43	Traction control plunger disconnected
44	Right front traction control valve
45	Left front solenoid
48	Left front traction control valve
51	Right rear solenoid
55	Left rear solenoid
62	Replenishing valve
63	Valve relay
64	Switch sequence
65	Switch sequence
66	Switch sequence
71	ECU

4.28 Trouble codes – 1990 through 1992 Cadillac Allante with Bosch 3

System service
Diagnosis

Trouble codes can be retrieved by flashing the red brake warning lamp on Chrysler models and early Allantes, and displayed on the driver information center screen on later Allantes.

Chrysler models

Refer to illustration 4.27

1   Turn the key to On (but don't start the engine). Don't turn the key off, or you'll clear the stored code.

2   Make sure the parking brake is fully released (the parking brake light switch will illuminate the same warning lamp you're trying to use to read codes).

3   Either the red brake warning lamp or the amber ABS lamp should stay on to indicate a code. If not, the system may be okay. Test drive the vehicle carefully in a safe area to make sure.

4   If one or both of the warning lights stays on, press the brake pedal firmly and hold it down. The red lamp will start to flash a code after 5 seconds. If you need to see the code more than once, just hold the brake pedal down and the code will repeat. To interpret the code, refer to the accompanying table **(see illustration)**.

5   The ECU stores only one code at a time. Once you've read the code, turn the ignition off to clear it. To display any additional codes, you'll need to repair the problem that caused the first one, then drive the vehicle to set the code for any remaining problem.

1987 through 1989 Allante

Refer to illustration 4.28

6   Turn the key to On (but don't start the engine). Don't turn the key off, or you'll clear the stored code.

7   Make sure the parking brake is fully released (the parking brake light switch will illuminate the same warning lamp you're trying to use to read codes).

8   Press the WARMER and OFF buttons on the climate control panel simultaneously and hold them down for about five seconds. Code numbers will display on the screen. The system will run through engine codes (starting with E), body codes (starting with B) and lighting codes (starting with L). Press the LO button to skip ahead to the ANTI-LOCK BRAKES? display, then press the HI button. The screen will flash KEEP BRAKE DEPRESSED; when it does, hold the pedal down until it reads COUNT LAMP FLASHES. At this point, count the flashes of the red brake warning lamp.

9   To interpret the code, refer to the accompanying table **(see illustration)**.

10   The ECU stores only one code at a time. Once you've read the code, turn the ignition off to clear the code from memory. To display any additional codes, you'll need to repair the problem that caused the first one, then drive the vehicle to set the code for any remaining problem.

1990 through 1992 Allante

11   Turn the key to On (but don't start the engine).

12   Make sure the parking brake is fully released.

13   Press the WARMER and OFF buttons on the climate control panel simultaneously and hold them down for about

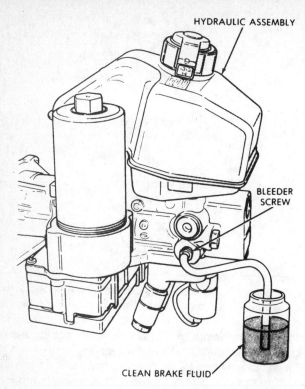

HYDRAULIC ASSEMBLY

BLEEDER SCREW

CLEAN BRAKE FLUID

4.29 Bleeding a Bosch 3 hydraulic assembly

five seconds. Code numbers will display on the screen. The system will run through engine codes (starting with E), body codes (starting with B), lighting codes (starting with L) and restraint codes (starting with R). After this display, press the LO button to skip ahead to the ABS/TCS display.

14 Locate the ALDL connector under the dash and connect a short jumper wire between the A and H terminals **(see illustration 4.17)**. At this point, count the flashes of the red brake warning lamp. The first code will be a code 12, indicating that the system is ready. Any trouble codes will flash next, each code displaying three times. This version of the system can store multiple codes.

15 To interpret the codes, refer to the accompanying table **(see illustration 4.28)**.

16 Once you've read the codes, press the RESET button to end the diagnostic mode. Remove the jumper wire form the ALDL connector. To clear any codes from memory, either disconnect the battery or remove the 20-amp brake fuse for 20 seconds.

System pressure relief

Due to the high pressure in this system, the system pressure must be relieved before disconnecting any hydraulic lines. Make sure the ignition key is in the Off position, then press the brake pedal firmly (with at least 50 pounds of pressure) as far as it will go at least 25 times. There will be a distinct increase in pedal effort as pressure in the accumulator is discharged. Once this happens, press

the pedal a few more times to make sure all pressure in the accumulator is depleted.

Brake fluid fill procedure

Because the system's accumulator acts as a fluid reservoir, it must be discharged to get an accurate fluid level. Depressurize the system as described above, then fill the fluid reservoir in the normal way.

System bleeding

Refer to illustration 4.29

Warning 1: *Wear eye protection when bleeding the brake system. If the fluid comes in contact with your eyes, immediately rinse them with water and seek medical attention.*

Warning 2: *Never use old brake fluid. It contains moisture which can boil, rendering the brake system inoperative.*

Warning 3: *If, after bleeding the system you do not have a firm brake pedal, or if the ABS light on the instrument panel does not go off, or if you have any doubts whatsoever about the effectiveness of the brake system, have it towed to a dealer service department or other repair shop equipped with the necessary tools for bleeding the hydraulic modulator.*

Caution: *Brake fluid will damage paint. Cover all painted surfaces and be careful not to spill fluid during this procedure.*

1 If a booster hose has been disconnected (for example, to replace the hoses or the pump), or if the brake fluid reservoir has been emptied or replaced, the booster must be bled. Otherwise, bleeding is done at the wheel brake bleed valves in the conventional way. Bleed in the following order: left rear, right rear, left front, right front.

2 To bleed the booster, first make sure the fluid reservoir is full, then depressurize the system as described above.

3 Connect a clear plastic hose to the bleeder screw on the hydraulic assembly and place its other end in a container **(see illustration)**.

4 Open the bleeder screw 1/2 to 3/4 turn and have an assistant turn the key to On (but don't start the engine). The pump should run and fluid should flow from the bleeder screw. Let this continue until the fluid coming from the valve is free of bubbles. **Caution:** *The pump should not be allowed to run for more than 60 seconds at a time. If clear brake fluid hasn't flowed after 60 seconds, turn the key to Off and let the pump cool for several minutes before bleeding again.*

5 Once clear fluid flows from the valve, shut off the key, close the valve and remove the hose.

6 Turn the key to On and let the pump run until it stops, about 30 seconds. This will pressurize the system.

Component replacement

The following components can be replaced separately:

a) *Electronic control unit*
b) *Hydraulic assembly, including the valve block, sensor block and reed block*

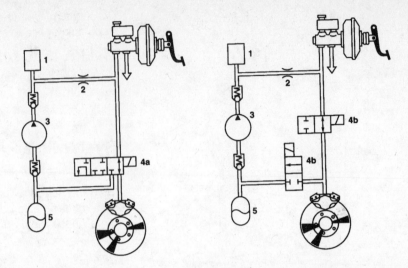

4.30 Bosch 2 and Bosch 5 hydraulic circuits

1. *Damper chamber*
2. *Throttle*
3. *Return pump*
4a. *Three-position solenoids*
4b. *Two-position solenoids*
5. *Accumulator chamber*

c) Pump and motor assembly (including new hoses and heat shield)
d) Pump hoses (new hoses include a new heat shield)
e) Fluid level sensor
f) Proportioning valves
g) Pump relay
h) Over-voltage protection relay
i) Wheel speed sensors

The front tone wheels are replaced as part of the CV joints. The rear tone wheels are replaced as part of the hubs.

Be sure to depressurize the hydraulic system as described above before undoing any lines.

Bosch 5, 5.3 and Delco-Bosch

Refer to illustration 4.30

Bosch 5 and its variants, 5.3 and Delco-Bosch, are improved versions of Bosch 2. Delco-Bosch 5 is a version used in a number of General Motors vehicles. Bosch 5.3 is a compact version of Bosch 5. The most significant changes from Bosch 2 are:

a) *Dual processors. Both processors receive the input signals from all of the wheel sensors, and should produce identical output signals. If they don't, the electronic control unit shuts the ABS off and illuminates the warning lamp.*
b) *A simplified solenoid design, with only two solenoid positions instead of three* **(see illustration).**

Bosch 5 comes in three-channel and four-channel versions. Vehicles with a front-rear split between the hydraulic circuits use either a three- or four-channel version, with one hydraulic channel at each front wheel and a single channel for both rear wheels. Each front wheel has its own wheel speed sensor. On some models, there's a separate speed sensor for each rear wheel. On others, a single speed sensor in the differential monitors both rear wheels. Vehicles with diagonally split hydraulic circuits (one front brake and the diagonally opposite rear brake on each circuit) use a four-channel version with four wheel sensors.

Bosch 5.3 achieves its smaller size and reduced weight by using a smaller pump motor and a more compact arrangement of components than Bosch 5.0. Its solenoids are made in two parts, with the hydraulic portion in the hydraulic modulator and the coils in the ECU, which plugs onto the hydraulic modulator.

Some versions of the system include traction control, and some include a lateral acceleration sensor and/or a yaw sensor.

System components

Components of the Bosch 5 ABS are the control unit, hydraulic modulator, solenoids, pumps and accumulators (contained within the hydraulic modulator), wheel speed sensors and tone wheels, solenoid relay, pump relay, brake light switch and ABS warning lamp.

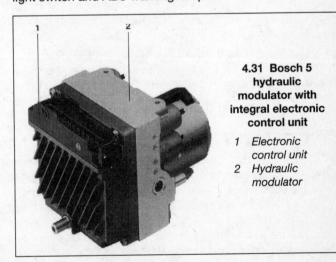

4.31 Bosch 5 hydraulic modulator with integral electronic control unit

1. *Electronic control unit*
2. *Hydraulic modulator*

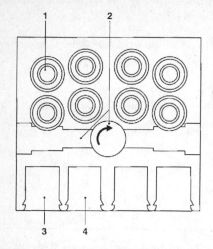

4.32 Bosch 5 hydraulic modulator (four-channel system)

1   Solenoid
2   Pump element
3   Damping chamber
4   Accumulator chamber

Electronic control unit

Refer to illustration 4.31

The electronic control unit (ECU) is installed in the vehicle either separately from the hydraulic modulator or as a combined unit, depending on model (see illustration). The control unit contains two microprocessors, which use a single control program. One of the microprocessors also has an electronically erasable programmable read only memory (EEPROM) chip, which stores diagnostic trouble codes. This chip will retain any stored codes even if the vehicle's battery is disconnected. A separate module in the ECU supplies stabilized voltage for ABS operation and controls the relays that operate the solenoids and pump. It also monitors system operation and illuminates the ABS warning lamp if an error occurs. The module stores error codes for as long as operating voltage is available.

The ECU obtains a reference speed from the fastest-moving wheel and uses this as a standard of comparison to determine when ABS operation is needed.

Hydraulic modulator

Refer to illustrations 4.32 and 4.33

The hydraulic modulator is part of the modular design of the Bosch 5 system, which means it can be mounted separately or combined with the ECU. The hydraulic modulator contains the solenoids, a pump for each of the two hydraulic circuits, an accumulator for each of the two hydraulic circuits and the noise damping chamber (see illustration).

The solenoids are two-position types, which move to the hold position or the release position as commanded by the ECU. There are either six or eight solenoids, two for each hydraulic channel (see illustration). One solenoid is an inlet and the other is an outlet.

The two pumps share a single motor. The pump is activated during ABS braking, and during traction control system operation on models so equipped.

Wheel speed sensors

The wheel sensors send the ECU a variable AC voltage signal as described in Chapter 1. Four-channel systems have a sensor at each wheel. Three-channel systems have a single sensor for the rear brakes, mounted on the transmission or in the differential.

Speed sensor air gaps are not adjustable with Bosch 5 systems.

Brake light switch

The brake light switch tells the ECU that the brake has been applied.

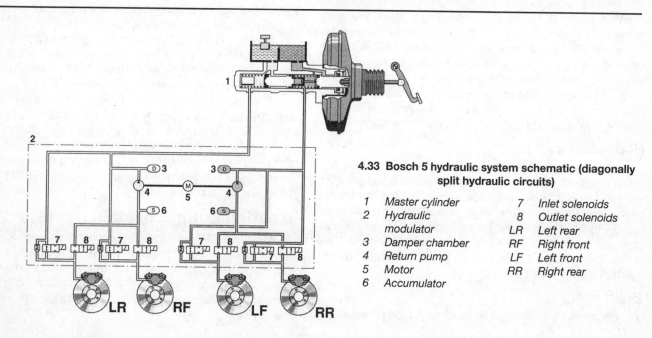

4.33 Bosch 5 hydraulic system schematic (diagonally split hydraulic circuits)

1	Master cylinder	7	Inlet solenoids
2	Hydraulic modulator	8	Outlet solenoids
		LR	Left rear
3	Damper chamber	RF	Right front
4	Return pump	LF	Left front
5	Motor	RR	Right rear
6	Accumulator		

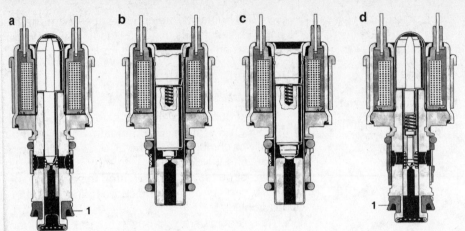

4.34 Bosch 5 ABS/ASR solenoids

a) Inlet solenoid
b) Outlet solenoid
c) Suction valve
d) Pilot valve
1 Non-return valve seal

System operation

On startup and again during drive-off, the ECU performs a self-test to check the system for faults. The test includes briefly powering the solenoids and pump motor. If a fault is detected, the ECU shuts the system off and illuminates the ABS warning lamp.

Under normal braking, the inlet solenoid in each hydraulic channel is open, allowing pedal pressure to flow unimpeded from the master cylinder to the calipers and wheel cylinders. The outlet solenoid in each channel is closed.

During ABS braking, the ECU controls hydraulic pressure at the brakes by cycling the solenoids in the HCU as many as 15 times per second, depending on the conditions. The cycles occur in three stages: pressure hold, pressure reduction and pressure build.

Hold cycle

When a wheel begins to lock, the impending lockup is detected by the ECU. The ECU then closes the inlet valve in the wheel's hydraulic channel, cutting off pedal pressure to the wheel. The outlet solenoid remains closed. As a result, hydraulic pressure at the wheel remains steady, neither increasing nor decreasing. This is called the hold or isolation cycle. If the driver releases the pedal at this point, hydraulic pressure will force the inlet valve's internal check valve open, allowing the release of hydraulic pressure at the wheel.

Reduction cycle

If the lockup condition continues, the ECU opens the outlet solenoid, releasing hydraulic pressure. Since the inlet solenoid is still being held closed by the ECU, hydraulic pressure at the wheel is reduced. This is called the decay or release cycle. The released brake fluid is temporarily stored in an accumulator (there's one for each brake circuit). The pump then returns the fluid from the accumulator to the master cylinder reservoir.

Build cycle

Once the lockup condition ceases and the wheel starts to turn at a rate the ECU considers acceptable, the outlet valve closes and the inlet valve opens. This allows pedal pressure to again build in the hydraulic circuit.

To restore pedal height, which drops during the decay cycle, the pump switches on, returning brake fluid to the master cylinder and increasing fluid pressure in the brake lines.

Traction control

Refer to illustration 4.34

Traction control systems used with Bosch 5 ABS are similar in operation to those used with Bosch 2. Since Bosch 5 ABS with traction control is widely used in General Motors vehicles, the following section discusses several General Motors variations.

The Bosch name Acceleration Slip Regulation (ASR) is used in some GM vehicles, while the same system in other GM vehicles is called the Traction Control System, or TCS. For example, the traction control lamp on some Camaro instrument panels is labeled ASR, while the equivalent Firebird system lamp is labeled TCS.

Bosch 5 TCS in General Motors vehicles can be turned off by a switch on the instrument panel. When this is done, the "OFF" lamp will light. Switching off TCS does not switch off the anti-lock brake system, however.

The hydraulic control unit used with traction control uses the same pump as the ABS. It contains additional solenoids for traction control operation **(see illustration)**. These are called the pilot valve and suction valve by Bosch, and the isolation solenoid and pump prime solenoid by General Motors. These solenoids are always installed in pairs, one of each type.

Traction control system operation

Bosch 5 ASR retards ignition timing and reduces fuel flow to reduce engine power. It starts by retarding the timing. In General Motors vehicles, timing retard doesn't go beyond zero degrees (Top Dead Center) and is limited to a few seconds' duration to prevent overheating the catalytic converter(s).

If this isn't enough, the system restricts fuel supply to the engine. On General Motors E- and K-body models, it shuts off up to half of the fuel injectors, one at a time. On D- and Y-body models and 1998 and later F-body models, the TCS takes over control of the throttle valve from the driver. Throttle control in GM vehicles is accomplished through a throttle relaxer. This is a uni-directional electric motor that operates the throttle cable adjuster, closing the throttle valve. While this is occurring, the driver will feel an unusual amount of freeplay in the accelerator. After TCS disengages, the throttle adjuster's internal adjuster spring returns it to the normal position.

Braking control in Bosch 5 TCS systems is accomplished by the TCS solenoids and the pump. The ECU monitors the wheel speed sensors, just as it does for ABS operation. When the sensor voltage at one drive wheel increases disproportionately, the ECU registers this as wheelspin due to acceleration. In response, it closes the isolation solenoid to prevent master cylinder pressure from reaching the wheel. At the same time, it opens the pump prime solenoid, which allows the pump to pull brake fluid from the master cylinder reservoir, and activates the pump. The pump supplies hydraulic pressure to the brake at the spinning wheel. Pressure delivery is controlled in hold, release and increase cycles, just like ABS, using the ABS solenoids. A pressure relief valve in the isolation solenoid prevents pump pressure from over-applying the brake by opening at a predetermined pressure. This allows excess brake fluid to return to the master cylinder.

Lateral accelerometer

This sensor is basically the same as the one used with Bosch 2 ABS/ASR in the 1992 through 1994 Corvette and 1995 Corvette LT5. The ECU uses the sensor signal in controlling the rear brakes. It also disables yaw control (if equipped) if the g-force exceeds a specified amount.

Yaw rate sensor

This sensor, installed in late 1998 and later Corvettes, is used together with the lateral acceleration sensor as part of the Active Handling system. It incorporates an oscillating tuning fork to produce a gyroscopic effect and produces an output voltage of 2.5 volts at zero yaw. Voltage ranges from 0.25 to 4.75 volts, which corresponds to a range of +/-64 degrees per second.

The Active Handling system uses readings from the wheel speed sensors, lateral acceleration sensor and steering sensor to calculate the degree to which the vehicle should yaw (rotate around its vertical axis). If this doesn't match the actual yaw rate indicated by the yaw rate sensor, the system engages traction control.

System service

Diagnosis

Diagnostic code retrieval requires the use of a scan tool. Follow the tool manufacturer's instructions to retrieve codes.

Bleeding

Warning 1: *Wear eye protection when bleeding the brake system. If the fluid comes in contact with your eyes, immediately rinse them with water and seek medical attention.*

Warning 2: *Never use old brake fluid. It contains moisture which can boil, rendering the brake system inoperative.*

Warning 3: *If, after bleeding the system you do not have a firm brake pedal, or if the ABS light on the instrument panel does not go off, or if you have any doubts whatsoever about the effectiveness of the brake system, have it towed to a dealer service department or other repair shop equipped with the necessary tools for bleeding the hydraulic modulator.*

Caution: *Brake fluid will damage paint. Cover all painted surfaces and be careful not to spill fluid during this procedure.*

Bleeding the regular brake system on a Bosch 5 vehicle is done by conventional methods. On Bosch 5 and Delco-Bosch systems, bleeding the secondary circuits in the HCU, or bleeding the system when the HCU has been replaced, requires a scan tool and pressure bleeding equipment. Follow the equipment manufacturer's instructions.

Wheel speed sensors

The wheel speed sensors on most GM models are bolt-in replacements. However, some, such as 1997 and later Corvette front sensors, are integrated with the wheel hub and can't be replaced separately. The sensor gap is non-adjustable on all GM models.

ECU and HCU

The electronic control unit and the hydraulic control unit can be replaced separately from each other. However, neither of these units can be disassembled for replacement of internal parts. The solenoid power relay and pump motor relay are part of the ECU and can't be replaced separately. The pump, motor, accumulators and solenoids are part of the HCU and can't be replaced separately.

Notes

Chapter 5
Delphi Chassis
(Delco Moraine) systems

General information

Delphi Chassis, formerly known as Delco Moraine, is a General Motors division that produces anti-lock braking systems, among other components. Two Delphi Chassis systems are used in GM vehicles: Delco Powermaster III and Delphi Chassis ABS VI.

Delco Powermaster III

This system is used in the 1989 through 1991 Buick Regal, Olds Cutlass and Pontiac Grand Prix. It's an integrated anti-lock brake system that combines the master cylinder and hydraulic boost unit into one assembly. The unit provides power brake assist as well as the boost needed for ABS operation.

The system uses three channels, one for each front wheel and one for both rear wheels. There are four wheel speed sensors, one at each wheel. The rear wheels are controlled together, using the select low principle.

The main brake system in vehicles equipped with Delco Powermaster III is conventional, with the exception of the hydraulic brake booster. All models use disc brakes at the front and disc or drum brakes at the rear, depending on model. The hydraulic system is split into front and rear circuits.

The Delco III system can be identified by the combined master cylinder/brake booster in the left rear corner of the engine compartment.

System components

Components of the Delco III ABS are the integrated modulator assembly (master cylinder, brake booster, accumulator, solenoids and pump), electronic control module and four wheel speed sensors. Relays, fuses and fusible links are located on the left side of the engine compartment, on or near the strut tower.

Electronic Brake Control Module (EBCM)

The central component of the Delco III system is the electronic control unit, which GM calls the Electronic Brake Control Module (EBCM). On most applications the EBCM is located under the passenger seat. The EBCM contains a microprocessor that receives input signals from the wheel sensors, switches, pump and hydraulic modulator.

The EBCM also receives diagnostic inputs from the system components and stores any problems as diagnostic codes, which can be retrieved with a scan tool.

The EBCM processes the input signals and then uses output signals to control the relays, the amber ABS warning lamp and the solenoids in the pressure modulator.

Master cylinder and booster

The master cylinder and hydraulic booster are part of the hydraulic modulator assembly. The boost valve is controlled by the driver through the brake pedal, opening to allow brake boost or ABS operation only when needed. The necessary high hydraulic pressure is supplied by the pump, which is located in the integrated modulator unit.

A fluid level switch in the reservoir indicates to the EBCM if the brake fluid level is low, causing the EBCM to illuminate the red warning light.

Hydraulic modulator assembly

The hydraulic modulator assembly is made in one piece with the master cylinder. The modulator contains three solenoids, one for each hydraulic channel. The two-position solenoids have release and hold positions. Each solenoid has two valves and two sets of electromagnetic windings, one for the hold function and one for the release function. During ABS braking, the hold windings close the spool valve at the output end of the solenoid, which is normally open to allow master cylinder pressure to operate the wheel brakes. This blocks master cylinder pressure to the brake, holding braking pressure at the wheel steady. If that isn't enough to keep the wheel from locking, the EBCM opens the poppet valve at the other end of the solenoid, releasing brake pressure back to the master cylinder reservoir.

Boost pump

The pump supplies hydraulic boost for normal braking, as well as the pressure needed for ABS operation. It's attached to the bottom of the hydraulic assembly. A pressure switch closes when accumulator pressure drops below 2200 psi, which energizes the pump relay, turning on the pump motor. The motor runs until pressure reaches approximately 2700 psi, when the switch opens. A relief valve opens if the pump pressure reaches approximately 3400 psi.

Accumulator

The bladder-type accumulator supplies hydraulic pressure for brake boost, as well as for ABS operation. The accumulator is pre-charged with nitrogen gas and stores brake fluid at a pressure of approximately 2200 to 2700 psi. A low pressure switch, which is normally open, grounds to the vehicle body when accumulator pressure drops below 2200 psi. Another low pressure switch illuminates the red brake warning lamp when accumulator pressure drops below 1800 psi.

Wheel speed sensors and tone wheels

The front wheel speed sensors are attached to the steering knuckles. The front tone wheels are integral with the outer CV joints. The rear sensors and tone wheels are integral with the rear hubs.

System operation

Under normal (non-ABS) braking, the solenoid in each hydraulic channel is in the release position, allowing pedal pressure to flow unimpeded from the master cylinder to the calipers and wheel cylinders. The pump maintains the accumulator charge between 2200 and 2700 psi so that accumulator pressure is available when needed for ABS braking. Current for the pump flows from the ABS power center, through the pump motor relay to the pump. The EBCM monitors the pump current at terminal 1C12.

During ABS braking, the EBCM closes the hold solenoid, cutting off hydraulic pressure from the master cylinder to the wheel. It then opens the release solenoid to release hydraulic pressure, preventing the wheel from locking. The released pressure returns to the master cylinder reservoir. When the ECU determines that more brake pressure is needed, it reopens the hold solenoid and closes the release solenoid, allowing pressure from the master cylinder into the caliper or wheel cylinder. Pressure at the rear wheels comes from the master cylinder boost chamber. Pressure at either front wheel comes from one of the master cylinder piston chambers, which have a smaller volume of fluid. For this reason, a displacement cylinder and isolation valve are employed in each of the front channels to prevent the fluid in the master cylinder piston chamber from being depleted.

System service

Diagnosis

System faults will cause the amber warning light to flash if the fault is not serious enough to disable the ABS, or illuminate steadily if a fault causes the ABS to be disabled. Identification of specific faults requires a bi-directional scan tool. Refer to the scan tool manufacturer's instructions for diagnostic procedures.

System pressure relief

Due to the high pressure in this system, the system pressure must be relieved before disconnecting any hydraulic lines. Make sure the ignition key is in the Off position, then press the brake pedal firmly as far as it will go at least 40 times.

System bleeding

Warning 1: *Wear eye protection when bleeding the brake system. If the fluid comes in contact with your eyes, immediately rinse them with water and seek medical attention.*

Warning 2: *Never use old brake fluid. It contains moisture which can boil, rendering the brake system inoperative.*

Warning 3: *If, after bleeding the system you do not have a firm brake pedal, or if the ABS light on the instrument panel does not go off, or if you have any doubts whatsoever about the effectiveness of the brake system, have it towed to a dealer service department or other repair shop equipped with the necessary tools for bleeding the hydraulic modulator.*

Caution: *Brake fluid will damage paint. Cover all painted surfaces and be careful not to spill fluid during this procedure.*

1   Relieve the system pressure.

2   With the ignition off, be sure the fluid reservoir is full.

3   Connect a clear hose to the bleeder valve on the right front brake caliper and submerge the other end of the hose in a container of brake fluid. Open the bleeder valve.

4   Have an assistant slowly depress the brake pedal. As the fluid flows from the caliper, tap on the caliper housing to free trapped air.

5   Close the bleeder valve and have the assistant release the brake pedal.

6   Repeat this step until air is no longer seen in the hose.

7   Repeat this procedure for the left front caliper.

8   Before bleeding the rear brakes, turn the ignition On and allow the pump motor to charge the system. The pump motor should stop running within one minute.

9   With the reservoir full, connect the hose to the bleeder

valve on the right rear caliper and submerge the other end of the hose in a container of clean brake fluid.

10 Open the bleeder valve.

11 Have an assistant slowly depress the brake pedal, part way only. Allow the fluid to flow for 15 seconds, while lightly tapping on the caliper housing to free trapped air.

12 Close the bleeder valve and have the assistant release the brake pedal.

13 Repeat this step until air is no longer seen in the hose.

14 Check the brake fluid level, then repeat this procedure for the left rear caliper.

15 Once all the calipers have been bled, the isolation valves on the ABS unit should be bled. Connect the bleeder hose to the inner side of the ABS unit and submerge the other end in the container of clean brake fluid. With the ignition still On, have an assistant apply light pressure to the brake pedal. Slowly open the bleeder valve and allow the fluid to flow until no more air bubbles are seen.

16 Repeat this procedure to the bleeder valve on the outer side of the unit.

17 Depressurize the system and check the brake fluid, adding as necessary.

18 Before turning the key On, sharply apply the brake pedal three times, using full force.

19 Turn the ignition key On and allow the pump motor to run. When the motor stops, turn the key Off. **Note:** *If the pump runs for more than 60 seconds, check the brake fluid level and look for leaks.*

20 Depress the brake pedal, using moderate pressure, then turn the ignition key on for three seconds. Repeat this procedure ten times.

21 Depressurize the system and recheck the fluid level.

Delphi Chassis ABS VI

This is a simple, low-cost integrated ABS widely used in General Motors front wheel drive vehicles. It was first used in the 1991 Buick Skylark, Olds Cutlass Calais, Pontiac Grand Am and Saturn vehicles. The system operates three channels with input from four wheel speed sensors. It uses three motor-driven pistons in the hydraulic unit to control brake line pressure.

Most ABS designs include electrically operated solenoid valves to cut off the wheel brake from master cylinder pressure, release brake pressure to prevent wheel lockup, and reopen the wheel brake to additional pressure. The additional pressure during an ABS stop is usually supplied by a pump (or by accumulators that have previously been charged by a pump). The solenoids are extremely fast-responding precision-machined devices that are relatively expensive to produce. The pump must be extremely reliable, and in some systems capable of generating nearly 3000 psi. All of this adds to the cost of the system.

ABS VI uses only two solenoids and no pump. In addition, the wheel speed sensors are made of plastic rather than stainless steel, further reducing the cost.

The main brake system used with ABS VI is conventional, with a vacuum booster.

System components

The system components are the electronic brake control module (EBCM), hydraulic modulator (which contains the motors, pistons and solenoids), four wheel speed sensors and tone rings, a system enable relay, lamp driver module and two indicator lights, one indicating ABS and the other indicating ABS ACTIVE.

Electronic Brake Control Module (EBCM)

The EBCM is located inside the vehicle, generally under the passenger seat. It receives inputs from the four wheel speed sensors and the brake light switch. It controls ABS operation by controlling the motors and solenoids in the hydraulic modulator.

Hydraulic modulator

Refer to illustration 5.1

The hydraulic modulator and its motor pack are mounted on the side of the master cylinder **(see illustration)**. It contains two solenoids, three electric motors and four pistons. There's a motor and piston for each front brake. The pistons for the two rear brakes are controlled by a single motor that operates them both in unison.

Wheel speed sensors

The front wheel speed sensors are mounted on the steering knuckles and their tone rings are permanently pressed onto the outer CV joints. The rear wheel speed

5.1 This top view of the hydraulic modulator/motor pack assembly shows the solenoids (arrows)

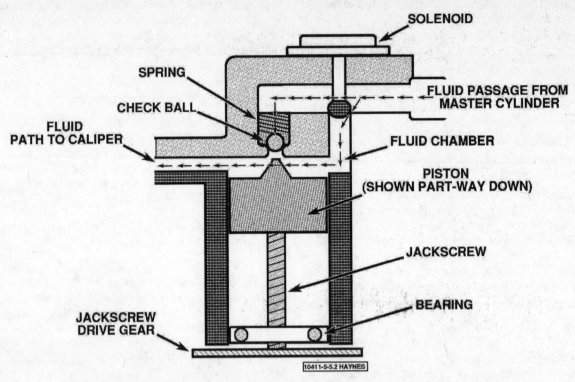

5.2 Here's a cutaway of one of the modulator pistons; this one operates a front brake

sensors are mounted in the rear suspension knuckles and their tone rings are integral with the rear hubs.

Indicator lights

The system has two lights, an amber one to indicate problems and a blue ABS ACTIVE light to indicate when the system is operation. A red light indicates problems with the main brake system.

System operation

Refer to illustrations 5.2 and 5.3

When the ignition is turned to the On position, the ABS and ABS ACTIVE lights illuminate for three seconds, then go out. The red brake warning light should flash once. When the key its turned to Start, the blue light should go out, the amber light should stay on and the red brake warning light should glow steadily. The lights should go out when the engine starts.

The EBCM positions the modulator pistons in their uppermost, or "home" position when the vehicle reaches about 5 mph. This can be heard as a clicking sound, and will be felt if the driver has a foot on the brake pedal.

During normal braking, the master cylinder transmits brake pressure to the wheel brakes through the modulator. The pistons are in the home positions. A probe on the tip of each piston pushes up the check ball in the fluid passage,

opening the route from the master cylinder to the wheel brake **(see illustration)**. The pistons are held in the home position by an expansion spring brake on the shaft of each motor. Hydraulic pressure in each ABS channel tries to push the piston downward. This causes torque to be applied through the jackscrew, to the gear, to the motor shaft. The torque expands the spring inside its housing, which locks the gear so it can't turn. When the motor turns during ABS operation, it contracts the spring, freeing the gear so it can be turned.

If the ABS should fail - by losing electrical power, for example - with a front piston out of the home position, the piston tip will not be up far enough to hold the check ball open. In this case, brake fluid from the master cylinder will flow past the open solenoid, so normal braking will still be available.

When the EBCM initiates anti-lock braking at a front wheel, the process starts out like many other ABS designs; the solenoid closes off the passage between the affected front wheel brake and the master cylinder, isolating the brake from pressure applied by the driver. There are no isolation solenoids for the rear passage; as the pistons move downward to start rear ABS operation, the protruding tips of the pistons stop pressing on the spring-loaded check balls, which then move downward under spring pressure to close the fluid passage to each rear brake.

The operation of the hydraulic modulator from this

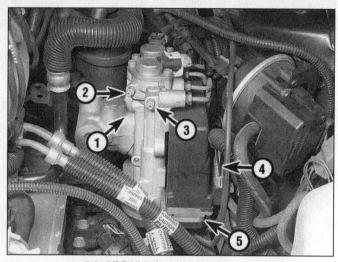

5.3 ABS VI hydraulic modulator details

1. Hydraulic modulator
2. Modulator rear bleed valve
3. Modulator front bleed valve
4. Motor pack
5. Gear cover and gears (on bottom of motor pack)

point on is what makes ABS VI different from every other ABS design in current use. The EBCM operates a bi-directional electric motor, which turns a jackscrew **(see illustration 5.2)**. The jackscrew raises or lowers an internally threaded piston inside a chamber, which is located in the hydraulic channel for the affected brake. This changes the internal volume of the chamber, which in turn changes the pressure in the brake line. When the piston rises, the chamber volume becomes smaller and brake line pressure increases. When the piston lowers, the chamber volume becomes larger and brake line pressure decreases. The motor rotates back and forth at the command of the EBCM, raising and lowering the piston. This change in pressure is used to "pump" the brakes just as the driver's foot on the pedal would do, but it happens much more rapidly.

The motors operate the jackscrews through gears, which are located inside a cover on the bottom of the hydraulic modulator **(see illustration)**. The motors are contained in a motor pack, which is attached to the side of the hydraulic modulator.

System service

Diagnosis

Diagnosis of ABS VI requires a General Motors TECH 1 scan tool or equivalent. Refer to the scanner manufacturer's instructions.

Bleeding

Warning 1: *Wear eye protection when bleeding the brake system. If the fluid comes in contact with your eyes, immediately rinse them with water and seek medical attention.*

Warning 2: *Never use old brake fluid. It contains moisture which can boil, rendering the brake system inoperative.*

Warning 3: *If, after bleeding the system you do not have a firm brake pedal, or if the ABS light on the instrument panel does not go off, or if you have any doubts whatsoever about the effectiveness of the brake system, have it towed to a dealer service department or other repair shop equipped with the necessary tools for bleeding the hydraulic modulator.*

Caution: *Brake fluid will damage paint. Cover all painted surfaces and be careful not to spill fluid during this procedure.*

1 The manufacturer specifies that it will be necessary to bleed the entire system whenever air is allowed into any part of the system.

2 The pistons in the hydraulic modulator must be raised to the home position before bleeding the system. This can be done with a scan tool if available; if not, use the following procedure.

3 To raise the pistons to the home position without a scan tool, start the engine and let it run for 10 seconds. Watch the ABS light - it should turn off after three seconds or so. **Warning:** *If the light doesn't go off, a scan tool must be connected to diagnose the problem. Have the vehicle towed to a dealer service department or other repair shop equipped with the necessary tool.*

4 If the light turned off like it is supposed to, turn the ignition off and repeat the procedure. If the light goes off again after three seconds, the brakes can now be bled.

5 Have an assistant on hand, as well as a supply of new brake fluid, an empty clear container, a length of clear plastic tubing to fit over the bleeder valve and a wrench to open and close the bleeder valve.

6 Remove the cap from the brake fluid reservoir and add fluid, if necessary (see Chapter 1). Don't allow the fluid level to drop too low during this procedure - check it frequently. Reinstall the cap.

7 Bleed the master cylinder as follows:

Models without bleeder valves on the hydraulic modulator

8 Disconnect the two forward brake lines from the master cylinder with a flare-nut wrench.

9 Fill the reservoir with brake fluid until fluid begins to flow from the two forward outlets.

10 Reconnect the forward lines to the master cylinder and tighten the tube nut fittings.

11 Slowly depress and hold down the brake pedal.

12 Loosen the fittings again and allow any air in the fluid to be purged, then retighten the fittings.

13 Slowly release the pedal and wait 15 seconds.

14 Repeat this procedure until all air is removed from the two front outlets.

5.4 Typical front wheel speed sensor

5.5 Typical rear wheel speed sensor

15 Disconnect the two rear tube nut fittings and repeat this procedure until all air is expelled from those ports as well. Proceed to Step 17.

Models with bleeder valves on the hydraulic modulator

16 Attach the bleeder hose to the rearmost bleeder valve on the modulator assembly **(see illustration 5.3)**. With the other end of the hose in a jar partially filled with clean brake fluid, open the valve slowly and have an assistant depress the brake pedal. Keep the pedal down until fluid flows. Close the valve and release the brake pedal. Repeat this until no air is evident as the fluid enters the jar, then repeat the procedure for the forward bleeder valve. After bleeding the hydraulic modulator assembly, bleed the rest of the braking system as described below.

All models

17 Check the fluid level again, adding fluid as necessary. When bleeding, make sure the fluid coming out of the bleeder is not only free of bubbles, but clean also.

18 Raise the vehicle and support it securely on jackstands.

19 Beginning at the right rear brake, loosen the bleeder screw slightly, then tighten it to a point where it's snug but can still be loosened quickly and easily.

20 Place one end of the tubing over the bleeder screw and submerge the other end in brake fluid in the container.

21 Open the bleeder screw and have your assistant slowly depress the brake pedal and hold the pedal firmly depressed. Watch for air bubbles to exit the submerged end of the tube. When the fluid flow slows, tighten the

screw, then have your assistant slowly release the pedal. Wait five seconds before proceeding.

22 Repeat Step 21 until no more air is seen leaving the tube, then tighten the bleeder screw and proceed to the left rear brake, right front brake and left front brake, in that order. Be sure to check the fluid in the master cylinder reservoir frequently.

23 After bleeding the right rear wheel brake, repeat Steps 19 through 22 on the left rear brake, right front brake and the left front brake, in that order.

24 Lower the vehicle and check the fluid level in the brake fluid reservoir, adding fluid as necessary.

25 Check the operation of the brakes. The pedal should feel solid when depressed, with no sponginess. If necessary, repeat the entire process. **Warning:** *Do not operate the vehicle if you are in doubt about the effectiveness of the brake system.*

Component replacement

Refer to illustrations 5.4 and 5.5

The hydraulic modulator, gears and motor pack can be replaced separately. Internal components of the hydraulic modulator, such as solenoids and pistons, are replaced as part of the modulator assembly. Individual motors in the motor pack are also replaced as part of the motor pack assembly. **Warning:** *To prevent injury, the tension of the gears must be relieved before removing them. This requires a scan tool, and must be done before the unit is removed from the vehicle.*

Wheel speed sensors are bolt-in replacements **(see illustrations)**. Be sure to free the wiring harnesses from any retaining clips.

Chapter 6
Kelsey-Hayes
(Lucas Varity) systems

General information

Kelsey-Hayes is a manufacturer of anti-lock braking systems that was bought by Lucas Varity in 1997, at which time the name of the ABS was changed to Lucas Varity.

Kelsey-Hayes (Lucas Varity) rear-wheel-only anti-lock systems are used in Chrysler Corporation, Ford and General Motors pick-up trucks and vans, as well as by Geo, Isuzu and Mazda. The system is called Rear Anti-lock Braking System (RABS) by Ford, and Rear Wheel Anti-lock (RWAL) by Chrysler and General Motors.

The company also produced a hybrid four-wheel system, in which a separate front-wheel system is added to vehicles equipped with a rear-only system. Finally, Kelsey-Hayes produces several versions of a complete four-wheel anti-lock system.

Kelsey-Hayes EBC2 (RABS or RWAL)

EBC2 is a non-integrated, one-channel system that works on the rear brakes only. Hydraulic pressure for ABS operation is supplied by the driver's foot on the brake pedal. There is no pump or other source of hydraulic pres-

sure. On 4WD vehicles, the system works only when the vehicle is in 2WD.

A system that works on the rear wheels only is especially useful in pick-up trucks because of the varying amount of weight in the cargo bed. The rear brakes on a truck with a fully loaded cargo bed need to be more powerful than those on a truck with an empty bed. Since there's only one set of brakes at the rear, it's not possible to have both.

Vehicle manufacturers have tried to find a compromise by designing rear proportioning valves to respond to the amount of load in the vehicle. This helps, but is not a complete solution.

Rear anti-lock brake systems are a simple, effective answer. They allow the use of rear brakes powerful enough for a full load, but keep this powerful braking system from prematurely locking the rear wheels when the bed is lightly loaded.

System components
Refer to illustrations 6.1 through 6.6

System components are a control module, a speed sensor and a combination valve. The valve contains a dump solenoid and an isolation solenoid. General Motors vehicles also include a digital ratio adapter controller (DRAC) module.

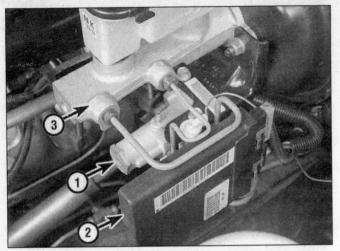

6.1 EBC2 system components (Chevy/GMC pick-ups)

1   Isolation/dump valve   3   Master cylinder
2   Control module

**6.2 Location of the EBC2 system components
(Dodge Durango)**

A   Controller, Anti-lock   B   RWAL valve
Brake (CAB)

Control module

The control module is mounted in various locations in the engine or passenger compartment **(see illustrations)**. It monitors the vehicle speed through a single sensor.

Speed sensor

The speed sensor is mounted in the differential in Ford and Chrysler vehicles **(see illustration)**. On General Motors vehicles, it's mounted in the transmission or transfer case. It works just like a wheel speed sensor, with a permanent magnet in the fixed portion of the sensor and a tone ring attached to the differential ring gear or the transmission or transfer case output shaft.

Combination valve

This valve, called the RABS valve by Chrysler and Ford

systems and RWAL valve by GM, is mounted in the brake lines between the master cylinder and rear brakes. Locations differ from model to model; in some cases it's next to the master cylinder **(see illustration)**, while in others it's mounted inside the frame rail under the vehicle **(see illustration)**. It contains an isolation valve, which is normally open, and a dump valve, which is normally closed.

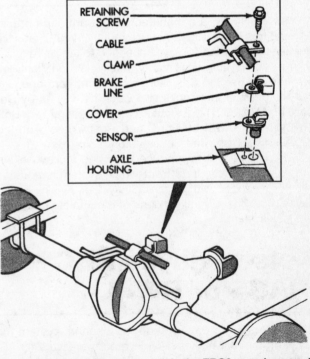

6.4 On Ford and Chrysler models the EBC2 speed sensor is mounted on top of the differential housing

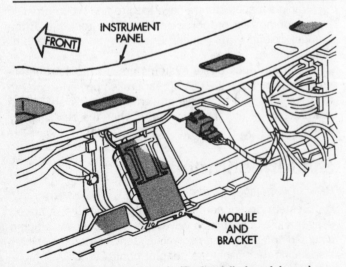

6.3 EBC2 control module (Dodge full-size pick-ups)

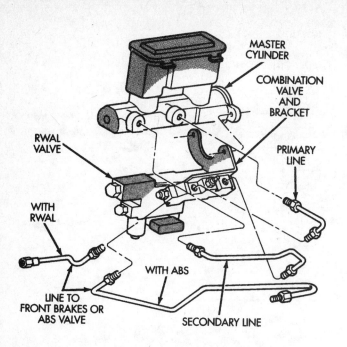

6.5 Here's a typical master cylinder, main brake combination valve and RWAL valve

6.6 On some Ford models, the hydraulic (RABS) valve is mounted on the rear frame rail (arrow)

Digital ratio adapter controller

This module, used on GM vehicles, converts the analog signal from the speed sensor into a digital signal that the ABS can use. The DRAC module also produces signals for other vehicle systems, such as cruise control and the engine management system. The module can be recalibrated or replaced with one of a different calibration if rear tire size is changed.

System operation

Refer to illustrations 6.7 through 6.11

During normal braking, hydraulic pressure from the master cylinder passes through the open isolation valve to the rear brakes **(see illustration)**. The control module monitors the rear wheel speed. When the rear wheel speed drops at an excessive rate, indicating wheel lockup, the control module initiates ABS braking.

During ABS braking, the isolation solenoid closes to cut off master cylinder pressure from the

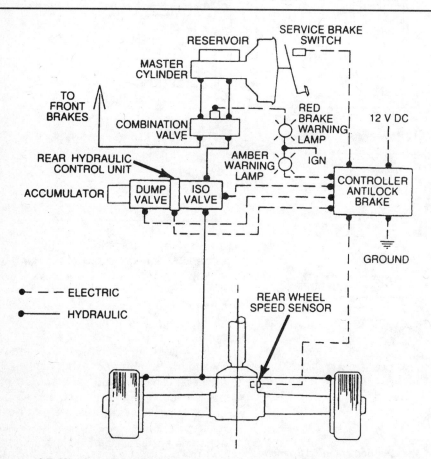

6.7 Here's a typical hydraulic and electrical schematic for EBC2 systems

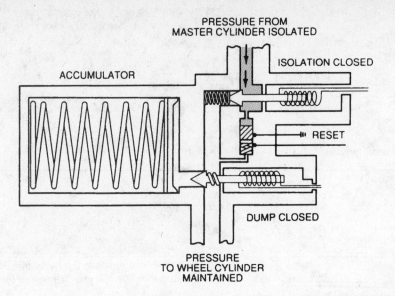

PRESSURE FROM MASTER CYLINDER ISOLATED

ISOLATION CLOSED

ACCUMULATOR

RESET

DUMP CLOSED

PRESSURE TO WHEEL CYLINDER MAINTAINED

6.8 When an ABS stop begins, the isolation valves closes to cut off master cylinder pressure from the rear brakes . . .

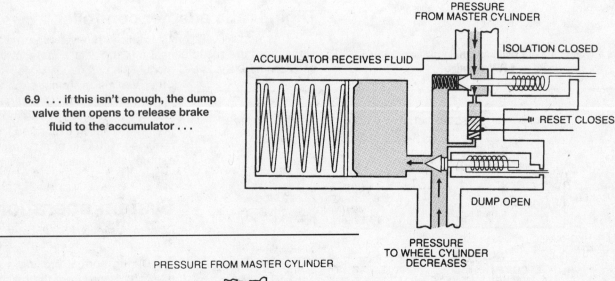

6.9 . . . if this isn't enough, the dump valve then opens to release brake fluid to the accumulator . . .

PRESSURE FROM MASTER CYLINDER

ISOLATION CLOSED

ACCUMULATOR RECEIVES FLUID

RESET CLOSES

DUMP OPEN

PRESSURE TO WHEEL CYLINDER DECREASES

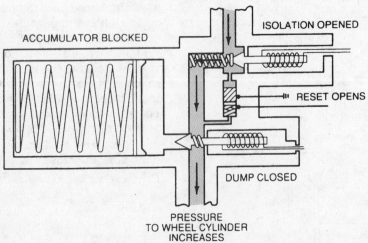

PRESSURE FROM MASTER CYLINDER

ISOLATION OPENED

ACCUMULATOR BLOCKED

RESET OPENS

DUMP CLOSED

PRESSURE TO WHEEL CYLINDER INCREASES

6.10 . . . when the wheel can be braked again, the isolation solenoid opens to allow master cylinder pressure to reach the rear brakes . . .

brakes **(see illustration)**. If this "hold" stage isn't enough to prevent rear wheel lockup, the control module opens the dump valve, which releases brake pressure to an accumulator in the combination valve **(see illustration)**. The module opens and closes the dump valve in very short pulses (milliseconds). A specific maximum number of dump cycles is allowed in any one ABS stop; if this number is exceeded, the ECU sets a trouble code. When enough pressure has been released to correct the lockup, the speed sensor indicates to the ECU that the rear wheel deceleration is no longer excessive,

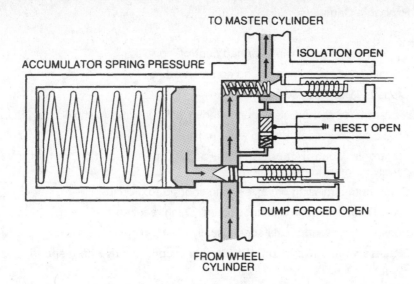

6.11 . . . and when the pedal is released at the end of the stop, the accumulator pushes stored fluid past the dump solenoid and back to the master cylinder

or locked up. The ECU then opens the isolation valve and closes the dump valve, allowing hydraulic pressure from the master cylinder to continue applying the rear brakes **(see illustration)**.

When the driver releases the brake pedal, the reset switch opens, sending a signal to the ECU. The ECU removes voltage from both of the solenoids, which then return under spring pressure to their normal positions (isolation valve open; dump valve closed) **(see illustration)**. This removes fluid pressure from the accumulator, which uses spring pressure to return the brake fluid to the master cylinder. The reset switch also resets the counter that records the number of dump cycles.

If a fault occurs, the control module will illuminate the warning lamp and disengage the ABS. Some models have a separate ABS warning lamp; others use the red brake warning lamp to indicate ABS problems. Note that a stored trouble code on Ford vehicles will be cleared if the engine is shut off before retrieving codes. The code may reappear if the engine is restarted, but you may have to drive the vehicle to try to reset it. It's a good idea to try to access codes before shutting off the engine whenever the light comes on .

System service

Diagnosis

Refer to illustration 6.12

A common cause of problems in this system is the speed sensor magnet picking up fine metal particles from inside the transmission, transfer case or differential. Removing and cleaning the speed sensor is a good place to start when diagnosing EBC2 problems.

The system can store trouble codes, but only one at a time. It displays codes by flashing the warning light in a series of long and short flashes. **Note:** *Trying to retrieve*

codes when there aren't any stored can cause a false code 9 to set. The code is indicated by a long flash, followed by a series of short flashes. For example, a long flash followed by two short flashes is a code 3 (not a code 12, as it would be with other systems). The flash sequence may start partway through, so wait until the first long flash to start counting the flashes. Let the sequence repeat as many times as necessary to be sure you've read the flashes correctly.

To retrieve codes, locate the diagnostic connector. The procedure from this point varies by manufacturer, as follows:

Ford: Do not shut off the engine when retrieving codes or the code will be cleared. Locate the diagnostic connector (single-pin connector with a black/orange wire) in the passenger compartment. Ground the connector for one second. When you're done reading the code, shut off the engine. This will clear the code.

Dodge: Turn on the ignition switch if isn't on already. Ground the test connector briefly with a jumper wire (it's located near the control module). When the code sequence begins to flash, disconnect the jumper wire. To clear the code once you're done, disconnect the electrical connector from the control module for 10 seconds.

General Motors: Only some GM vehicles equipped with RWAL can be diagnosed with flash codes, and not all codes can be retrieved by the flash method. A scanner is required on all models built after August 1994. For models built between August 1990 and August 1994, a scanner is required to retrieve codes 6, 9 and 10. To retrieve flash codes where possible, locate the ALDL connector and connect pins A and H together with a jumper wire for 20 seconds **(see illustration 4.17 in Chapter 4)**. When you're done reading the code, remove the ABS fuse or disconnect the negative cable from the vehicle's battery. This will clear the code.

Code	Probable Cause
1	Not used
2	Open isolation valve wiring or bad control module
3	Open dump valve wiring or bad control module
4	Closed RWAL valve switch
5	More than 16 dump pulses generated in 2WD vehicles (disabled for 4WD)
6	Erratic speed sensor reading while rolling
7	Electronic control module fuse pellet open, isolation output missing, or valve wiring shorted to ground
8	Dump output missing or valve wiring shorted to ground
9	Speed sensor wiring/resistance (usually high reading)
10	Speed sensor wiring/resistance (usually low reading)
11	Brake switch always on, RWAL light comes on when speed exceeds 40 mph
12	Not used
13	Electronic control module phase lock loop failure
14	Electronic control module program check failure
15	Electronic control module RAM failure

6.12 Kelsey-Hayes EBC2 trouble codes

Once you've read the code, use the accompanying table to identify the problem **(see illustration)**.

Bleeding

Warning 1: *Wear eye protection when bleeding the brake system. If the fluid comes in contact with your eyes, immediately rinse them with water and seek medical attention.*

Warning 2: *Never use old brake fluid. It contains moisture which can boil, rendering the brake system inoperative.*

Warning 3: *If, after bleeding the system you do not have a firm brake pedal, or if the ABS light on the instrument panel does not go off, or if you have any doubts whatsoever about the effectiveness of the brake system, have it towed to a dealer service department or other repair shop equipped with the necessary tools for bleeding the hydraulic modulator.*

Caution: *Brake fluid will damage paint. Cover all painted surfaces and be careful not to spill fluid during this procedure.*

Start by bleeding the modulator, then bleed the brakes in the normal way. If there's a bleed valve on the modulator, use it; if not, loosen a modulator hydraulic line.

Component replacement

The speed sensor gap is not adjustable. If the gap is too small or too large, the problem may be damage to the sensor or the housing it's mounted in. Speed sensor replacement is a bolt-in job. Be sure to clean the area around the sensor thoroughly before removing it, and detach the wiring harness from any retainers. The tone ring is integral with the component it's mounted on.

The combination valve and control module are replaced as assemblies.

Kelsey-Hayes EBC4

Refer to illustration 6.13

This is a non-integrated, three channel system with three or four wheel speed sensors. It was first used on 1990 General Motors M and L series mini-vans (Chevy Astro and Pontiac Safari), then added to the S- and T-series (compact) Blazer and Jimmy, as well as the Olds Bravada, for 1991. The system was also used on 1992 through 1994 Suburbans and added to the 1993 G series van. On 4WD models, the system works while the vehicle is in four wheel drive.

The system can be identified by the combined electronic and hydraulic control unit **(see illustration)**. The shape of the unit differs slightly from model to model, but all have five metal brake lines, two inlet from the master cylinder and three outlet, attached to one side of the unit. On pick-up trucks, the unit is mounted on the left inner fender. On M and L-series vans, it's mounted directly below the master cylinder. On G-series vans, it's mounted on the bracket attached to the passenger side frame rail.

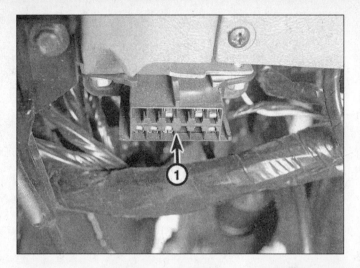

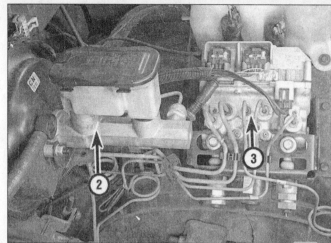

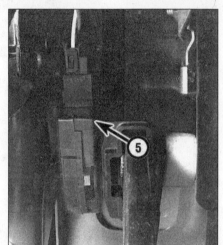

6.13 Kelsey-Hayes EBC4 (4WAL) components

1	Assembly Line Diagnostic Link (ALDL)	5	Brake pedal switch
2	Master cylinder	6	Parking brake switch
3	Brake Pressure Modulator Valve (called the Electro-Hydraulic Control Unit in early models)	7	Wheel speed sensor
		8	Warning light
4	Combination valve		

System components

Brake Pressure Modulator Valve (BPMV)

The electronic and hydraulic control unit combines both the electronic and hydraulic functions, which are handled by separate units in many systems, into a single unit. On models through 1992, this unit is called the Electro-Hydraulic Control Unit (EHCU). Beginning in 1993, the component was renamed the Brake Pressure Modulator valve (BPMV). This Section uses the term BPMV for all model years.

The BPMV contains the Electronic Brake Control Module (EBCM), which is the brain of the system. The EBCM receives electronic inputs and uses them to control the BPMV. It also operates the ABS warning lamp and stores diagnostic codes.

The BPMV contains the solenoids, accumulators, accumulator bypass valve, reset switches (models through February, 1993) and a dual-piston pump.

Solenoids and valves

Solenoids control two types of valves; isolation valves and pulse width modulation valves. Isolation valves are normally open, and close to cut off the master cylinder from the wheel brakes during an ABS stop. Pulse width modulation valves are normally closed, and open to release hydraulic pressure from the wheel brake during an ABS stop.

Low-pressure accumulators

These are spring-loaded storage containers that receive the fluid that bleeds off from the brakes during an ABS stop. All models through 1991, and all 1992 models except C- and K-series trucks, use two low-pressure accumulators. 1992 C- and K-series trucks, and all 1993 and later models, use three low-pressure accumulators, one for each front ABS channel and one for the rear channel.

Pump

The pump transfers fluid from the low-pressure accumulators to the high-pressure accumulators. The pump uses one electric motor with an eccentric shaft on one end to operate two pistons, one for each hydraulic circuit. An inlet check valve in the pump keeps the pump primed; this check valve opens at 12 to 14 psi. The outlet check valve opens during pump operation.

High-pressure accumulators

These receive fluid from the pump and store it at high pressure for use during the pressure increase stage of an ABS stop. A bypass valve releases excess accumulator pressure so the pump isn't overloaded. There are two high-pressure accumulators, one for both front channels and one for the rear channel.

Speed sensors

All versions of 4WAL use a separate wheel speed sensor for each front wheel. C- and K-series trucks through 1991, and all others through 1992, use a separate wheel speed sensor at each rear wheel. Beginning in 1992 for C- and K-series trucks, and 1993 for the other models, a single vehicle speed sensor is used at the rear, mounted in the transmission or transfer case.

Speed sensor calibrator

Vehicles with a single rear speed sensor also have a speed sensor calibrator. This converts the AC output of the speed sensor into a square-wave DC signal, which the EBCM can use. The calibrator adjusts the signal frequency for different sizes of wheels and tires, and allows the speed sensor to be used for several other systems besides ABS. To accommodate different sizes of tires, the calibrator can be adjusted in some models, and in other models replaced with a different version. The calibrator is mounted behind the glove compartment on all except G-series vans. On these models, it's clipped to the parking brake pedal bracket.

System operation

Electrical circuits

The BPMV receives power for the pump and solenoids through terminal B of the 2-pin connector. The other pin of this connector goes to ground. During ABS operation, the BPMV uses an internal relay to switch the pump on.

The BPMV receives wheel speed sensor signals through an 8-pin connector. On models with four wheel speed sensors, all eight terminals of the connector are used. On models with a vehicle speed sensor (which have only two wheel speed sensors), only terminals B, C, F and G are used.

A 10-pin connector is used for the remaining inputs and outputs. These include: EBCM power (terminal A); the amber ABS warning lamp (terminal B); the brake pedal switch (terminal C); the transfer case switch on 4x4 models (terminal D); diagnostic output (terminal F); and the red brake warning lamp (terminal H).

Terminal J of the 10-pin connector provides ground. On models that use a vehicle speed sensor for the rear channel, the VSS signal is first modified by the calibrator, then sent to terminal E of the 10-pin connector.

On models with reset switches (produced through February 1992), the metal brake lines provide ground for the switches. Therefore, it's important that the BPMV be securely bolted to the vehicle.

Circuit protection

A fusible link protects the pump motor and solenoid circuit (terminal A of the 2-pin connector). A 20-amp fuse protects the warning lamp circuits (terminals B and H of the

10-pin connector). A 15-amp fuse protects the EBCM power circuit (terminal A of the 10-pin connector).

Self-diagnosis

On startup, the EBCM conducts a test of the ABS warning lamp by lighting the bulb briefly and checking its circuit for opens and shorts. If it finds a problem, it stores a trouble code. It also checks the red brake warning lamp circuit, looking for problems both in the lamp and in the main braking system. The EBCM also checks the speed sensor circuits for continuity and checks its own internal circuitry.

If no problems are found during the startup check, the EBCM turns off the warning lamp. The entire check takes about three seconds. If a problem is found, the EBCM keeps the amber warning lamp on by grounding terminal B of the 10-pin connector. It also disengages the ABS and stores a trouble code.

When the vehicle is first driven off and reaches 8 mph, the EBCM operates the components in the hydraulic portion of the BPMV, including the solenoids, pump and relay. This produces sounds, which the driver may hear. This is normal, especially on 1992 and earlier models.

If the driver's foot is on the brake pedal during the 8 mph check, the EBCM will delay the check until the pedal is released.

While the vehicle is in operation, the EBCM checks the wheel sensors; circuit continuity while the vehicle is standing still, and speed sensor output when the vehicle is moving above 3 mph. During braking, the EBCM monitors the signals from the reset switches (vehicles built through February 1992) to make sure the switch circuits are good.

Normal braking

During normal braking, the isolation solenoids are open, allowing free passage of hydraulic pressure from the master cylinder to the wheel brakes. The pulse width modulation (release) solenoids are closed, so hydraulic pressure can increase when the brakes are applied. The accumulators, both high and low pressure, remain empty and the pump does not run. The wheel speed sensors and the brake pedal switch send continuous signals to the EBCM, which monitors them to determine when anti-lock braking is necessary.

Anti-lock braking

The EBCM needs specific signals from the speed sensors and the brake pedal switch to decide that anti-lock braking is needed. The pedal switch signal must indicate that the brakes have been applied, and one or more speed sensor signals must be dropping fast enough to indicate that a wheel is about to lock up.

Anti-lock braking begins with the isolation solenoids. These normally open solenoids are closed by the EBCM, which cuts off master cylinder pressure from the wheel brakes. The pulse width modulator solenoids, which are normally closed, stay closed. This holds brake pressure steady.

If the EBCM concludes that holding a steady pressure isn't enough to prevent wheel lock-up, it opens the pulse width modulation solenoid, which releases brake fluid from the wheel brake. This causes brake pressure to drop. The released fluid flows to the low-pressure accumulator, where it is retrieved by the pump and pumped to the high-pressure accumulator. The EBCM causes the pump to run by grounding the pump relay, which is located inside the BPMV.

When the EBCM decides that the wheel is no longer about to lock up, meaning that its brake can receive more hydraulic pressure, the check valve opens, allowing pressurized fluid from the high-pressure accumulator into the hydraulic circuit to increase brake pressure. If still more pressure increase is needed, the EBCM opens the isolation solenoid, allowing master cylinder pressure back into the brake circuit.

System service
Diagnosis

Refer to illustration 6.14

The EBCM memory stores a number of trouble codes that can help identify problems. Codes fall into three different categories, which General Motors has assigned the names hard, condition-latched soft, and ignition-latched soft.

Condition-latched soft codes disengage the ABS and turn on the amber light only as long as the condition, or problem, exists.

Ignition-latched soft codes cause the EBCM to disengage the ABS until the ignition is shut off and turned back on; if the problem has gone away, ABS will be reactivated and the warning lamp turned out when the key is turned back on.

Hard codes cause the EBCM to disengage the ABS and not re-engage it until the problem is repaired.

Some codes may fall into more than one category, depending on how many times they occur.

Trouble codes can be retrieved by flashing the ABS warning lamp to indicate the number of the code. To retrieve codes, locate the ALDL connector and connect pins A and H together with a jumper wire **(see illustration 4.17 in Chapter 4)**. Turn the ignition key to On (but don't start the engine) and watch the ABS warning lamp. After two or three seconds, the ABS warning lamp will begin to flash in a pattern that indicates the code.

The initial code is always code 12 (2WD) or code 13 (4WD and all-wheel drive). This is indicated by a single flash, then two more flashes close together (code 12) or a single flash and four flashes (code 14). This indicates that the system is ready. **Note:** *If the brake pedal is pressed during the check, the ABS lamp will flash code 13 (2WD) or code 15 (4WD and all-wheel drive). This does not indicate a problem.*

The initial code will flash three times, then any trouble codes will be flashed three times each. The sequence of codes will repeat itself, starting with the initial code, once it has displayed all of the stored codes.

When you're done reading the codes, disconnect the jumper wire from terminal H of the ALDL connector. Leave it connected to terminal A, since you'll shortly need to reconnect it between terminals A and H.

Once you've read the codes, use the accompanying table to identify the problem (see illustration).

To clear codes, turn the ignition to Off, then back to On (but as before, don't start the engine). Reconnect the wire between terminals A and H for two seconds, then disconnect it from terminal H, then reconnect it again for two sec-

onds. **Note:** *Don't wait more than 10 seconds between the times you connect the wire, and don't connect the wire more than twice.* This should cause both the amber ABS lamp and the red brake warning lamp to illuminate for two seconds. When this happens, the codes have been cleared.

Bleeding

Warning 1: *Wear eye protection when bleeding the brake system. If the fluid comes in contact with your eyes, immediately rinse them with water and seek medical attention.*

Warning 2: *Never use old brake fluid. It contains moisture which can boil, rendering the brake system inoperative.*

Warning 3: *If, after bleeding the system you do not have a firm brake pedal, or if the ABS light on the instrument panel does not go off, or if you have any doubts whatsoever about the effectiveness of the brake system, have it towed to a dealer service department or other repair shop equipped with the necessary tools for bleeding the hydraulic modulator.*

Caution: *Brake fluid will damage paint. Cover all painted surfaces and be careful not to spill fluid during this procedure.*

Bleeding is conventional, unless one of the lines at the BPMV has been opened or the BPMV has been replaced. In this case, you'll need to bleed the BPMV as well. If you can't obtain a firm pedal, pressure bleeding equipment, special adapters, and a scan tool will be required.

Component replacement

Speed sensor replacement is a bolt-in job. Be careful to route the sensor harness correctly, and secure it in all of its retainers. Sensor rings are integral with the component they're mounted on and are replaced as an assembly.

The entire brake pressure modulator valve (BPMV), including the hydraulic components and the electronic brake control module (EBCM), is replaced as a single assembly. The EBCM and hydraulic components can't be replaced separately.

Kelsey-Hayes EBC310

Refer to illustrations 6.15, 6.16 and 6.17

This system is used in GM pick-ups and vans, beginning with the 1995 model year. It's also used in Chrysler products such as the 1997 and later Dodge Dakota.

The system uses three hydraulic channels, one at each front wheel and one for both rear wheels. It can be recognized by its combined electronic and hydraulic control assembly (see illustration). Dodge calls this a Controller, Anti-lock Brake (CAB). GM calls it an electro-hydraulic control unit (EHCU).

The General Motors version is very similar to the EBC4 system described earlier. However, it no longer uses high-

Code	Probable cause
12	Initialization code (2WD)
13	Initialization code with brake pedal pressed (2WD)
14	Initialization code (4WD)
15	Initialization code with brake pedal pressed (4WD)
21	Right front wheel speed sensor circuit open
22	No signal from right front wheel speed sensor
23	Intermittent signal from right front wheel speed sensor
25	Left front wheel speed sensor circuit open
26	No signal from left front wheel speed sensor
27	Intermittent signal from left front wheel speed sensor
28	Loss of signal from both front wheel speed sensors at once
29	Loss of signal from all speed sensors at once
31	Right rear wheel speed sensor circuit open (four-sensor system)
32	No signal from right rear wheel speed sensor (four-sensor system)
33	Intermittent signal from right rear wheel speed sensor (four-sensor system)
35	Left rear wheel speed sensor or vehicle speed sensor circuit open
36	No signal from left rear wheel speed sensor or vehicle speed sensor
37	Intermittent signal from left rear wheel speed sensor or vehicle speed sensor
38	Excessive difference in speed sensor signals
41 through 66	Internal failure in BPMV
67	Open pump circuit or shorted EBCM pump output

6.14 EBC4 trouble codes

pressure accumulators to provide hydraulic pressure during the build cycle of an ABS stop. Instead, pump pressure is used, aided by master cylinder pressure if this isn't enough.

The Dodge truck version is also similar to the EBC4, but rather than eliminating both high-pressure accumulators, only the rear one has been eliminated. The high-pressure accumulator for the front circuit remains. In place of the high-pressure accumulator in the rear circuit, there is an attenuator, a separate spring-loaded chamber that damps pressure pulses to reduce pedal feedback during an ABS stop **(see illustrations)**.

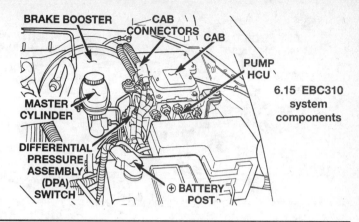

6.15 EBC310 system components

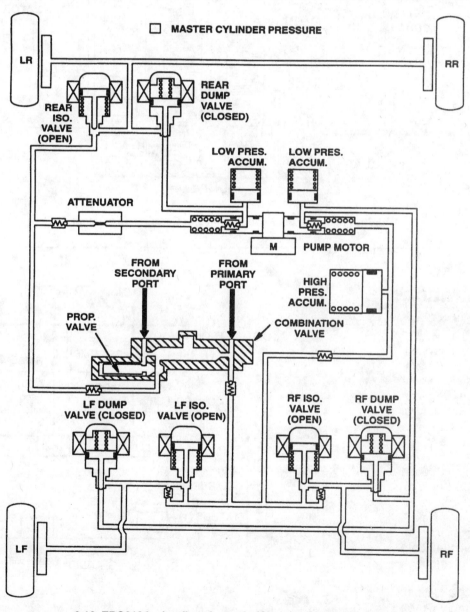

6.16 EBC310 hydraulic schematic (Chrysler Corporation version)

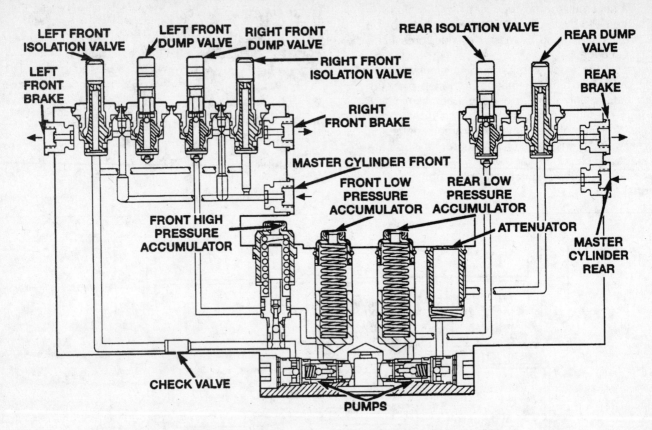

6.17 EBC310 hydraulic control unit (Chrysler Corporation version)

System operation

Refer to illustrations 6.18, 6.19, 6.20 and 6.21

Operation of the GM system is very similar to the EBC4 system described earlier, except that build pressure isn't stored in high-pressure accumulators. This section discusses the system used in Dodge trucks.

The system receives power from the ignition switch through terminal 1-C2 **(see illustrations)**. This input is protected by a 20 amp fuse in the junction block. A second power input for the pump is protected by a 40 amp fuse in the power distribution center.

At startup, the CAB tests its random access memory (RAM) and read-only memory (ROM). If

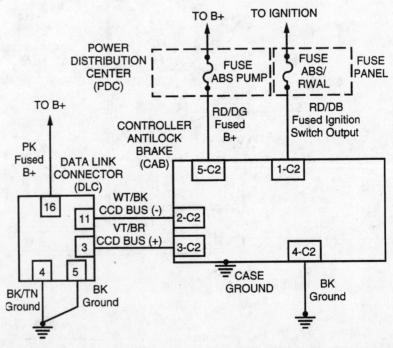

6.18 EBC310 power and CCD bus connections (Chrysler Corporation version)

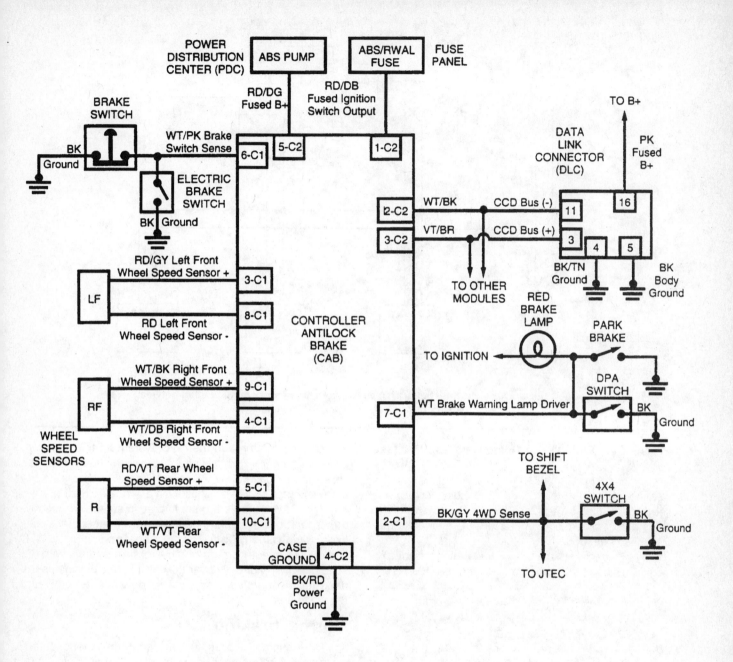

6.19 EBC310 electrical schematic (Chrysler Corporation version)

there's a problem in either type of memory, the CAB disengages ABS, sets a code and turns on the ABS warning lamp.

When the vehicle is driven off, the CAB operates the solenoids and pump briefly to test them. This will occur at a speed below 4 mph if the brake pedal has been released. If the pedal is being pressed, the test will occur when the vehicle reaches 4 mph. If there's a problem, the CAB disengages

ABS, sets a code and turns on the ABS warning lamp.

Wheel speed signals are provided by three speed sensors, one at each front wheel and on at the differential in the rear axle. Besides the wheel speed sensors, the CAB receives inputs from the brake lamp switch, 4WD switch (if equipped), and the warning lamps for the ABS and main braking system. The CAB can also communicate with other control modules, such as the "smart" instrument cluster,

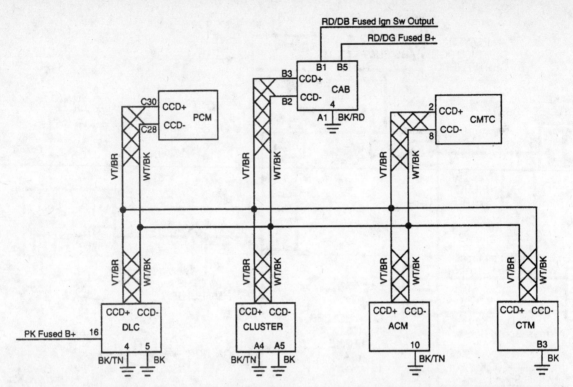

6.20 Chrysler Collision Detection (CCD) bus system, used for communication between the various control modules on the vehicle

through the Chrysler Collision Detection (CCD) bus **(see illustration)**.

The speed sensor signals let the CAB know if a wheel is decelerating rapidly, which indicates impending lockup.

The brake lamp switch lets the CAB know that the brake has been applied, so it doesn't initiate anti-lock braking when it isn't needed.

The 4WD switch lets the CAB know that the front axle is engaged, which means that the front and rear wheels are

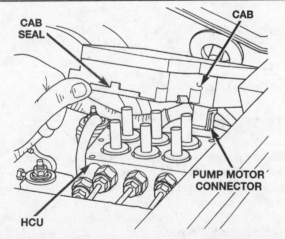

6.21 The electronic control unit (called a CAB by Chrysler Corporation and an EBCM by General Motors) can be replaced separately from the hydraulic control unit

locked together through the 4WD system. In this situation, braking at the front wheels affects the rear wheels, and vice versa. In response, the CAB increases the number of pressure decrease cycles it will allow in any one ABS stop.

The CAB controls the six hydraulic solenoids directly, rather than through wiring harnesses from a separate control unit **(see illustration)**. The electronic portion of the CAB is mounted directly on top of the hydraulic portion, with the solenoids fitting directly over the valves. This eliminates the need for a separate wiring harness between the CAB and the solenoids.

Normal braking

During normal braking, the isolation solenoids are open, allowing free passage of hydraulic pressure from the master cylinder to the wheel brakes. The dump solenoids are closed, so hydraulic pressure can increase when the brakes are applied. The accumulators, both high and low pressure, remain empty and the pump does not run. The wheel speed sensors and the brake pedal switch send continuous signals to the CAB, which monitors them to determine when anti-lock braking is necessary.

Anti-lock braking

The CAB needs specific signals from the speed sensors and the brake pedal switch to decide that anti-lock braking is needed. The pedal switch signal must indicate that the brakes have been applied, and one or more speed

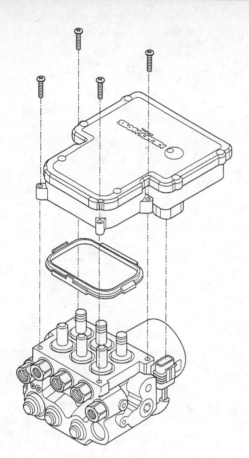

6.22 The two control units are screwed together with a seal between them

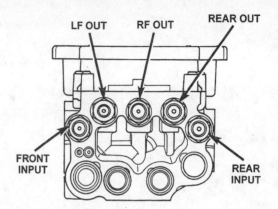

6.23 Here's the brake line arrangement on an EBC310 hydraulic control unit

sensor signals must be dropping fast enough to indicate that a wheel is about to lock up.

Anti-lock braking begins with the isolation solenoids. These normally open solenoids are closed by the CAB, which cuts off master cylinder pressure from the wheel brakes. The dump solenoids, which are normally closed, stay closed. This holds brake pressure steady.

If the CAB concludes that holding a steady pressure isn't enough to prevent wheel lock-up, it opens the dump solenoid, which releases brake fluid from the wheel brake. This causes brake pressure to drop. The released fluid flows to the low-pressure accumulator. In the front channels, it is retrieved by the pump and pumped to the high-pressure accumulator.

When the CAB decides that the wheel is no longer about to lock up, meaning that its brake can receive more hydraulic pressure, the isolation solenoid opens, allowing pressurized fluid from the high-pressure accumulator (front channels) or pump (rear channels) into the hydraulic circuit to increase brake pressure. If still more pressure increase is needed, master cylinder pressure is allowed back into the brake circuit. This may cause pedal pulsation or a drop in pedal height during an ABS stop, but does not indicate a problem.

System service
Diagnosis and bleeding

Warning 1: *Wear eye protection when bleeding the brake system. If the fluid comes in contact with your eyes, immediately rinse them with water and seek medical attention.*

Warning 2: *Never use old brake fluid. It contains moisture which can boil, rendering the brake system inoperative.*

Warning 3: *If, after bleeding the system you do not have a firm brake pedal, or if the ABS light on the instrument panel does not go off, or if you have any doubts whatsoever about the effectiveness of the brake system, have it towed to a dealer service department or other repair shop equipped with the necessary tools for bleeding the hydraulic modulator.*

Caution: *Brake fluid will damage paint. Cover all painted surfaces and be careful not to spill fluid during this procedure.*

Chrysler Corporation specifies the use of a DRB III scan tool or equivalent to retrieve codes from the CAB. A scan tool is also required to bleed the hydraulic control unit if air manages to find its way into it. Bleeding the remainder of the system is conventional.

Component replacement

Refer to illustrations 6.22 and 6.23

Speed sensor replacement is a bolt-in job. Be careful to route the sensor harness correctly, and secure it in all of its retainers. Sensor rings are integral with the component they're mounted on and are replaced as an assembly.

The electronic and hydraulic control units can be separated from each other and replaced separately **(see illustration)**. Be sure to reconnect the fluid lines to the correct ports if the HCU is replaced **(see illustration)**.

The system relay is mounted inside the electronic control unit and is replaced as a unit with it. The pump is mounted inside the HCU and is replaced as a unit with it.

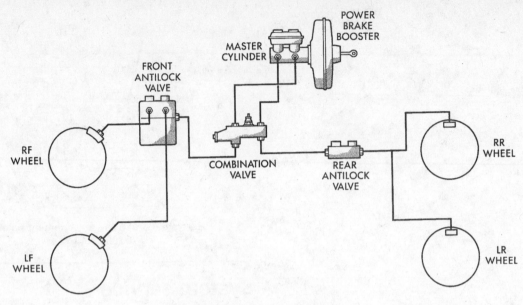

6.24 EBC5H hydraulic schematic

Kelsey Hayes EBC5H

Refer to illustrations 6.24 and 6.25

This system is a hybrid used in some Dodge pick-up trucks. It consists of an EBC2 (RWAL) system at the rear, combined with a separate front wheel anti-lock system **(see illustration)**. It can be identified by its two hydraulic units, one for the front brakes and one for the rear **(see illustrations)**.

System components

The system consists of the front and rear hydraulic control units, relays, 4WD switch (4WD models), three

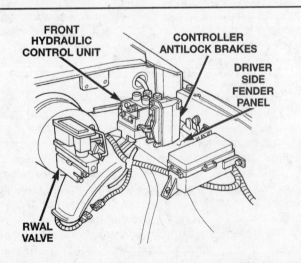

6.25 Typical EBC5H component locations

speed sensors and the electronic control unit - which Chrysler calls the Controller, Anti-lock Brake (CAB).

The front HCU contains two isolation and two dump solenoids, as well as a pump, low-pressure accumulator, high-pressure accumulator, switches and check valves.

The rear HCU contains one isolation and one dump solenoid and one accumulator.

The ABS main relay is mounted in the engine compartment near the HCU on 1993 through 1995 vans, and in the power distribution center on all other models. The ABS fuse is installed in the fuse block or power distribution center.

System operation

Refer to illustrations 6.26, 6.27 and 6.28

The front and rear systems function differently. The rear system is the same as the EBC2 system described earlier in this chapter. It has no pump and no means of increasing pressure during an ABS stop beyond the pressure supplied by the driver at the brake pedal.

The front system employs an electric pump to increase pressure during an ABS stop and to move released brake fluid from the low-pressure accumulator to the high-pressure accumulator, where it is used to increase brake line pressure during the build cycle of an ABS stop.

The system receives power for the warning lamp and main relay coil from the ignition switch **(see illustrations)**. This input is protected by a fuse. Power for the pump and solenoids, which flows through the main relay when it is energized by its coil, comes directly from the battery and is protected by a fusible link.

When the ignition is turned to On, the CAB tests its random access memory (RAM) and read-only memory (ROM).

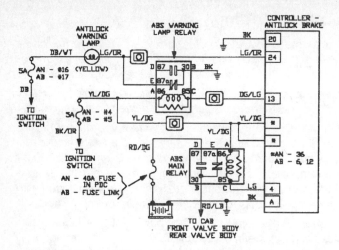

6.26 EBC5H power inputs - 1993 Dakota and 1993-1/2 vans

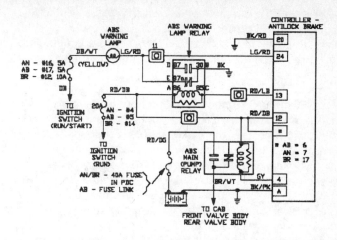

6.27 EBC5H power inputs - 1994 through 1996 Dakota and 1994 through 1997 Dodge pick-ups and vans

If there's a problem in either type of memory, the CAB disengages ABS, sets a code and turns on the ABS warning lamp. It also check the warning lamps bulbs and circuits.

When the vehicle is driven off, the CAB operates the solenoids and pump briefly to test them as soon as vehicle speed reaches 8 mph. If there's a problem, the CAB disengages the ABS, sets a code and turns on the ABS warning lamp.

Wheel speed signals are provided by three speed sensors, one at each front wheel and on at the differential in the rear axle. Besides the wheel speed sensors, the CAB receives inputs from the brake lamp switch, 4WD switch (if equipped), and the warning lamps for the ABS and main braking system.

The speed sensor signals let the CAB know if a wheel is decelerating rapidly, which indicates impending lockup.

The brake lamp switch lets the CAB know that the brake has been applied, so it doesn't initiate anti-lock braking when it isn't needed.

The 4WD switch lets the CAB know that the front axle is engaged, which means that the front and rear wheels are locked together through the 4WD system. In this situation, braking at the front wheels affects the rear wheels, and vice versa. In response, the CAB increases the number of pressure decrease cycles it will allow in any one ABS stop.

Normal braking

During normal braking, the isolation solenoids are open, allowing free passage of hydraulic pressure from the master cylinder to the wheel brakes. The dump solenoids are closed, so hydraulic pressure can increase when the brakes are applied. The accumulators, in both the front and rear HCUs, remain empty and the front HCU's pump does not run. The wheel speed sensors and the brake pedal switch send continuous signals to the CAB, which monitors them to determine when anti-lock braking is necessary.

Anti-lock braking

The CAB needs specific signals from the speed sensors and the brake pedal switch to decide that anti-lock braking is needed. The pedal switch signal must indicate that the brakes have been applied, and one or more speed sensor signals must be dropping fast enough to indicate that a wheel is about to lock up.

Anti-lock braking begins with the isolation solenoids **(see illustration)**. These normally open solenoids are closed by the CAB, which cuts off master cylinder pressure from the wheel brakes. The dump solenoids, which are normally closed, stay closed. This holds brake pressure steady. The same thing happens in both the front and rear HCUs.

If the CAB concludes that holding a steady pressure isn't enough to prevent wheel lock-up, it opens the dump

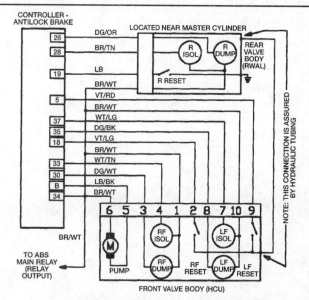

6.28 EBC5H power outputs to solenoids

solenoid at the affected wheel, which releases brake fluid from the wheel brake. This causes brake pressure to drop. The released fluid flows to the low-pressure accumulator (front) or single accumulator (rear). In the front channels, it is retrieved by the pump and pumped to the high-pressure accumulator.

When the CAB decides that a front wheel is no longer about to lock up, meaning that its brake can receive more hydraulic pressure, the isolation solenoid opens, allowing pressurized fluid from the high-pressure accumulator into the hydraulic circuit to increase brake pressure. If still more pressure increase is needed, master cylinder pressure is allowed back into the brake circuit. This may cause pedal pulsation or a drop in pedal height during an ABS stop, but does not indicate a problem.

In the rear system, there is no means of increasing hydraulic pressure during the ABS stop beyond that supplied by the driver's foot on the brake pedal. The brake fluid released from the rear brakes during the ABS stop is stored in the accumulator and returned to the master cylinder after the ABS stop is complete.

System service

Diagnosis

Chrysler Corporation specifies the use of a DRB III scan tool or equivalent to retrieve codes from the CAB.

Brake bleeding

Warning 1: *Wear eye protection when bleeding the brake system. If the fluid comes in contact with your eyes, immediately rinse them with water and seek medical attention.*

Warning 2: *Never use old brake fluid. It contains moisture which can boil, rendering the brake system inoperative.*

Warning 3: *If, after bleeding the system you do not have a firm brake pedal, or if the ABS light on the instrument panel does not go off, or if you have any doubts whatsoever about the effectiveness of the brake system, have it towed to a dealer service department or other repair shop equipped with the necessary tools for bleeding the hydraulic modulator.*

Caution: *Brake fluid will damage paint. Cover all painted surfaces and be careful not to spill fluid during this procedure.*

Bleeding of the main brake system is conventional. Bleeding the HCU requires a DRB III scan tool or equivalent. Follow the tool manufacturer's instructions. After the HCU is bled, bleed the main brake system again.

Component replacement

Speed sensor replacement is a bolt-in job. Be careful to route the sensor harness correctly, and secure it in all of its retainers. Sensor rings are integral with the component they're mounted on and are replaced as an assembly.

The CAB and the front and rear hydraulic control units can be replaced separately.

Chapter 7
Nippondenso, Nissin and Sumitomo systems

Nippondenso (Subaru)

1990 and later Subaru models with anti-lock brakes use one of several different Nippondenso systems (except the 1990 through 1992 Legacy, which has a Bosch system). All of these are four-channel systems with four wheel speed sensors. The front wheels are controlled independently, while the "select low" principle is used at the rear. All-wheel drive models use a G-switch that lets the electronic control unit know the rate of deceleration. This allows the ECU to change the ABS operation to compensate for different friction characteristics of the road surface.

Subaru Nippondenso 2L

This system is used on 1990 through 1992 Legacy turbo models, the 1993 Legacy with automatic transaxle, and the 1992 through 1997 SVX.

The system is similar is design and function to Bosch 2 systems, described in Chapter 4. The electronic control unit, which is mounted in the passenger compartment, controls the hydraulic control unit, which is mounted in the right front corner of the engine compartment.

System components

Refer to illustration 7.1

System components are the electronic control unit, hydraulic control unit, four wheel speed sensors, brake light switch, and ABS warning lamp **(see illustration on following page)**. The hydraulic control unit contains three solenoids and the pump. There's one wheel speed sensor at each wheel, with a tone wheel mounted on each hub.

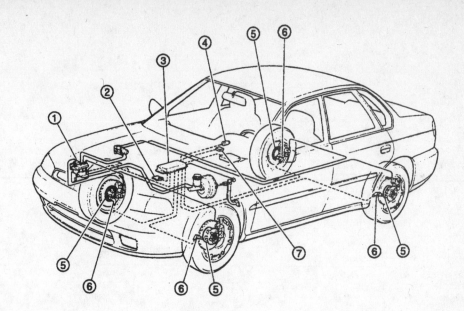

7.1 Nippondenso 2L ABS components (1994 Subaru Legacy shown)

1   Hydraulic control unit
2   G-sensor
3   Electronic control unit
4   ABS warning lamp
5   Tone wheel
6   Wheel speed sensor
7   Diagnostic connector

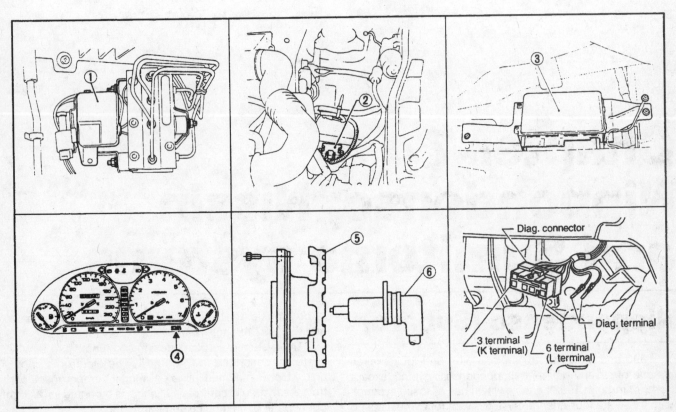

System operation

Refer to illustration 7.2

The battery supplies fuse-protected voltage to the ignition switch, which in turn supplies power to the brake light switch, G sensor (if equipped), ABS warning lamp, and automatic transmission control module **(see illustration)**. The ECU receives power from the ignition switch at terminal 1. Power for the pump and solenoid relays is supplied directly to the relays and does not flow through the ignition switch.

The ECU monitors the input voltage signals from the wheel speed sensors, When one of them drops too rapidly, indicating that a wheel is about to lock up, it initiates anti-lock braking. The ECU grounds the solenoid and pump relays, operating the solenoids and pump to maintain brake line pressure at a level that will prevent the wheel from locking up.

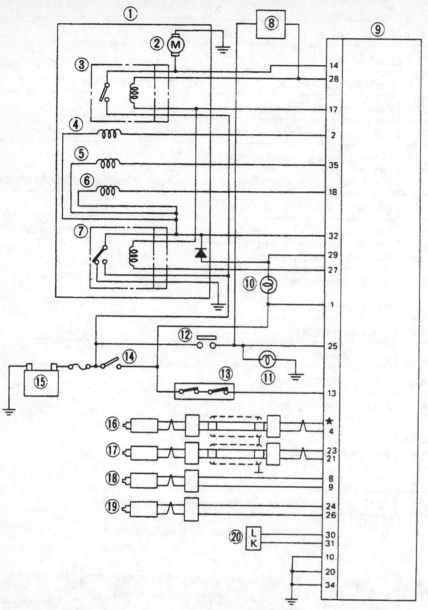

7.2 Nippondenso 2L ABS electrical schematic (1994 Subaru Legacy shown)

1 Hydraulic control unit
2 Pump motor
3 Pump relay
4 Left front solenoid
5 Right front solenoid
6 Rear solenoid
7 Solenoid relay
8 Automatic transaxle control module
9 Electronic control unit
10 ABS warning lamp
11 Brake light
12 Brake light switch
13 G-sensor
14 Ignition switch
15 Battery
16 Left front wheel speed sensor
17 Right front wheel speed sensor
18 Left rear wheel speed sensor
19 Right rear wheel speed sensor
20 Diagnostic connector

★FWD: 5
AWD: 22

System service

Diagnostics

Refer to illustrations 7.3 and 7.4

The system can store up to three trouble codes at a time. If more than three problems occur, the system will store the most recent three. These will stay in memory until they are cleared.

Trouble codes can be retrieved by flashing the ABS warning lamp as follows:

1 Locate the diagnostic connector under the driver's side of the instrument panel (**see illustration**). With the key in the Off position, connect one of the diagnosis terminals to connector terminal 6 (L).

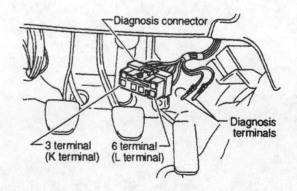

7.3 Nippondenso 2L diagnostic connector

2 Turn the key on and watch the ABS warning light. It will flash a long flash, then a short flash. This indicates code 11, the start code (not a trouble code). If no trouble codes are stored, only code 11 will flash.

3 If trouble codes are stored, the warning lamp will flash them in order, starting with the code most recently stored. Each code consists of a series of long and short flashes. A code 22, for example, would be two long flashes followed by two short flashes. A code 31 would be three long flashes followed by one short flash.

4 The codes will continue to flash in order for up to five minutes. While the codes are flashing, read them and write them down.

5 To interpret the codes, refer to the accompanying table **(see illustration)**.

6 To clear codes from the ECU memory, disconnect the diagnosis terminal from terminal 6. Reconnect and disconnect the connector three more times, all within a total of 12 seconds. Each connection and disconnection should last at least 1/2-second.

7 To make sure the codes are

Code	Problem area
11	Start code
21	Right front wheel speed sensor (open circuit or excessive input voltage)
22	Right front wheel speed sensor
23	Left front wheel speed sensor (open circuit or excessive input voltage)
24	Left front wheel speed sensor
25	Right rear wheel speed sensor (open circuit or excessive input voltage)
26	Right rear wheel speed sensor
27	Left rear wheel speed sensor (open circuit or excessive input voltage)
28	Left rear wheel speed sensor
29	Sensor tone wheel
31	Right front solenoid
33	Left front solenoid
39	Rear solenoid
41	Electronic control unit
42	Low source voltage
51	Solenoid relay
52	Pump or pump relay
54	Brake light circuit
56	Defective g-sensor or incorrect electronic control unit

7.4 Nippondenso 2L trouble codes

7.5 Here's a typical Nippondenso wheel speed sensor installed in a Subaru

7.6 The speed sensor tone rings are bolted to the hubs at the front and rear of the vehicle

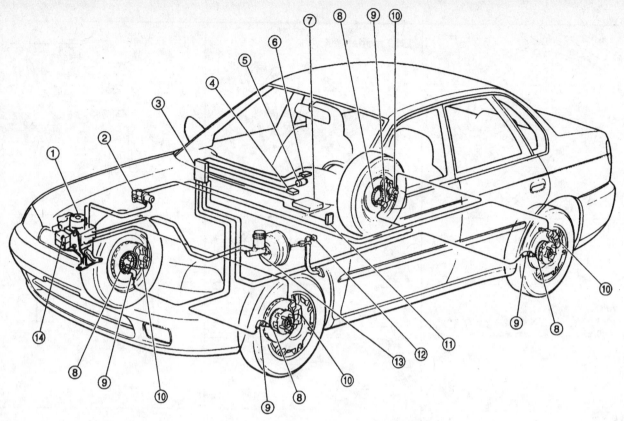

7.7 Nippondenso 5.3 ABS components - part 1 of 2 (1996 Subaru Legacy shown)

1	Hydraulic control unit	8	Tone wheel
2	Proportioning valve	9	Wheel speed sensor
3	Electronic control unit	10	Caliper
4	Diagnostic connector	11	G-sensor (all-wheel drive)
5	ABS warning lamp	12	Brake light switch
6	Data link connector (for Subaru scan tool)	13	Master cylinder
7	Transmission control module (automatic transaxle)	14	Relay box

cleared, reconnect the diagnosis terminal to terminal 6 and watch the ABS lamp. It should now flash only a code 11, the start code.

Wheel sensor adjustment

Measure the gap between the wheel speed sensor and the tone ring with a non-magnetic (brass or plastic) feeler gauge. It should be 0.035 to 0.055-inch at the front wheels and 0.028 to 0.047-inch at the rear wheels. If it's incorrect, it can be adjusted with spacers.

Component replacement

Refer to illustrations 7.5 and 7.6

Wheel sensor replacement is a bolt-in job **(see illustration)**. Be sure to check the air gap as described above.

Tone wheel replacement is also a bolt-in job **(see illustration)**. Tighten the mounting bolts to 84 to 144 in-lbs.

The hydraulic control unit and electronic control unit are replaced as assemblies.

Subaru Nippondenso 5.3

This system is used on the 1996 Subaru Legacy and Impreza. Similar in operation to the Bosch 5 systems described in Chapter 4, it uses a pair of two-position solenoids per hydraulic channel. The system has four wheel speed sensors and four hydraulic channels.

The electronic control unit, which is mounted behind the right side of the instrument panel, controls the hydraulic control unit, which is mounted in the right front corner of the engine compartment.

System components

Refer to illustrations 7.7 and 7.8

System components are the electronic control unit, hydraulic control unit, four wheel speed sensors, brake light switch, and ABS warning lamp **(see illustrations)**. The hydraulic control unit contains eight two-position solenoids (one inlet solenoid and one outlet solenoid per channel) and

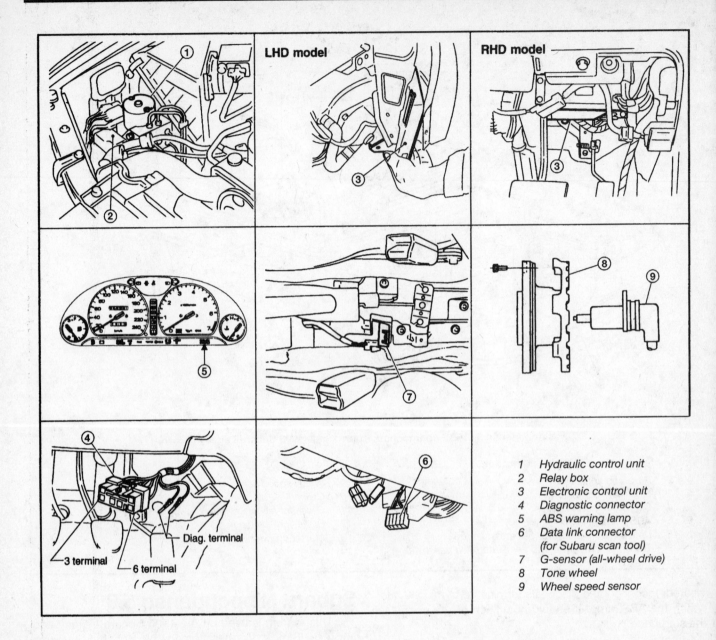

LHD model

RHD model

Diag. terminal

3 terminal

6 terminal

1 Hydraulic control unit
2 Relay box
3 Electronic control unit
4 Diagnostic connector
5 ABS warning lamp
6 Data link connector
   (for Subaru scan tool)
7 G-sensor (all-wheel drive)
8 Tone wheel
9 Wheel speed sensor

7.8 Nippondenso 5.3 ABS components - part 2 of 2 (1996 Subaru Legacy shown)

the pump. There's one wheel speed sensor at each wheel, with a tone wheel mounted on each hub.

System operation

Refer to illustrations 7.9 through 7.13

The electronic control unit receives system power from the ignition switch, through a fuse-protected circuit, at terminal 28.The ECU supplies power for the pump and solenoid relays at terminal 54, and for diagnostic output at

terminal 13 **(see illustration)**.

The ECU monitors the input voltage signals from the wheel speed sensors, When one of them drops too rapidly, indicating that a wheel is about to lock up, it initiates anti-lock braking. The ECU grounds the solenoid and pump relays, operating the solenoids and pump to maintain brake line pressure at a level that will prevent the wheel from locking up.

During normal braking, the inlet solenoids are open and

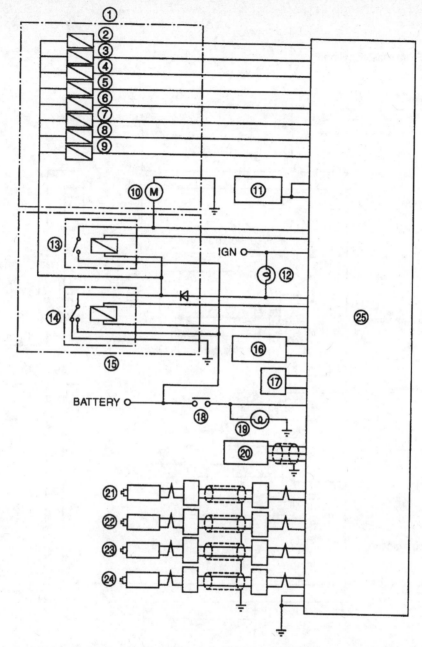

7.9 Nippondenso 5.3 ABS electrical schematic (1996 Subaru Legacy shown)

1	Hydraulic control unit	14	Solenoid relay
2	Left front inlet solenoid	15	Relay box
3	Left front outlet solenoid	16	Data link connector
4	Right front inlet solenoid	17	Diagnostic connector
5	Right front outlet solenoid	18	Brake light switch
6	Left rear inlet solenoid	19	Brake light
7	Left rear outlet solenoid	20	G-sensor
8	Right rear inlet solenoid	21	Left front wheel speed sensor
9	Right rear outlet solenoid	22	Right front wheel speed sensor
10	Pump motor	23	Left rear wheel speed sensor
11	Automatic transaxle control module	24	Right rear wheel speed sensor
12	ABS warning lamp	25	Electronic control unit
13	Pump relay		

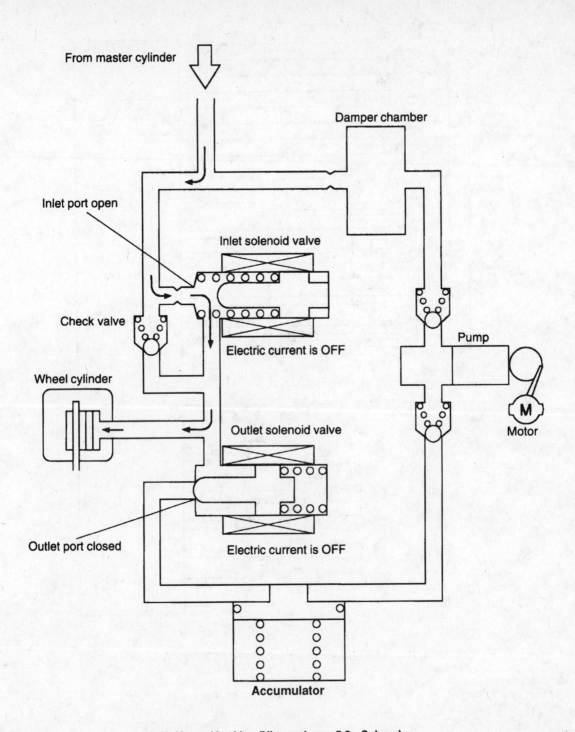

From master cylinder

Damper chamber

Inlet port open

Inlet solenoid valve

Check valve

Electric current is OFF

Wheel cylinder

Pump

Outlet solenoid valve

Motor

Outlet port closed

Electric current is OFF

Accumulator

7.10 Normal braking (Nippondenso 5.3 - Subaru)

the outlet solenoids are closed **(see illustration)**. Braking pressure flows through the open inlet solenoid. Since the outlet solenoid is closed, the brake fluid flows to the caliper and applies the brake. The pump remains off.

During the first phase of anti-lock braking, the inlet solenoid closes, cutting off master cylinder pressure from the brake **(see illustration)**. The pump starts to run. If the ECU decides the wheel is still decelerating too quickly, it

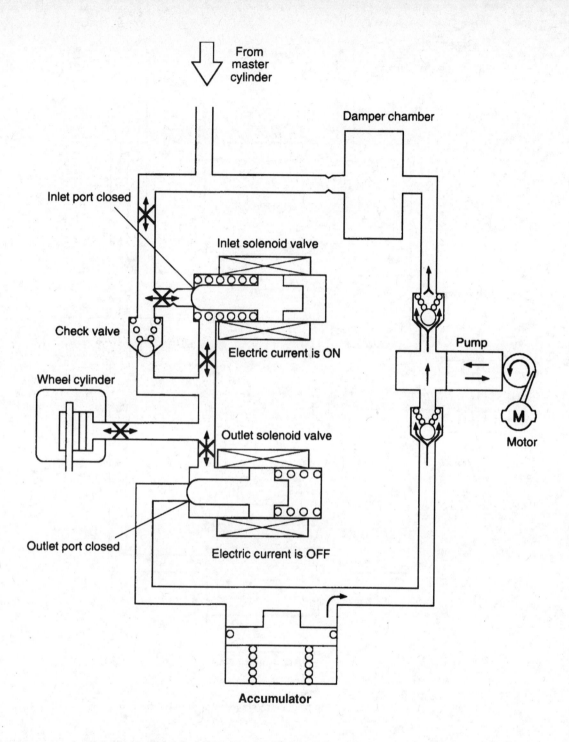

7.11 Anti-lock braking hold cycle (Nippondenso 5.3 - Subaru)

opens the outlet solenoid, releasing hydraulic pressure into a spring-loaded accumulator **(see illustration)**. The pump collects this fluid from the reservoir and returns it to the master cylinder, passing it through a damper chamber to reduce pedal pulsations felt by the driver.

When the ECU decides that more braking pressure can be applied to the wheel, it opens the inlet solenoid again, allowing pedal pressure to reach the brake **(see illustration)**.

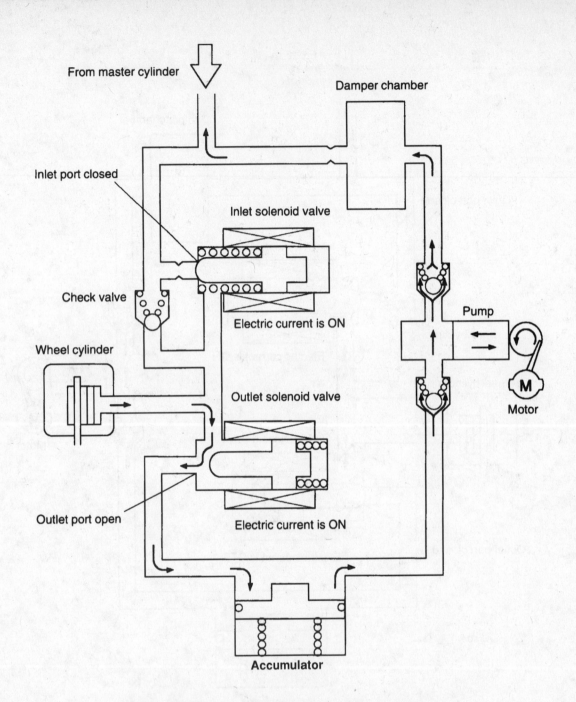

7.12 Anti-lock braking release cycle (Nippondenso 5.3 - Subaru)

System service

Diagnosis

The system can store up to three trouble codes at a time. If more than three problems occur, the system will store the most recent three. These will stay in memory until they are cleared.

Trouble codes can be retrieved and cleared in the same way as for the Nippondenso 2L system described earlier in this chapter. To interpret the codes, refer to the accompanying table (**see illustration 7.4**).

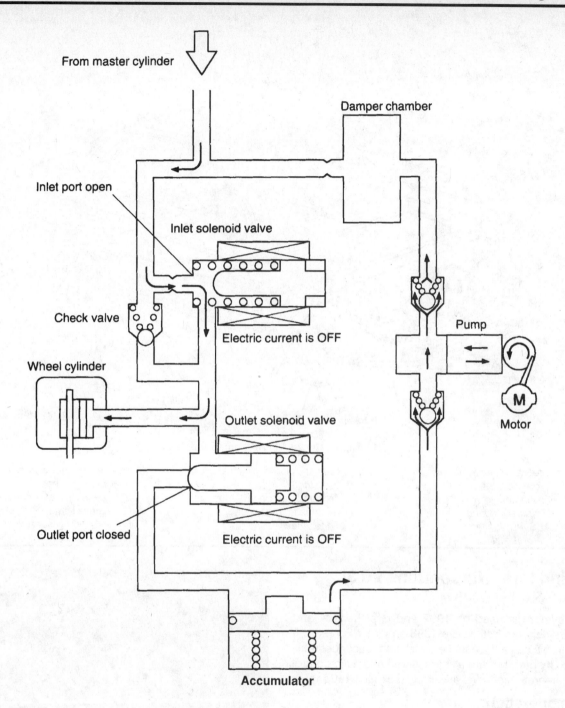

7.13 Anti-lock braking pressure build cycle (Nippondenso 5.3 - Subaru)

Wheel sensor adjustment

Procedures and specifications are the same as for the Nippondenso 2L system.

Component replacement

Wheel sensor replacement is a bolt-in job **(see illustra-**tion 7.5)**. Be sure to check the air gap as described previously in this Chapter (it's the same as for the 2L system).

Tone wheel replacement is also a bolt-in job **(see illustration 7.6)**. Tighten the mounting bolts to 84 to 132 in-lbs.

The hydraulic control unit and electronic control unit are replaced as assemblies.

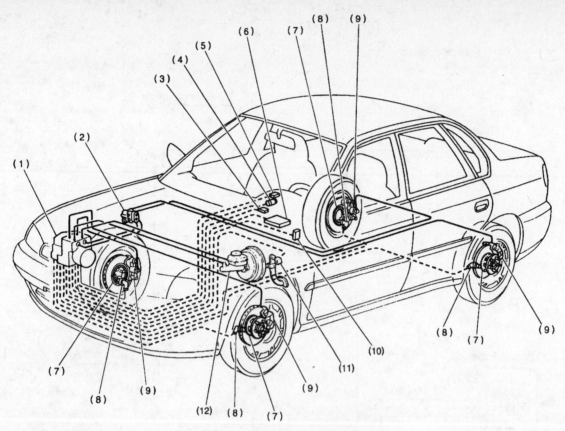

7.14 Nippondenso 5.3i ABS components

1	Integrated electronic and hydraulic control unit	5	Data link connector (for Subaru scan tool)	8	Wheel speed sensor
2	Proportioning valve	6	Transmission control module (automatic transaxle)	9	Brake caliper
3	Diagnostic connector			10	G-sensor (all-wheel drive)
4	ABS warning lamp	7	Tone wheel	11	Brake light switch
				12	Master cylinder

1997 and later Nippondenso 5.3i

Refer to illustrations 7.14 and 7.15

This system is used on 1997 and later Legacy and Impreza models, as well as the 1998 and later Forester. It operates in the same way as the 5.3 system described earlier in this Chapter, but the electronic and hydraulic control units are integrated into one assembly **(see illustrations)**.

System operation

The system receives power from the ignition switch, through a fuse-protected circuit, at terminal 1. System ground is supplied through terminal 23. Operation of the ABS hydraulics (solenoids and pump) is the same as for the

System service

Diagnosis and service of the 5.3i system are the same as for the 5.3 system, but the electronic and hydraulic control units are replaced as a single assembly. Refer to **illustration 7.4** to interpret trouble codes.

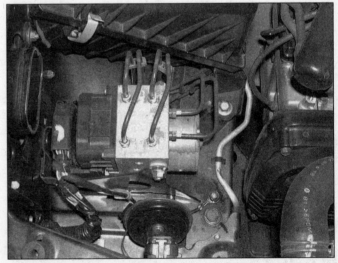

7.15 Integrated electronic and hydraulic control unit - Nippondenso 5.3i

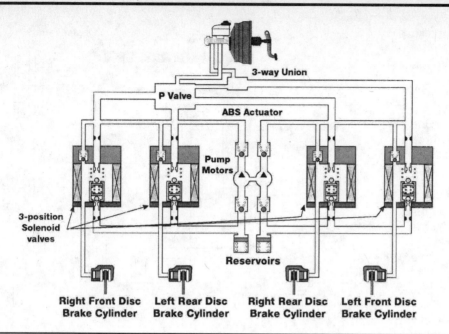

7.16 Hydraulic schematic - Nippondenso Toyota system

Right Front Disc Brake Cylinder Left Rear Disc Brake Cylinder Right Rear Disc Brake Cylinder Left Front Disc Brake Cylinder

Nippondenso (Toyota)

Some Toyota models use a Nippondenso system with three-position solenoids. The system comes in three-channel and four-channel versions, with one solenoid per channel. The three-channel version controls the front wheels independently and the rear wheels together, while the four-channel version controls all four wheels independently.

System components

Refer to illustration 7.16

The system includes an electronic control unit, hydraulic control unit and three or four wheel speed sensors. The hydraulic control unit contains the solenoids (one for each ABS channel), two pumps (one for each hydraulic circuit), and two accumulators **(see illustration)**. Most models use a wheel speed sensor at each wheel, but Cressidas and Supras through 1993 use a single rear sensor mounted on the transmission.

System operation

Refer to illustrations 7.17, 7.18, 7.19 and 7.20

During normal braking, each solenoid's inlet valve is open and its outlet port is closed **(see illustration)**.

Pedal pressure enters the solenoid through the inlet port. Of the three possible outlets - to the caliper, to the accumulator and to the pump - only the outlet to the caliper is open. The outlet to the accumulator is blocked by the outlet valve, and the line to the pump is blocked by the no. 1 check valve. As a result, pedal pressure flows unimpeded from the master cylinder to the caliper.

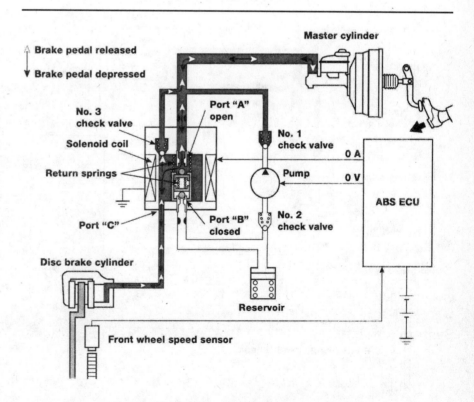

7.17 Nippondenso Toyota system in normal braking mode

When the pedal is released, brake fluid returns to the master cylinder through the inlet valve and through the no. 3 check valve.

During ABS braking, the ECU controls hydraulic pressure at the brakes by cycling the solenoids in the HCU. The cycles occur in three stages: pressure hold, pressure reduction and pressure build.

Hold cycle

When a wheel begins to lock, the impending lockup is detected by the ECU. The ECU then applies a holding current (about 2 amps) to the solenoid. The solenoid closes the inlet valve in the wheels' hydraulic channel, cutting off pedal pressure to the wheel **(see illustration)**. The outlet passage in the solenoid remains closed. Pedal pressure holds closed the two remaining possible outlets, the no. 1 and no. 3 check valves. As a result, hydraulic pressure at the wheel remains steady, neither increasing or decreasing. This is called the hold or isolation cycle.

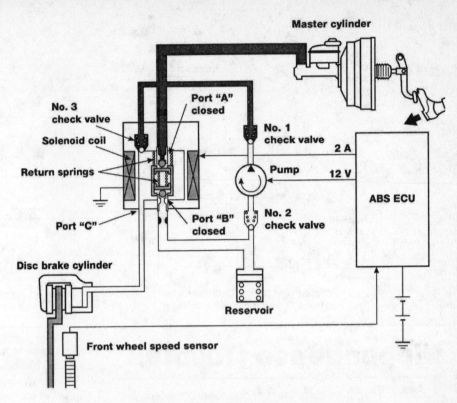

7.18 Nippondenso Toyota system in ABS hold cycle

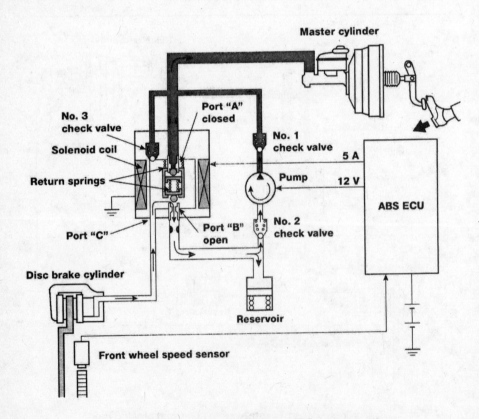

7.19 Nippondenso Toyota system in ABS release cycle

Reduction cycle

If the lockup condition continues, the ECU applies full current (about 5 amps) to the solenoid. This opens the outlet passage, releasing hydraulic pressure to the accumulator **(see illustration)**. Since the inlet passage is still closed, hydraulic pressure at the wheel is reduced. The pump begins to run, collecting the released brake fluid and returning it to the master cylinder.

Build cycle

Once the lockup condition ceases and the wheel starts to turn at a rate the CAB considers acceptable, the ECU returns the solenoid to its at-rest position, with the inlet valve open and the outlet valve closed **(see illustration)**. This once again allows pedal pressure to reach the caliper. The pump returns fluid from the accumulator to the master cylinder, restoring brake pedal height that was lost during the reduction cycle.

System service

Diagnosis

Refer to illustrations 7.21 and 7.22

Trouble codes can be retrieved by flashing the ABS warning lamp as follows:

1 Locate the diagnostic connector **(see illustration)**. On most models it can be found in the engine compartment, mounted to the firewall or along one of the inner fender panels. Depending on model, either disconnect the check connector (early models) or remove the short-circuit pin that's installed between two of the terminals in the data link connector (later models). Then install a short jumper wire or a bent paper clip between terminals Tc and E1.

2 Turn the key on and watch the ABS warning light. If there are no trouble codes stored, the light will start to flash after two seconds, then it will flash steadily, once every half-second.

3 If trouble codes are stored, the warning lamp will flash them in order, starting with the lowest code number. Each code consists of two sets of flashes separated by a 1.5-second pause. The first set of flashes indicates the first digit of the code and the second set indicates the second digit of the code. A code 22, for example, would be two flashes, then a 1.5-second pause, then two more flashes. A code 31 would be three flashes, then a 1.5-second pause, then one flash.

4 If more than one code is stored, there will be a 2.5-second pause between the codes. Then the code with the next higher number will flash. While the codes are flashing, read them and write them down.

5 To interpret the codes, refer to the accompanying table **(see illustration on next page)**.

6 To clear codes from the ECU memory, press the brake pedal and let it all the way back up eight times within 3 seconds (under the test conditions described in Step 1).

7 To make sure the codes are cleared, watch the ABS lamp. It should now flash only a steady flash every half-second, indicating that the codes have been cleared.

Component replacement

Due to the wide variety of vehicles using this system, consult a vehicle-specific service manual for details of replacement procedures. In general, the wheel speed sensors can be replaced separately. The electronic and hydraulic control units are replaced as assemblies.

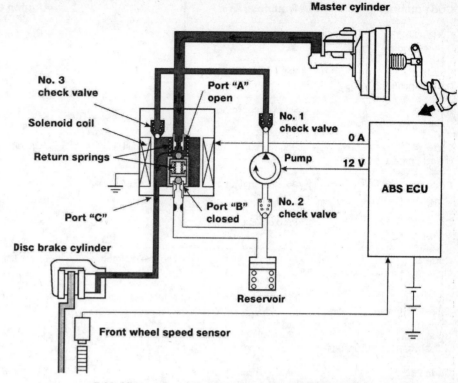

7.20 Nippondenso Toyota system in ABS build cycle

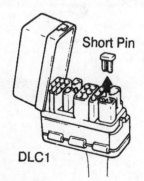

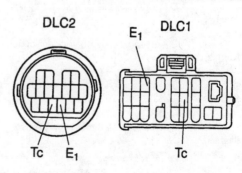

7.21 Diagnostic connector - Nippondenso Toyota

Haynes ABS Manual

Code number	Trouble area	Action to take
Code 11 (1 flash, pause, 1 flash)	Open circuit in solenoid relay circuit	Check the solenoid relay and the relay circuit
Code 12 (1 flash, pause, 2 flashes)	Short circuit in solenoid relay circuit	Check the solenoid relay and the relay circuit
Code 13 (1 flash, pause, 3 flashes)	Open circuit in ABS motor relay circuit	Check the pump motor relay and circuit
Code 14 (1 flash, pause, 4 flashes)	Short circuit in ABS motor relay circuit	Check the solenoid relay and the relay circuit
Code 21 (2 flashes, pause, 1 flash)	Problem in right front wheel solenoid circuit	Check the actuator solenoid and circuit
Code 22 (2 flashes, pause, 2 flashes)	Problem in left front wheel solenoid circuit	Check the actuator solenoid and circuit
Code 23 (2 flashes, pause, 3 flashes)	Problem in right rear wheel solenoid circuit	Check the actuator solenoid and circuit
Code 24 (2 flashes, pause, 4 flashes)	Problem in left rear wheel solenoid circuit	Check the actuator solenoid and circuit
Code 25 (2 flashes, pause, 5 flashes)	SMC1 circuit open or shorted	Check the ABS actuator and circuit
Code 26 (2 flashes, pause, 6 flashes)	SMC2 circuit open or shorted	Check the ABS actuator and circuit
Code 27 (2 flashes, pause, 7 flashes)	SRC1 circuit open or shorted	Check the ABS actuator and circuit
Code 28 (2 flashes, pause, 8 flashes)	SRC2 circuit open or shorted	Check the ABS actuator and circuit
Code 31 (3 flashes, pause, 1 flash)	Sensor signal problem - right front wheel	Check the speed sensor, sensor rotors, wire harness and connector of the speed sensor
Code 32 (3 flashes, pause, 2 flashes)	Sensor signal problem - left front wheel	Check the speed sensor, sensor rotors, wire harness and connector of the speed sensor
Code 33 (3 flashes, pause, 3 flashes)	Sensor signal problem - right rear wheel	Check the speed sensor, sensor rotors, wire harness and connector of the speed sensor
Code 34 (3 flashes, pause, 4 flashes)	Sensor signal problem - left rear wheel	Check the speed sensor, sensor rotors, wire harness and connector of the speed sensor
Code 35 (3 flashes, pause, 5 flashes)	Open circuit - right front speed sensor or circuit	Check the speed sensor, wire harness and electrical connector
Code 36 (3 flashes, pause, 6 flashes)	Open circuit - left front speed sensor or circuit	Check the speed sensor, wire harness and electrical connector
Code 37 (3 flashes, pause, 7 flashes)	Speed sensor rotor has incorrect number of teeth	Check for a damaged sensor rotor
Code 38 (3 flashes, pause, 8 flashes)	Open circuit - right rear speed sensor or circuit	Check the speed sensor, wire harness and electrical connector
Code 39 (3 flashes, pause, 9 flashes)	Open circuit - left rear speed sensor or circuit	Check the speed sensor, wire harness and electrical connector

7.22 ABS trouble codes - Nippondenso Toyota

Code number	Trouble area	Action to take
Code 41 (4 flashes, pause, 1 flash)	Abnormally low battery voltage	Check the charging system (alternator, battery and voltage regulator) for any problems
Code 43 (4 flashes, pause, 3 flashes)	ABS control system malfunction	Check all wiring and connections associated with the ABS system
Code 44 (4 flashes, pause, 4 flashes)	NE signal circuit open or shorted	Check wiring harness and connectors between ABS ECU and PCM
Code 49 (4 flashes, pause, 9 flashes)	Open circuit - brake light switch or circuit	Check the brake light switch or circuit
Code 51 (5 flashes, pause, 1 flash)	Pump motor locked	Check the pump motor, relay and battery for shorts or abnormalities
Code 53 (5 flashes, pause, 3 flashes)	PCM communication circuit malfunction	Check wiring harness and connectors between ABS ECU and PCM
Code 58 (5 flashes, pause, 8 flashes)	Open circuit - brake light switch or circuit	Check the brake light switch or circuit
Code 61 (6 flashes, pause, 1 flash)	Engine control system malfunction	Check for engine control system trouble codes
Code 62 (6 flashes, pause, 2 flashes)	ECU malfunction	ECU problem
Light always ON	ECU malfunction	ECU problem

7.22 ABS trouble codes - Nippondenso Toyota (continued)

Sumitomo I (Ford and Mazda)

Refer to illustration 7.23

This system was used in the Ford Probe and the Mazda 626, MX-6 and RX-7 from 1988 through early 1991. It is variously known as Sumitomo I and (by Ford) as Sumitomo (Mazda Old Generation). The system can be identified by the brake fluid reservoir on top of the hydraulic control unit **(see illustration)**.

System components

The system consists of an electronic control unit, hydraulic control unit, four wheel speed sensors and associated wiring and brake hoses. The hydraulic control unit contains four solenoids, three control valves, a pump and an accumulator.

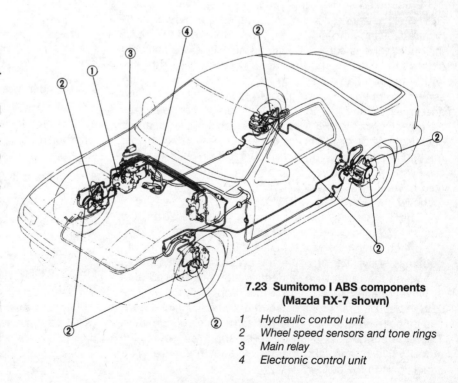

7.23 Sumitomo I ABS components (Mazda RX-7 shown)

1   *Hydraulic control unit*
2   *Wheel speed sensors and tone rings*
3   *Main relay*
4   *Electronic control unit*

Lamp flashes	Voltmeter sweeps	Condition
1	1	Right front wheel speed sensor
1	2	Left front wheel speed sensor
1	3	Rear wheel speed sensor
1	4	Right front tone ring
1	5	Left front tone ring
1	6	Right rear tone ring
1	7	Left rear tone ring
Stays on	1	Modulator or wiring harness
4	1	Modulator or wiring harness
Stays on or flashes	2, 3, or 4	Relay or modulator
Stays on or flashes	5	Modulator or ECU
Stays on or flashes	6	ECU
Stays on	None	ECU or low system voltage

7.24 Sumitomo I trouble codes

System operation

The four solenoids operate the three control valves, which in turn modulate brake pressure during an ABS stop. The solenoids are controlled electrically; the modulators are controlled hydraulically by the action of the solenoids. During normal braking, master cylinder pressure flows through the modulator to the wheel brakes; during an ABS stop, the solenoids open up a passage that lets high pressure from the pump and accumulator flow to the modulator.

Each solenoid contains two valves, an inlet from the HCU reservoir and an outlet from the high pressure accumulator. During normal braking, the inlet valve is open and the outlet valve is closed. During an ABS stop, the solenoid closes the inlet valve and opens the outlet valve. This isolates the modulator from the HCU reservoir, and at the same time opens the modulator to high pressure from the accumulator and pump. This high pressure does two things: it closes the cutoff valve inside the modulator, and it causes the slide piston inside the modulator to rise against the spring pressure that normally holds it down. The rising slide piston opens up a space beneath it, into which brake fluid flows from the caliper. This reduces braking pressure at the wheel, preventing wheel lockup.

The electronic control unit can hold pressure at a steady level by closing the solenoid inlet valve and keeping the outlet valve closed, so that the brake is cut off from both master cylinder pressure and accumulator pressure.

When the rate of wheel deceleration has slowed (that is, wheel rotating speed is no longer dropping too fast), the ABS increases braking pressure at the wheel again. It does this by opening the inlet valve and closing the outlet valve. The slide piston is pushed down by spring pressure, the cutoff valve opens, and master cylinder pressure once again flows to the caliper.

System service
Diagnosis

Refer to illustration 7.24

Trouble codes can be retrieved with the ABS warning lamp and an analog voltmeter. Unlike the usual flash code method, where the ABS lamp flashes to indicate the number of a trouble code, the ABS lamp flashes and sweeps of the voltmeter needle must be used in combination to determine the problem.

1   Set the voltmeter on the 0 to 20-volt DC scale.

2   Locate the ABS check connector in the wiring harness near the electronic control unit. This is a four-pin connector with green/red, green/black and black wires. Connect a short jumper wire between the terminals for the green/black and black wires.

3   Turn the key on and watch the ABS warning light. Note whether it stays on constantly, flashes steadily, flashes once only, or flashes four times. Write this down.

4   Set the voltmeter to the 0-20 volt DC range. Connect its positive lead to the green/red wire's terminal and the negative lead to a good body ground. The needle should sweep from zero to 12 volts, then back to zero. Write down the number of sweeps.

5   To interpret the combination of flashes and voltmeter needle sweeps, refer to the accompanying table **(see illustration)**.

6   If more than one code is stored, the first code's cause will have to be repaired, then the code cleared, before the next code will be displayed.

7   To clear codes from the ECU memory, connect a short

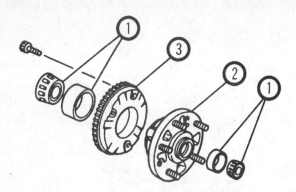

7.25 Sumitomo I front wheel tone ring (Mazda RX-7 shown)

1	Wheel bearing and race	2	Wheel hub
		3	Tone ring

7.26 Sumitomo I rear wheel tone ring (Mazda RX-7 shown)

jumper wire between the green/red and green/black wires' terminals in the check connector. Turn the key to On, but don't start the engine, and watch the ABS lamp. It should come on. If it does, let it stay on for about two seconds, then shut the key off and disconnect the jumper wire.

Component replacement

Refer to illustrations 7.25 and 7.26

Wheel speed sensor and tone ring replacement are bolt-in jobs (see illustrations).

The electronic control unit and the hydraulic control unit are replaced as assemblies.

Sumitomo II (Ford and Mazda)

Refer to illustration 7.27

This system was used in the Ford Probe and the Mazda 626, MX-6 and RX-7 from late 1991 through 1997, as well as in the 1995 through 1997 Mazda Protege. It is variously known as Sumitomo II, Compact Sumitomo and (by Ford) as Sumitomo (Mazda New Generation). The system can be identified by the hydraulic control unit (see illustration).

System components

Refer to illustrations 7.28 and 7.29

The system consists of an electronic control unit, hydraulic control unit, four wheel speed sensors and associated wiring and brake hoses (see illustration). The

7.27 The Sumitomo II hydraulic control unit (arrow) is located beneath the master cylinder

7.28 The electronic control unit (arrow) is under the left side of the instrument panel

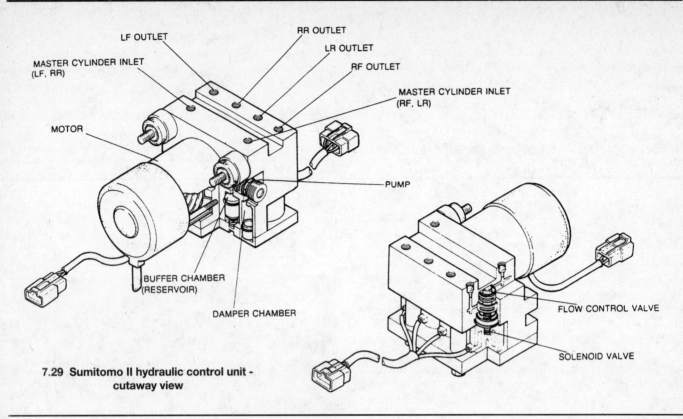

LF OUTLET
RR OUTLET
LR OUTLET
MASTER CYLINDER INLET
(LF, RR)
RF OUTLET
MASTER CYLINDER INLET
(RF, LR)
MOTOR
PUMP
BUFFER CHAMBER
(RESERVOIR)
DAMPER CHAMBER
FLOW CONTROL VALVE
SOLENOID VALVE

**7.29 Sumitomo II hydraulic control unit -
cutaway view**

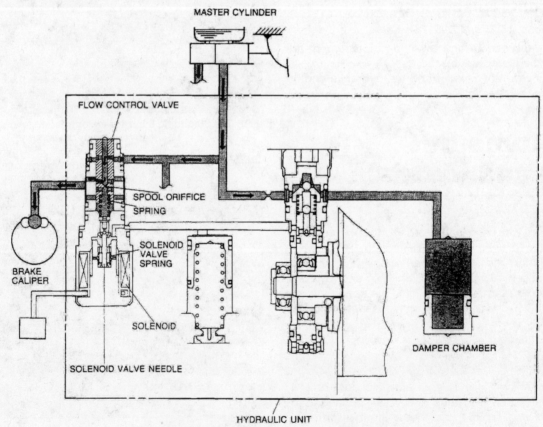

MASTER CYLINDER
FLOW CONTROL VALVE
SPOOL ORIFFICE
SPRING
SOLENOID
VALVE
SPRING
BRAKE
CALIPER
SOLENOID
DAMPER CHAMBER
SOLENOID VALVE NEEDLE
HYDRAULIC UNIT

7.30 Sumitomo II hydraulic schematic - normal braking mode shown

hydraulic control unit contains four solenoid/flow control valves, a pump, a buffer chamber and a damper chamber **(see illustration)**.

System operation

The four solenoids operate the flow control valves, which in turn modulate brake pressure during an ABS stop. The solenoids are controlled electrically; the flow control valves are controlled by the action of the solenoids.

Normal braking

Refer to illustration 7.30

During normal braking, master cylinder pressure flows through the flow control valves to the wheel brakes **(see illustration)**. The solenoid needle valve is closed. This maintains a steady hydraulic pressure above and below the spool valve in the flow control valve, so the flow control valve's passage is open between the master cylinder and caliper.

Anti-lock braking

The ECU monitors the signals from the wheel speed sensors continuously. When it detects that a wheel is about to lock up, it sends current to the solenoid. This causes the solenoid needle to push down against the spring pressure that normally holds it upward, which in turn opens up a passage in the flow control valve. The change in hydraulic pressure caused by the open passage pushes the spool valve downward, where it blocks the flow of hydraulic pressure from the master cylinder to the caliper.

When the ECU decides that the wheel speed is still dropping too fast, it moves the spool valve still farther down

the bore. This opens up a passage from the caliper to the buffer chamber, which brake fluid from the caliper then flows into. This reduces braking pressure in the caliper, releasing the brake.

When the rate of wheel deceleration has slowed (that is, wheel rotating speed is no longer dropping too fast), the ABS increases braking pressure at the wheel again. It does this by de-energizing the solenoid, which causes its needle to move upward and close the passage. The caliper is now re-opened to master cylinder pressure caused by the driver's foot on the pedal, so braking force is applied to the wheel again. The brake fluid that bled off to the buffer chamber is a returned to the master cylinder by the pump. The damper chamber in the hydraulic control unit reduces pedal feedback and ABS noise.

System service
Diagnosis

Refer to illustrations 7.31 and 7.32

Trouble codes can be retrieved with the ABS warning lamp and an analog voltmeter. The voltmeter indicates the number of the trouble code with sweeps of its needle. The ABS lamp either lights continuously to indicate a current problem or flashes in synchronization with the voltmeter needle to indicate a past problem.

1   Set the voltmeter on the 0 to 20-volt DC scale.

2   Early models equipped with this system have a check connector like that for Sumitomo I. Later models have a data link connector in the engine compartment **(see illustration)**.

3   If you're working on an early model, connect a short jumper wire between the terminals for the green/black and black wires. Connect the voltmeter positive lead to the green/red wire's terminal and the negative lead to a good body ground.

4   If you're working on a later model, connect a short jumper wire between terminals FSB and GND of the data link connector **(see illustration 7.31)**. Connect the voltmeter positive lead to terminal TBS and the voltmeter negative lead to a good body ground.

5   Turn the key on and watch the ABS warning light and voltmeter. Note whether the light stays on constantly or flashes. Watch the sweeps of the voltmeter needle and write the number down. The needle indicates the number of any trouble codes by the number of its sweeps. For example, a code 22 would be two sweeps, a 1.6-second pause, then two more sweeps. There's a four-second pause between codes. The codes are displayed one after another. Write them down.

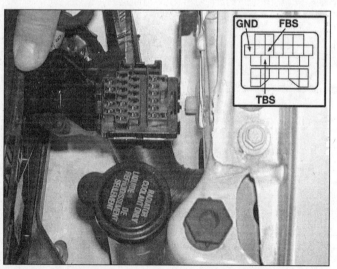

7.31 Typical Sumitomo II data link connector (1993 Ford Probe shown)

Code*	Problem area
11	Right front wheel speed sensor
12	Left front wheel speed sensor
13	Right rear wheel speed sensor
14	Left rear wheel speed sensor
15	Front and rear wheel speed sensors
22	Solenoid
51	Fail-safe relay
53	Pump or pump relay
61	Electronic control unit
None*	Electronic control unit
*If the ABS warning lamp is on constantly.	

7.32 ABS trouble codes - Sumitomo II

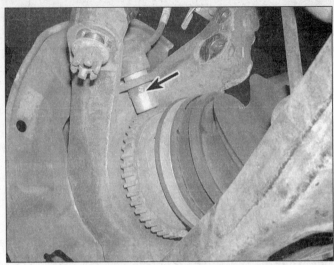

7.33 Here's a typical front wheel speed sensor on a vehicle equipped with a Sumitomo II ABS system

6 To interpret the codes, refer to the accompanying table **(see illustration).**

7 To clear codes from the ECU memory, pump the brake pedal 10 times, taking less than one second per pump. Then turn off the key, disconnect the voltmeter and remove the jumper wire.

Bleeding

Brake bleeding is conventional.

Component replacement

Refer to illustrations 7.33 and 7.34

Wheel speed sensor replacement is a bolt-in job **(see** illustrations). Tone rings are replaced as part of the component they're mounted on.

The electronic control unit and the hydraulic control unit are replaced as assemblies.

Nippondenso, Nissin and Sumitomo (Honda and Acura)

This Section covers one basic design manufactured by Sumitomo, Nippondenso and Nissin and used in a number of Acura and Honda vehicles starting in 1987. Use of this design continued through 1997 in some models.

7.34 Here's a typical rear wheel speed sensor on a vehicle equipped with a Sumitomo II ABS system

7.35 The ABS control unit (arrow) on many Honda and Acura vehicles is located in the trunk, or behind the seat back . . .

7.36 . . . or under a panel next to the rear seat

7.37 The hydraulic control unit is mounted in the right rear corner of the engine compartment . . .

System components

Refer to illustrations 7.35 through 7.40

The main system components are the electronic control unit, pump, accumulator, and hydraulic control unit **(see illustrations)**. The HCU contains four solenoids and three modulators. Fail-safe relays are mounted at various locations in the engine compartment **(see illustrations)**. There's a wheel speed sensor at each wheel.

System operation

Operation of the hydraulic solenoids and modulators is essentially the same as for the Sumitomo I system, described earlier in this Chapter. However, the pump and accumulator are contained in a separate unit from the modulator. The pump is controlled by a pressure switch independently of the electronic control unit.

7.38 . . . the HCU reservoir looks different from model to model, but the basic design is the same

7.39 The relays are mounted in the engine compartment in a box like this . . .

7.40 . . . lift the cover for access

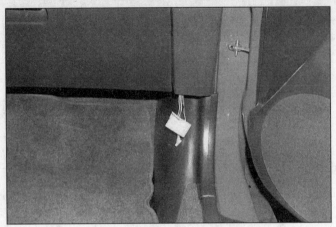

7.41 Here's a typical ABS check connector . . .

7.42 . . . use it together with the ABS warning lamp to read trouble codes

7.43 ABS trouble codes - 1990 through 1993 Integra, 1991 Accord

| TROUBLE CODE | | MALFUNCTIONING COMPONENT/ SYSTEM | WHEELS-AFFECTED | | | | OTHER COMPONENTS POSSIBLY INVOLVED |
MAIN CODE	SUB-CODE		FRONT RIGHT	FRONT LEFT	REAR RIGHT	REAR LEFT	
1	–	Hydraulic controlled components	–	–	–	–	ABS main relay fuse Motor relay (ON) Pressure switch (OFF) Accumulator Modulator
2		Parking brake switch-related problem	–	–	–	–	Brake fluid level switch [BRAKE] light
3	1	Pulser(s)	○				
	2			○			
	4				○	○	
4	1	Speed sensor	○				
	2			○			
	4				○		
	8					○	
5	–	Speed sensor(s) Rear wheel lock			○	○	Modulator Rear brake drag
	4				○		
	8					○	
6	–	Fail-safe relay (Open, short)		○	○		
	1			○			
	4				○		
7	1	Solenoid related problem (Open)	○				ABS B1 fuse
	2			○			Front fail-safe relay
	4				○	○	Rear fail-safe relay

2118-9-2.5 HAYNES

System service
Diagnosis

Refer to illustrations 7.41 through 7.45

On early models, remove the inspection cover for the ECU and look for a light emitting diode (LED). If there is one, it's used to flash trouble codes. If not, codes are flashed by the ABS warning light.

These systems flash two-digit trouble codes. The light starts by flashing the first digit of the code (for example, three flashes equal a number 3), then it flashes the second digit of the code (for example, four flashes equal a 4). The resulting code is a 3-4 (not a 34).

To read trouble codes on a system with an LED, simply switch the key to On (but don't start the engine) and watch the LED. After 10 seconds, it will start to flash any stored codes.

To read trouble codes on a system using the ABS warning lamp, connect a jumper wire between the terminals of the check connector **(see illustration)**. Make sure you use the 2-terminal check connector, not the three-terminal data link connector. Turn the key to On (but don't start the engine) and watch the ABS warning lamp **(see illustration)**. After 10 seconds, it will start to flash any stored codes.

TROUBLE CODE		MALFUNCTIONING COMPONENT/ SYSTEM	WHEELS-AFFECTED				OTHER COMPONENTS POSSIBLY INVOLVED
MAIN CODE	SUB-CODE		FRONT RIGHT	FRONT LEFT	REAR RIGHT	REAR LEFT	
1	—	Pump motor over-run	—	—	—	—	Motor fuse, motor relay Pressure switch
	2	Pump motor circuit problem	—	—	—	—	Motor relay, Unit fuse
	3	High pressure leakage	—	—	—	—	Solenoid
	4	Pressure switch	—	—	—	—	
	8	Accumulator gas leakage	—	—	—	—	
2	1	Parking brake switch-related problem	—	—	—	—	Brake fluid level switch BRAKE light
3	1	Pulser(s)	○				
	2			○			
	4				○	○	
4	1	Speed sensor	○				
	2			○			
	4				○		
	8					○	
5	—	Speed sensor(s)			○	○	Modulator
	4				○		
	8					○	
6	—	Fail-safe relay (Open, short)	—	—	—	—	Front or rear fail-safe relay
	1		—	—	—	—	Front fail-safe relay
	4		—	—	—	—	Rear fail-safe relay
7	1	Solenoid related problem (Open)	○				ALB 3 or ABS B3 fuse
	2			○			ALB 1 or ABS B1 fuse Front fail-safe relay
	4				○	○	Rear fail-safe relay

2118-9-2.5 HAYNES

7.44 ABS trouble codes - 1991 through 1995 Legend, 1992 through 1995 Civic and Del Sol

TROUBLE CODE		MALFUNCTIONING COMPONENT/ SYSTEM	WHEELS-AFFECTED				OTHER COMPONENTS POSSIBLY INVOLVED
MAIN CODE	SUB- CODE		FRONT RIGHT	FRONT LEFT	REAR RIGHT	REAR LEFT	
1	—	Pump motor over-run	—	—	—	—	Pressure switch
	2	Pump motor circuit problem	—	—	—	—	Motor relay, Unit fuse, Motor fuse
	3	High pressure leakage	—	—	—	—	Solenoid
	4	Pressure switch	—	—	—	—	
	8	Accumulator gas leakage	—	—	—	—	
2	1	Parking brake switch-related problem	—	—	—	—	Brake fluid level switch [BRAKE] light
3	1	Pulser(s)	○				
	2			○			
	4				○	○	
	12	Different diameter tire					
4	1	Speed sensor	○				
	2			○			
	4				○		
	8					○	
5	—	Speed sensor(s)			○	○	Modulator
	4				○		
	8					○	
6	—	Fail-safe relay (Open, short)	—	—	—	—	Front or rear fail-safe relay
	1		—	—	—	—	Front fail-safe relay
	4		—	—	—	—	Rear fail-safe relay
7	1	Solenoid related problem (Open)	○				ABS B1 fuse / Front fail-safe relay
	2			○			
	4				○	○	Rear fail-safe relay
8	1	ABS control unit problem	Faulty ABS unit				
	2						
	4						

2118-9-2.5 HAYNES

7.45 ABS trouble codes - 1994 through 1997 Integra

7.46 Here's a typical front wheel speed sensor . . .

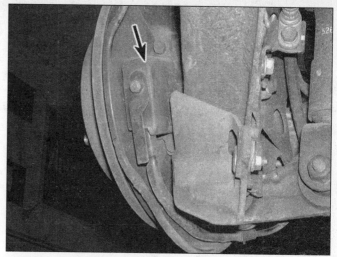

7.47 . . . and here's a typical rear sensor, hidden behind a protective cover

Codes are generally similar in all models equipped with this system, but there are slight variations. This Section includes typical examples of the codes used on most models. To interpret the codes, refer to the accompanying tables **(see illustrations)**.

Bleeding

Warning 1: *Wear eye protection when bleeding the brake system. If the fluid comes in contact with your eyes, immediately rinse them with water and seek medical attention.*
Warning 2: *Never use old brake fluid. It contains moisture which can boil, rendering the brake system inoperative.*
Warning 3: *If, after bleeding the system you do not have a firm brake pedal, or if the ABS light on the instrument panel does not go off, or if you have any doubts whatsoever about the effectiveness of the brake system, have it towed to a dealer service department or other repair shop equipped with the necessary tools for bleeding the hydraulic control unit.*
Caution: *Brake fluid will damage paint. Cover all painted surfaces and be careful not to spill fluid during this procedure.*

1   Remove any residual vacuum from the power brake booster by applying the brake several times with the engine off. Remove the master cylinder reservoir cover and fill the reservoir with brake fluid. Reinstall the cover. Also check the fluid level in the hydraulic control unit, adding as necessary. **Note:** *Check the fluid level often during the bleeding operation and add fluid as necessary to prevent the fluid level from falling low enough to allow air bubbles into the master cylinder or hydraulic control unit.*

2   If you have removed and installed (or replaced) the master cylinder, or if the fluid level in the master cylinder became too low and allowed air into the system, begin the procedure by bleeding the lines at the master cylinder. Have an assistant slowly depress the brake pedal and hold

it there, then loosen the brake line fittings (one at a time) at the master cylinder, allowing fluid and air to escape. Repeat this procedure until the fluid coming out is free of air, then proceed to the next step.

3   Now bleed the hydraulic control unit (HCU). Attach a snug-fitting bleed hose to the bleeder valve on the control unit. Start the engine to build up pressure in the HCU, then slowly open the bleeder valve 1/8 to 1/4 turn to allow fluid and air to escape; do this in small increments, repeating the procedure until the fluid coming out of the HCU is free of air. **Warning:** *The fluid in the HCU is under high pressure. Don't open the bleeder valve rapidly or more than 1/4 of a turn, or the brake fluid may squirt out with great force.* Turn off the engine and proceed to bleed the remainder of the system. **Note:** *If the ABS light on the instrument panel comes on, repeat this step.*

4   Bleeding the remainder of the system is conventional. Bleed the right rear brake first, followed by the left front, the left rear, and the right front, in that order.

5   Check the operation of the brakes. The pedal should feel solid when depressed, with no sponginess. If necessary, repeat the entire process.

Component replacement

Refer to illustrations 7.46 and 7.47

Wheel sensor replacement is a bolt-in job **(see illustrations)**. The sensor rings are replaced as part of the component they're mounted on.

The accumulator and pump can be replaced separately. Individual solenoids in the hydraulic control unit can also be replaced separately.
Warning: *Before any components of the hydraulic control unit are loosened or removed, the pressure inside the unit must be bled off by attaching a hose to the bleeder on the HCU, directing the end of the hose into a container, then slowly opening the bleeder until the pressure is relieved.*

Notes

Chapter 8
Teves systems

Teves Mark II

Teves Mark II is an integrated three-channel system that incorporates the booster, hydraulic actuator and master cylinder into one unit. Power assist for braking is provided by hydraulic pressure from the booster portion of the hydraulic actuator.

The system is used on 1986 through 1990 General Motors A-body, C-body, E-body and K-body vehicles:

A-body: *1986 through 1990 Pontiac 6000 STE (1989 and 1990 in 6000 STE fwd models).*

C body: *1986 through 1990 Buick Electra and Park Avenue; 1986 through 1990 Oldsmobile Ninety-Eight Regency and Brougham; 1986 through 1990 Cadillac Deville and Fleetwood.*

E-body: *1988 through 1990 Buick Riviera; 1988 through 1990 Oldsmobile Toronado;1988 through 1990 Cadillac Eldorado.*

H-body: *1987 through 1990 Oldsmobile Eight-Eight.*

K-body: *1988 through 1990 Cadillac Seville.*

The system can be identified by the combined master cylinder/booster/hydraulic modulator, mounted in the engine compartment in the standard master cylinder location. The Regular Production Option (RPO) code listed on the sticker (usually in the glove compartment) is JM4 or JL9.

System components

The system consists of the electronic brake control module (EBCM), two warning lamps, wheel speed sensors, associated wiring and the hydraulic assembly. The hydraulic assembly contains the master cylinder and booster, which are used for the main brake system as well as for the ABS. The hydraulic assembly also contains the accumulator, pump and valve block. The valve block contains the solenoids that cause brake line pressure to be held steady, reduced or increased during an anti-lock stop.

Electronic Brake Control Module (EBCM)

The EBCM is mounted in the trunk or in the passenger compartment, depending on model.

The EBCM receives the signals from the wheel speed sensors and uses them to decide whether or not to initiate anti-lock braking. In 1987 and later models, a brake pedal switch input is also required.

Master cylinder

The master cylinder operates the front brakes through a single piston (Pontiac STE) or two pistons (all others). The piston(s), aided by pressure from the booster, force brake fluid through the lines to provide braking pressure at the wheels.

Rear brake operation is unconventional. The rear brakes are operated during normal braking by booster pressure, rather than by their own piston. The driver's foot on the brake pedal regulates the amount of booster pressure applied to the rear wheels during non-ABS stops.

The master cylinder reservoir has a fluid level switch that illuminates the red brake warning lamp and the amber ABS lamp if fluid level drops too low.

Pump and accumulator

The pump and accumulator work together to provide the hydraulic pressure needed for both normal and anti-lock braking. The pump pressurizes the fluid and directs it to an accumulator, where it is stored at high pressure. The pump begins running when accumulator pressure drops to 2030 psi and shuts off when accumulator pressure reaches 2610 psi. A pressure switch senses the pressure, and switches the pump on or shuts it off as needed. A relief valve opens to direct fluid from the pump to the reservoir if accumulator pressure reaches 3340 psi.

If pump pressure drops below 1500 psi, the red brake warning lamp and amber ABS lamp will illuminate, and stay on until the pressure rises to 1900 psi.

Valve block

The valve block is part of the hydraulic assembly. It contains six solenoid-operated valves, three inlet and three outlet. The inlet valves are normally open, allowing brake pressure from the master cylinder to operate the wheel brakes. The outlet valves are normally closed.

Wheel speed sensors

There's a speed sensor at each wheel. These send AC voltage signals to the EBCM. If the voltage drops too quickly, indicating that a wheel is about to lock up, the EBCM initiates anti-lock braking.

Differential lock switch

On Pontiac 6000 STE models with all-wheel drive, locking the differential will send a signal to the EBCM that prevents ABS operation.

System operation

On startup, the EBCM receives 12 volts at terminal 2 when the key is turned to On. The EBCM conducts a diagnostic check, which includes checking the circuits of the wheel speed sensors, main valve solenoid, and the solenoids in the valve block, as well as the pressure switch and fluid level sensor circuit. It also checks its own internal circuits. During the startup period, the booster pump may run for as long as 30 seconds to pressurize the accumulator.

While the key is turned to Start, the EBCM either receives a cranking voltage signal at terminal 19, or discontinues the 12-volt signal at terminal 2, depending on model.

If the diagnostic check turns up a problem, the EBCM doesn't activate the ABS. Instead, it illuminates the ABS warning lamp. If the diagnostic check is OK and the key is turned to On, the EBCM receives power at terminals 3 and 20. While the vehicle is being driven, the EBCM continuously checks its internal circuits, as well as the wheel speed sensor circuits, for problems. If a problem is detected, the EBCM will disengage ABS. On later models, which have trouble code capability, the EBCM stores a trouble code which can be retrieved to identify the problem.

Normal braking

During normal braking, the inlet solenoids in the valve block are open, which allows brake fluid to flow through them to the wheel brakes. The driver's foot on the pedal controls the booster, which does two things. It applies power assist to the master cylinder piston(s) that control the two front brakes. It also uses the booster control valve to apply braking pressure directly to the rear brakes (there is no master cylinder piston for the rear brakes). The pressure that applies the rear brakes during normal braking comes from the accumulator (which is supplied by the pump) and is regulated by the booster control valve.

Anti-lock braking

The EBCM continuously monitors the voltage signals from the wheel speed sensors while the vehicle is being driven. If one or more of the signals drops too rapidly, indicating that a wheel is about to lock up, it initiates anti-lock braking. The EBCM opens the main valve in the valve block, which allows booster pressure to flow to the front brake lines.

Anti-lock braking starts by holding braking pressure steady. The EBCM closes the inlet solenoids in the valve block, which cuts off the wheel brakes from booster pressure. If that isn't enough, the EBCM opens the outlet valve at the affected wheel, which allows brake fluid to flow from the wheel to the reservoir, reducing braking pressure.

When the EBCM decides that the wheel has picked up enough speed that it can be braked again, it opens the inlet and outlet solenoids at once, which allows booster pressure to apply the brake at the affected wheel.

All of this occurs at up to 15 times per second, and can be heard (clicking sounds) and felt (pedal rise and pulsation) by the driver.

System service
Diagnosis

Early models do not have the ability to store trouble codes. Diagnosis on these models is done by starting, then driving the vehicle and noting the sequence of the red and amber warning lamps. Later models can store trouble codes. These are retrieved by flashing the ABS lamp in a sequence that indicates the number of the trouble code. The number is then compared to a code chart to determine the problem area.

Lamp sequence

This method must be used on the following models:

a) *Pontiac 6000 STE (all)*

b) *1986 through 1988 Buick Electra and Park Avenue; Oldsmobile Eighty-Eight; Oldsmobile Ninety-Eight Regency and Brougham; Cadillac Deville and Fleetwood.*

1 Since you'll need to take careful notes on what the red and amber lamps do while you're starting and driving the vehicle, it's a good idea to have a passenger write the information down.

2 If the ignition is on, turn the key to Off and leave it there for at least 15 seconds.

3 Make sure the parking brake is off. If it's on, it will cause the red brake warning lamp to stay on, which will give inaccurate test results.

4 Turn the key to On. The ABS lamp should come on for three to six seconds, then go out. The brake warning lamp should not come on. **Note:** *If the accumulator is discharged, the pump may run for up to 30 seconds while it recharges. During this time, both lamps will be on. If this happens, let the pump finish running, then shut the key off and start the test over.*

5 Turn the key to Start. Both lamps should now be on. When the engine starts and you let go of the key, the brake lamp should go out immediately and the ABS lamp should stay on for three to six seconds.

6 Take the vehicle for a short drive at a speed above 20 mph. Watch the lamps; if either one comes on, note its pattern (when it came on, whether it is continuous or intermittent, and which light came on). Have your passenger write this down.

7 Brake to a stop. Again, both lamps should stay out. If either one comes on, note which one and have your passenger write it down.

8 After stopping, let the engine idle and watch the lamps. If either one comes on, write its pattern down.

9 Compare the lamp pattern to the following:

a) *Brake lamp on only during cranking; ABS lamp on briefly during key on, all during cranking, briefly after engine starts: This is the normal pattern.*

b) *Brake lamp on only during cranking; ABS lamp on continuously: ABS problem.*

c) *Brake lamp on only during cranking; ABS lamp comes on after drive-off: Wheel speed sensor, main relay, or short in lamp circuit.*

d) *Brake lamp on only during cranking; ABS lamp on during key On, but not during cranking: Diode, main relay or main relay circuit*

e) *Brake lamp on only during cranking; ABS lamp does not come on at all: Bulb, bulb circuit, or ECBM.*

f) *Brake lamp on only during cranking; ABS lamp comes on intermittently while driving: Low fluid level, fluid level sensor, pressure sensor, or related circuits.*

g) *Both lamps on continuously: Low fluid level, fluid level sensor, or sensor circuits.*

h) *Both lamps normal at startup, but come on while braking: Low fluid level, fluid level sensor, pressure sensor, or related circuits.*

i) *Brake lamp on continuously, anti-lock lamp normal: Parking brake on, switch adjustment or defective switch; main brake system problem.*

Flash codes

Refer to illustrations 8.1 and 8.2

1 This method can be used in all of the models not listed under *Lamp sequence.*

2 Locate the ALDL connector under the dash. Connect terminal H or G depending on model, to terminal A with a short jumper wire **(see illustration)**.

3 Turn the key to On (but don't start the engine). If no trouble codes are stored, the lamp will light for four seconds, then go out.

4 If codes are stored, the ABS warning lamp will flash a sequence indicating the code number. To flash a code 21, for example, the lamp will flash twice, pause for three seconds, then flash once.

5 After each code is flashed, write it down. To see if there are additional codes stored, disconnect the jumper wire briefly, then reconnect it. If there's another code stored, its number sequence will flash. If not, the ABS warning lamp will light continuously to indicate the end of the stored codes.

6 Once you've read all of the stored codes, disconnect the jumper wire from the ALDL connector and turn the key to Off.

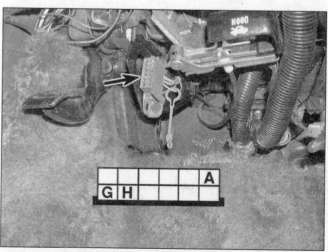

8.1 Here's a typical ALDL connector, and the terminals used for retrieving trouble codes in the Teves II system

7 To interpret the codes, refer to the accompanying table (**see illustration**).

System pressure relief

Because the accumulator operates at very high pressure, it's important for safety reasons to depressurize it before disconnecting any hydraulic lines. Make sure the ignition is off, then disconnect the negative cable from the battery. Press the brake pedal firmly at least 25 times, applying 50 lbs of force to the pedal each time. This should cause a distinct change in the feel of the pedal as the pressure in the accumulator is used up. To make sure, press the pedal several more times after the pedal feel changes.

Once you're done, reconnect the cable to the negative terminal of the battery.

Bleeding

Warning 1: *Wear eye protection when bleeding the brake system. If the fluid comes in contact with your eyes, immediately rinse them with water and seek medical attention.*

Warning 2: *Never use old brake fluid. It contains moisture which can boil, rendering the brake system inoperative.*

Warning 3: *If, after bleeding the system you do not have a firm brake pedal, or if the ABS light on the instrument panel does not go off, or if you have any doubts whatsoever about the effectiveness of the brake system, don't drive the vehicle. Have it towed to a dealer service department or other repair shop for diagnosis.*

Caution: *Brake fluid will damage paint. Cover all painted surfaces and be careful not to spill fluid during this procedure.*

Bleeding the front brakes on these models is conventional. The rear brakes require a different procedure, since rear brake pressure for normal braking is supplied by the booster.

1 Connect a length of clear plastic tubing to the bleed valve on the right rear brake and place the other end of the tube in a container. The container should have a capacity of about one quart.

2 Turn the key to ON (but don't start the engine). If the accumulator is discharged, the hydraulic pump will run until it fills (this should take no more than 30 seconds).

3 Open the bleed valve that the hose is attached to. With the key still in the On position, have an assistant depress the brake pedal a short distance (don't push it all the way and don't press hard), then hold it there. While the pedal is pressed, the booster pump will run, forcing fluid out through the bleed valve.

4 Keep holding the pedal in a slightly pressed position until the fluid flowing from the hose is free of air bubbles. This will take at least ten seconds. Once this happens, let up the brake pedal and close the bleed valve.

11	EBCM problem
12	EBCM problem
21	Main valve defective; hydraulic actuator problem
22	Left front solenoid valve circuit
23	Left front outlet valve circuit
24	Right front solenoid valve circuit
25	Right front outlet valve circuit
26	Rear solenoid valve circuit
27	Rear outlet valve circuit
31	Left front wheel speed sensor
32	Right front wheel speed sensor
33	Right rear wheel speed sensor
34	Left rear wheel speed sensor
35	Left front wheel speed sensor
36	Right front wheel speed sensor
37	Right rear wheel speed sensor
38	Left rear wheel speed sensor
41	Left front wheel speed sensor
42	Right front wheel speed sensor
43	Right rear wheel speed sensor
44	Left rear wheel speed sensor
45	Missing wheel speed sensor signals (left front)
46	Missing wheel speed sensor signals (right front)
47	Missing wheel speed sensor signals (rear)
48	Missing wheel speed sensor signals (all three)
51	Left front outlet valve
52	Right front outlet valve
53	Rear outlet valve
54	Rear outlet valve
55	Left front wheel speed sensor
56	Right front wheel speed sensor
57	Right rear wheel speed sensor
58	Left rear wheel speed sensor
61	EBCM circuit problem in low fluid/pressure warning loop
71	Left front outlet valve
72	Right front outlet valve
73	Rear outlet valve
74	Rear outlet valve
75	Left front wheel speed sensor
76	Right front wheel speed sensor
77	Right rear wheel speed sensor
78	Left rear wheel speed sensor

8.2 Teves II trouble codes (General Motors)

5 Recheck fluid level in the reservoir and top it up if necessary.

6 Move the hose and container to the left rear bleed valve. Repeat Step 3 until bubble-free air flows from the hose, then release the brake pedal and close the bleed valve.

7 Turn the key to Off and remove the hose and container. Check brake fluid level one more time and add fluid if necessary.

Component replacement

Electronic brake control module

The EBCM is replaced as an assembly. Depending on model, it is located in the trunk, beneath or behind the glove compartment, or screwed to the underside of the instrument panel above the pedals.

Hydraulic assembly

A number of the hydraulic assembly components can be replaced separately. These include the accumulator, fluid reservoir, pressure switch, high pressure hose, pump, valve block, master cylinder and bracket. Before any work is carried out on the hydraulic assembly, the system pressure must be relieved as described earlier in this Chapter.

Wheel speed sensors

1 Wheel sensor replacement is a bolt-in job. Be sure to route the sensor harness correctly and install it in all of its retainers. If the sensor is installed in an aluminum bracket, coat the sensor shaft (but not the tip) with anti-seize compound.

2 Sensors on early models are adjustable. Adjustable sensors come in two designs at the front and one design at the rear.

3 Type I front sensors are used at the front of 1986 A - body models, 1986 through 1988 C-body models, and 1987 and 1988 H-body models.

4 Type II front sensors are used at the front of 1988 and 1989 E-body models.

5 Adjustable rear sensors are used on 1986 through 1989 A-body models and 1986 C-body models.

6 If you're working on a Type I front sensor, measure the gap with a non-magnetic feeler gauge.

a) On 1986 A-body models (Pontiac 6000 STE) and C-body models (Buick Electra and Park Avenue; Oldsmobile Ninety-Eight Regency and Brougham; Cadillac Deville and Fleetwood), the gap should be 0.028-inch.

b) On 1987 and 1988 C-body models (Buick Electra and Park Avenue; Oldsmobile Ninety-Eight Regency and Brougham), and H-body models (Olds Eighty-Eight), the gap should be 0.040-inch.

7 If you're working on a Type II front sensor, measure the gap with a non-magnetic feeler gauge. On 1988 and 1989 E-body models (Buick Riviera; Oldsmobile Toronado; Cadillac Eldorado), the gap should be 0.020-inch.

8 If you're working on a rear sensor, measure the gap with a non-magnetic feeler gauge. It should be 0.028-inch on both the 1986 through 1989 A-body (Pontiac 6000 STE) and 1986 C-body (Buick Electra and Park Avenue; Oldsmobile Ninety-Eight Regency and Brougham; Cadillac Deville and Fleetwood).

Teves Mark IV

Refer to illustrations 8.3, 8.4 and 8.5

A three-channel version of Teves Mark IV 1992 through 1994 Jeep vehicles. A four-channel version of the system is used on the 1990 and later Lincoln Town Car and Continental, as well as the 1990 through 1995 Ford Taurus and Mercury Sable. The Town Car has rear drum brakes; the Continental, Taurus and Sable have rear disc brakes.

A four-channel version of Teves Mark IV is also used in a number of GM sedans from 1991 through 1998.

The following paragraphs discuss the details of the Mark IV system used in Jeeps. Ford and General Motors system operation is basically the same as for the Jeep systems, but it includes a separate hydraulic channel for each rear wheel. Each of the rear channels has its own inlet and outlet solenoids. This allows the electronic brake control module to control the rear brakes individually.

The Teves Mark IV used in 1992 through 1994 Jeep vehicles is a three-channel system, with one hydraulic channel at each front wheel and a single channel for both rear wheels. Each wheel has its own wheel speed sensor.

The main brake system in vehicles equipped with the Mark IV is conventional, with a dual-diaphragm vacuum booster and tandem master cylinder. Most models use front disc brakes and rear drum brakes. Some have optional rear disc brakes.

The Teves Mark IV system in Jeeps can be identified by the pedal travel sensor mounted on the brake booster, as well as the two brake lines running from the master cylinder reservoir to the hydraulic control unit **(see illustrations)**.

Components of the Mark IV ABS are the controller, anti-lock brakes (CAB), hydraulic control unit (HCU),

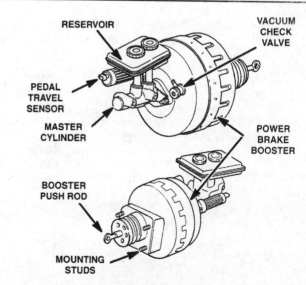

8.3 Pedal travel sensor, master cylinder and booster – Teves Mark IV

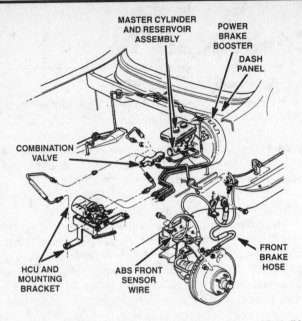

8.4 Anti-lock brake system components – Teves Mark IV

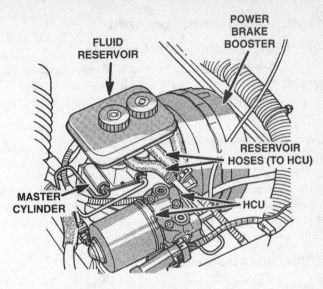

8.5 Reservoir-to-HCU hoses – Teves Mark IV

solenoids (contained within the HCU), pump and motor (also contained within the HCU), wheel speed sensors and tone wheels, main relay, pump relay, acceleration switch and ABS warning lamp.

System components

Controller, Anti-lock Brake (CAB)

Refer to illustrations 8.6 and 8.7

The central component of the Mark IV system is the Controller, Anti-lock Brake (CAB), which is mounted in various locations, depending on model **(see illustration)**. The CAB contains two identical microprocessors, both of which receive input signals from the wheel sensors, acceleration switch, pedal travel sensor, brake light switch and pump rotation sensor **(see illustration)**. The inputs are compared, and if they aren't identical, the CAB shuts down the ABS and sets a trouble code. The CAB also receives diagnostic inputs from the system components and stores any problems as diagnostic codes, which can be retrieved with a scan tool.

The CAB processes the input signals and then uses output signals to control the pump relay, the amber ABS warning lamp and the solenoids in the hydraulic control unit (HCU).

Hydraulic control unit

The hydraulic control unit (HCU) is mounted near the master cylinder and connected to it by hydraulic lines **(see illustration 8.5)**. The combination valve, part of the main brake system, is mounted in the lines that connect the master cylinder reservoir to the HCU.

The HCU contains six solenoids, two for each hydraulic channel. One of the solenoids in each channel is an inlet and the other is an outlet. It also contains an electric pump, which increases hydraulic pressure when needed.

Wheel speed sensors and tone wheels

Refer to illustrations 8.8, 8.9 and 8.10

The front wheel speed sensors are attached to the steering knuckles **(see illustration)**. The rear sensors are bolted to the brake backing plate **(see illustrations)**. The front and rear tone wheels are mounted at the outboard ends of the axleshafts.

8.6 Controller, Anti-lock Brake (CAB) – Teves Mark IV

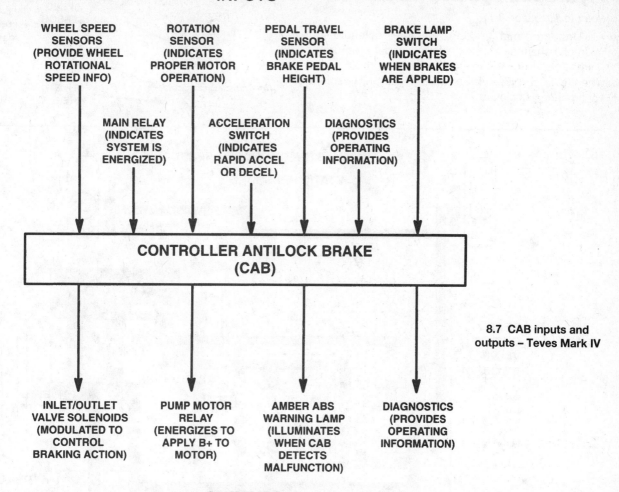

INPUTS

WHEEL SPEED SENSORS (PROVIDE WHEEL ROTATIONAL SPEED INFO)

ROTATION SENSOR (INDICATES PROPER MOTOR OPERATION)

PEDAL TRAVEL SENSOR (INDICATES BRAKE PEDAL HEIGHT)

BRAKE LAMP SWITCH (INDICATES WHEN BRAKES ARE APPLIED)

MAIN RELAY (INDICATES SYSTEM IS ENERGIZED)

ACCELERATION SWITCH (INDICATES RAPID ACCEL OR DECEL)

DIAGNOSTICS (PROVIDES OPERATING INFORMATION)

CONTROLLER ANTILOCK BRAKE (CAB)

8.7 CAB inputs and outputs – Teves Mark IV

INLET/OUTLET VALVE SOLENOIDS (MODULATED TO CONTROL BRAKING ACTION)

PUMP MOTOR RELAY (ENERGIZES TO APPLY B+ TO MOTOR)

AMBER ABS WARNING LAMP (ILLUMINATES WHEN CAB DETECTS MALFUNCTION)

DIAGNOSTICS (PROVIDES OPERATING INFORMATION)

OUTPUTS

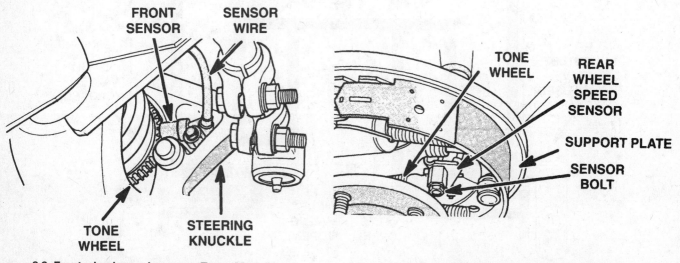

FRONT SENSOR

SENSOR WIRE

TONE WHEEL

STEERING KNUCKLE

TONE WHEEL

REAR WHEEL SPEED SENSOR

SUPPORT PLATE

SENSOR BOLT

8.8 Front wheel speed sensor – Teves Mark IV (Jeep installation shown)

8.9 Rear wheel speed sensor – Teves Mark IV (Jeep installation shown)

Hydraulic system operation

Refer to illustration 8.11

Under normal braking, the inlet solenoid in each hydraulic channel is open, allowing pedal pressure to flow unimpeded from the master cylinder to the calipers and wheel cylinders **(see illustration)**. The outlet solenoid in each channel is closed.

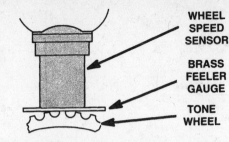

8.10 Measure speed sensor air gap with a non-magnetic (brass or plastic) feeler gauge

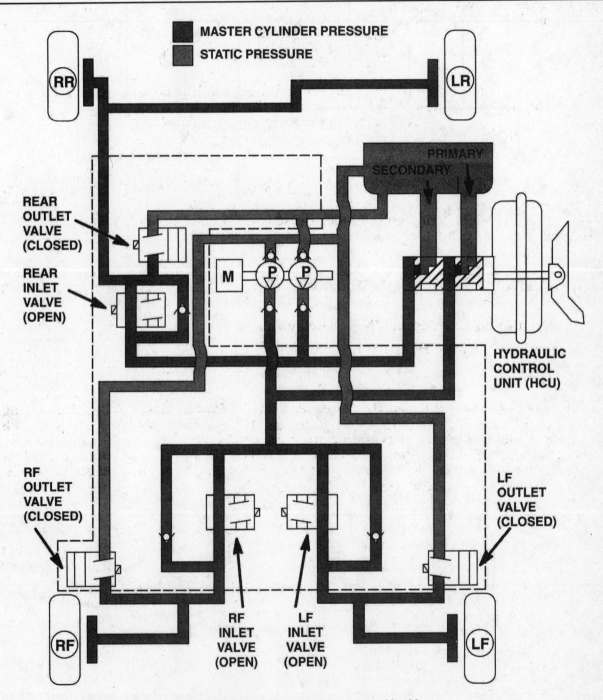

8.11 Teves Mark IV hydraulic schematic – normal braking

Hold cycle

Refer to illustration 8.12

When a wheel begins to lock, the impending lockup is detected by the CAB. The CAB then closes the inlet valve in the wheels' hydraulic channel, cutting off pedal pressure to the wheel **(see illustration)**. The outlet solenoid remains closed. As a result, hydraulic pressure at the wheel remains steady, neither increasing or decreasing. This is called the hold or isolation cycle. If the driver releases the pedal at this point, hydraulic pressure will force the inlet valve's internal check valve open, allowing the release of hydraulic pressure at the wheel.

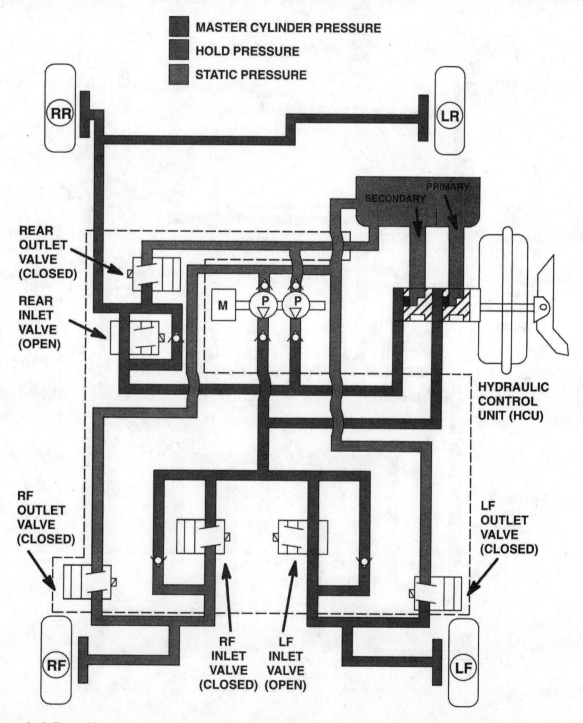

8.12 Teves Mark IV hydraulic schematic – anti-lock braking in hold cycle at right front wheel

Decay cycle

Refer to illustration 8.13

If the lockup condition continues, the CAB opens the outlet solenoid, releasing hydraulic pressure back to the master cylinder reservoir **(see illustration)**. Since the inlet solenoid is still being held closed by the CAB, hydraulic pressure at the wheel is reduced. This is called the decay or release cycle.

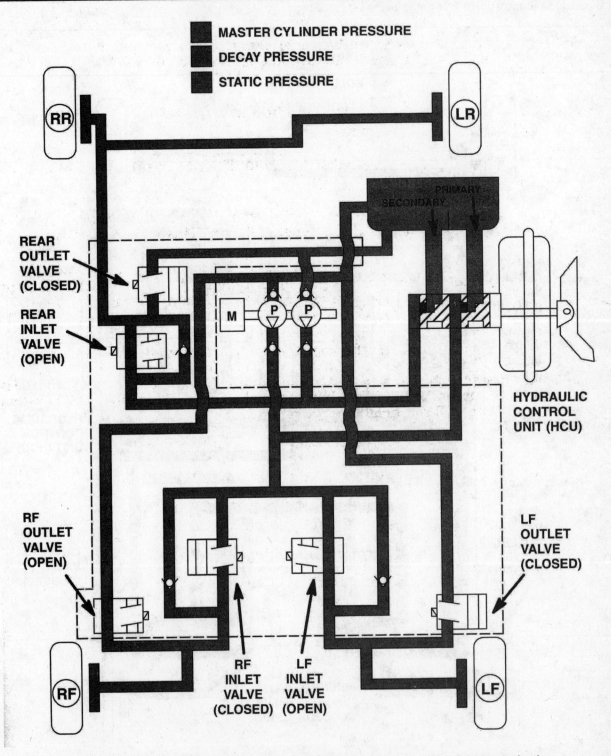

8.13 Teves Mark IV hydraulic schematic – anti-lock braking in decay cycle at right front wheel

Build cycle

Refer to illustration 8.14

Once the lockup condition ceases and the wheel starts to turn at a rate the CAB considers acceptable, the outlet valve closes and the inlet valve opens **(see illustration)**.

This allows pedal pressure to again build in the hydraulic circuit.

To restore pedal height, which drops during the decay cycle, the pump switches on, returning brake fluid to the master cylinder and increasing fluid pressure in the brake lines.

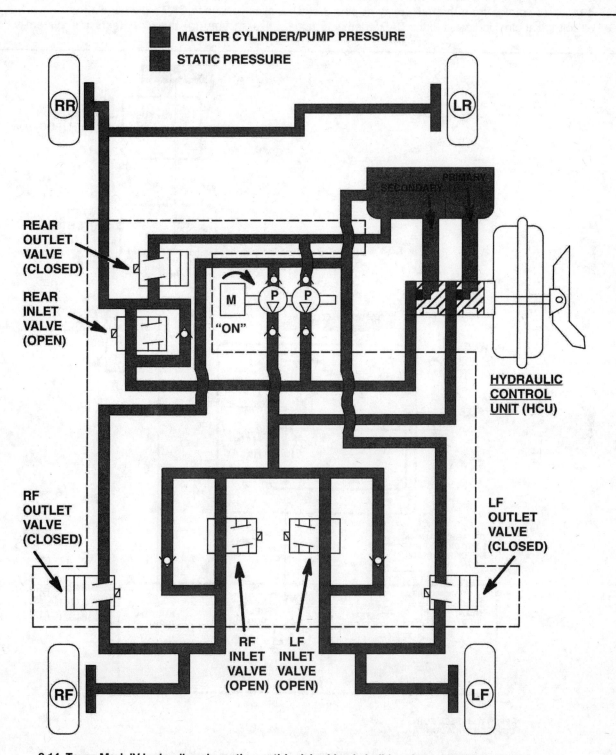

8.14 Teves Mark IV hydraulic schematic – anti-lock braking in build cycle at right front wheel

Electrical system operation
Controller, Anti-lock Brake (CAB)

Refer to illustrations 8.15 and 8.16

The CAB receives power for its internal operation from the ABS fuse in the fuse block **(see illustration)**. In addition, it receives voltage from the main relay at pins 3 and 33. The voltage at pin 3 indicates to the CAB whether or not there is correct system voltage. The CAB uses the voltage at pin 33 to provide reference voltage for the ABS sensors.

When the vehicle is started and the ignition switch is released to the Run position, the CAB receives input at terminal 53 **(see illustration)**. It then grounds the main relay coil through terminal 34, which closes the relay and supplies voltage to CAB pins 3 and 33.

On startup, the CAB tests the system with a static

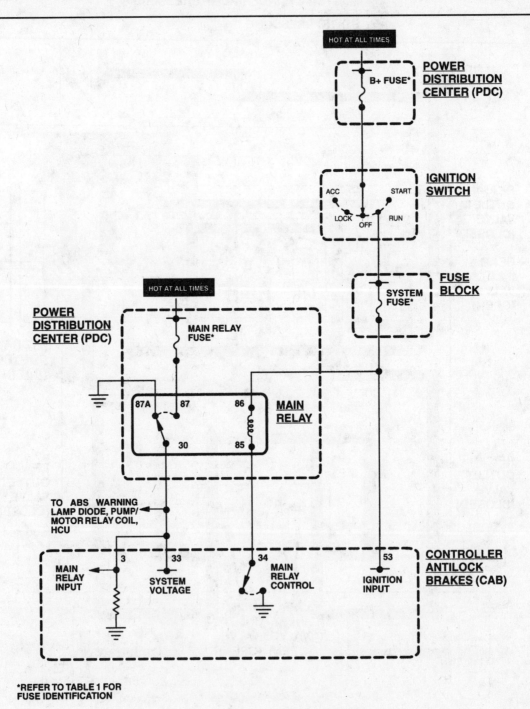

8.15 CAB power circuit – Teves Mark IV

check. This consists of:

a) A continuity check of the wheel sensor circuits, pedal travel sensor circuit, HCU circuit and acceleration switch

b) A voltage check at pin 3 of the CAB (9 to 16 volts DC is required to activate the system)

c) Cycling the solenoids in the HCU by grounding their ground circuits. This causes the brake pedal to pulsate rapidly, which will be felt by the driver if the pedal is applied during the check.

Once the vehicle reaches about six miles per hour, the CAB conducts a dynamic check. This consists of running

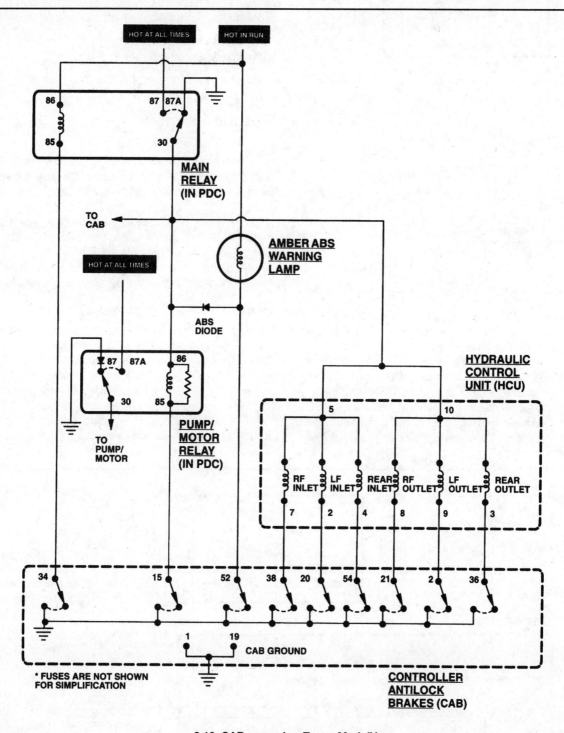

8.16 CAB grounds – Teves Mark IV

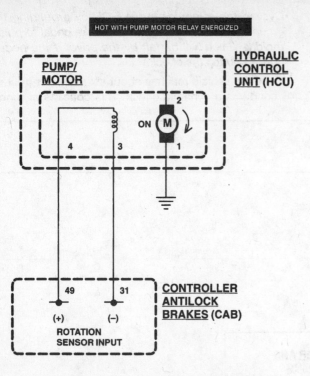

8.17 Rotation sensor circuit – Teves Mark IV

indicating that there's sufficient voltage to operate the system. Until these signals are received, the ABS system is dormant and the main brake system functions normally.

Once ABS operation starts, the CAB controls the inlet and outlet solenoids and the pump motor as described previously in *Hydraulic system operation*. The CAB controls all of these components by switching their ground circuits on (closed) or off (open). In the case of the pump, the CAB grounds the pump relay, which then supplies current to the pump.

Wheel sensors

The wheel sensors send the CAB a variable AC voltage signal as described in Chapter 1.

Rotation sensor

Refer to illustration 8.17

The rotation sensor is designed to tell the CAB whether or not the pump is working correctly **(see illustration)**. If the pump runs longer than it should, the CAB sets a trouble code.

The rotation sensor is mounted on top of the pump motor. When the motor spins, the rotation sensor produces a small amount of AC voltage. The voltage is sent alternately to pins 31 and 48 of the CAB, which records the signal as in indication that the pump motor is running.

Solenoids

There are two solenoids per hydraulic channel, one inlet and one outlet. The inlet solenoids are held open by spring pressure, and closed electrically by the CAB when anti-lock braking begins. Internal check valves in the inlet solenoids release when pedal is released, allowing hydraulic pressure in the brake lines to drop.

The outlet solenoids are held closed by spring pressure, and opened electrically by the CAB.

the pump for one to two seconds and checking the rotation sensor to make sure the pump operates.

If any part of the system fails during the static or dynamic check, the CAB shuts the ABS down, sets a diagnostic code and illuminates the amber ABS warning lamp.

The CAB needs three inputs to start ABS operation: the signals from the wheel sensors, indicating partial lockup; the signal from the brake light switch, indicating that the brake pedal has been applied; and the signal from the main relay,

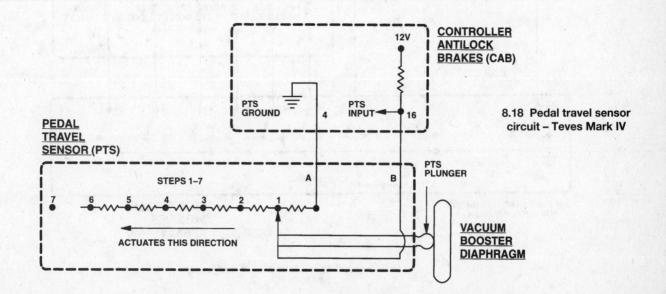

8.18 Pedal travel sensor circuit – Teves Mark IV

Pedal travel sensor

Refer to illustrations 8.18 and 8.19

The pedal travel sensor receives a reference voltage from pin 16 of the CAB, then increases its resistance, dropping the voltage in stages **(see illustration)**. The pedal travel sensor indicates to the CAB that the pedal has traveled far enough that pump operation is needed.

The pedal travel sensor is matched to the brake booster on each vehicle with a color code in red, white, green or blue. If you replace the booster or pedal travel sensor, it's critical to make sure the color code on the PTS plunger tip matches the dot on the outside of the booster **(see illustration)**.

Brake light switch

The brake light switch tells the CAB that the brake has been applied.

Acceleration switch

Refer to illustrations 8.20 through 8.25

This switch, sometimes called a g-switch, is used in Jeeps to let the CAB know how quickly the vehicle is decelerating, which indicates to the CAB how high the coefficient of friction of the road surface is. Ideally, the CAB should be able to vary the duty cycles (open vs. closed time) of the solenoids according to the coefficient of friction. The signals from the wheel speed sensor tell the CAB that ABS braking is necessary, but they don't provide information about the friction of the road surface. The acceleration switch does.

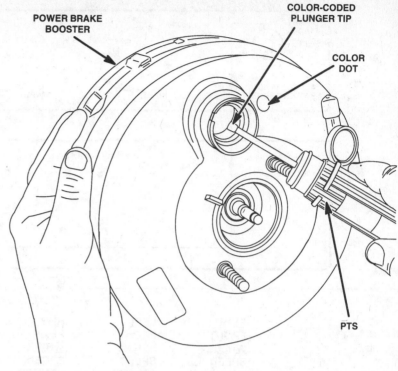

8.19 **The color dot on the booster must match the tip of the pedal travel sensor**

The switch consists of three mercury switches, contained in a single housing **(see illustration)**. Two of the mercury switches, designated G1 and G3, are designed to detect road friction during a forward stop. The third switch, designated G2, is designed to work during a rearward stop. All of the switches are normally closed. During a hard stop, the mercury inside the switch moves forward (G1 and G3) or rearward (G2) to open the switch.

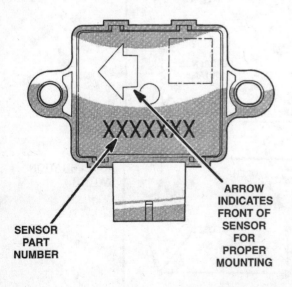

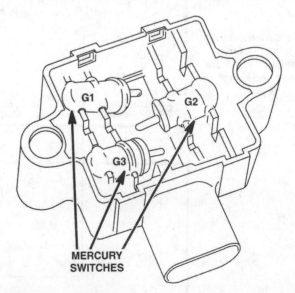

8.20 **Acceleration switch (g-switch) – Teves Mark IV**

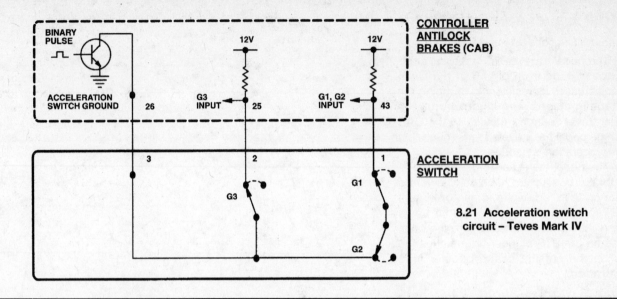

8.21 Acceleration switch circuit – Teves Mark IV

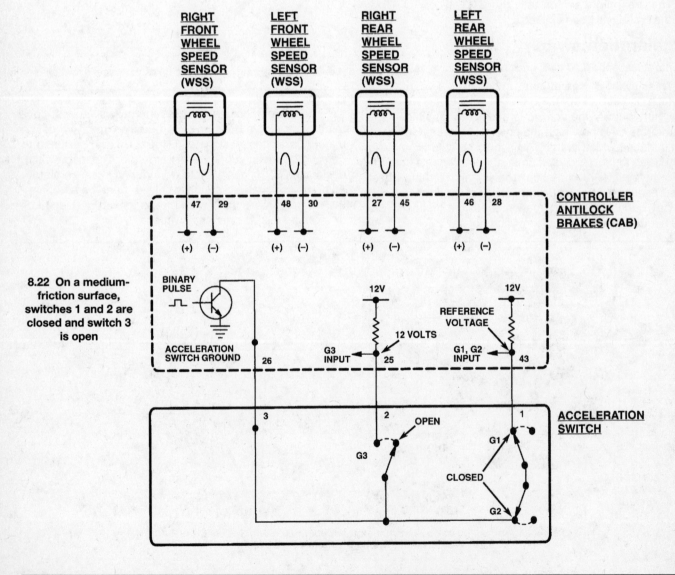

8.22 On a medium-friction surface, switches 1 and 2 are closed and switch 3 is open

The switch unit is connected to the CAB at pins 43 (input for switches G1 and G2) and 26 (input for G3) **(see illustration)**. The connection to the CAB at pin 26 provides ground for all three switches. While the switches are in their normal closed position, the CAB senses a reference voltage at pins 43 and 26.

During a hard forward stop on a medium-friction surface (such as loose dirt or gravel), only enough g-force is generated to open switch G3 (G3 opens at 0.21g, while G1 opens at 0.45g). The signal at CAB pin 25, the input for G3, steadies at 12 volts **(see illustration)**. While this is happening, the CAB receives signals from the wheel sensors telling

it to activate the ABS. Since it is receiving only the G3 signal at this time, it adjusts the duty cycle of the ABS solenoids for a medium-friction surface.

During a hard forward stop on a high-friction surface, such as smooth dry pavement, enough g-force is generated to open both G3 and G1 (again, G3 opens at .21g and G1 opens at .45g) **(see illustration)**. Now the CAB senses 12 volts at terminals 25 and 43, together with wheel sensor inputs telling it to activate the ABS. In response, it adjusts the duty cycle of the ABS solenoids for a high-friction surface.

During a hard forward stop on a low-friction surface,

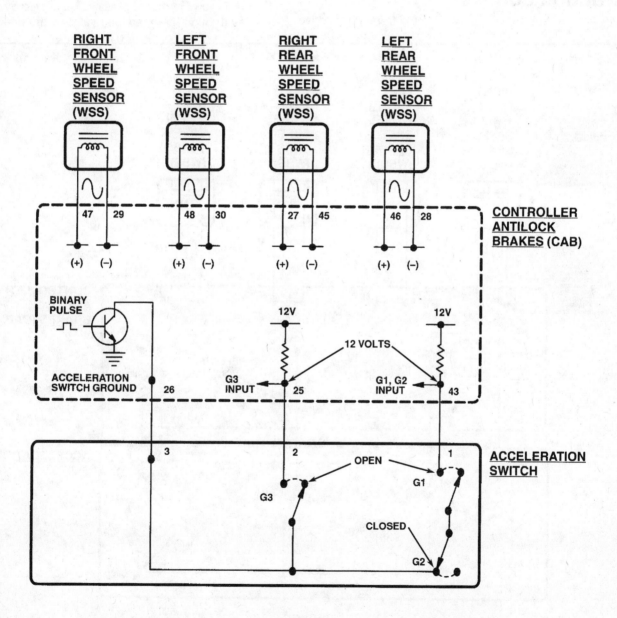

8.23 On a high-friction surface, switches 1 and 3 are open and switch 2 is closed

such as icy pavement, none of the switches closes **(see illustration)**. The CAB receives signals from the wheel sensors telling it to activate the ABS, while at the same time receiving reference voltage at pins 25 and 43. In response, it adjusts the solenoid duty cycle for a low-friction surface.

During a hard rearward stop – for example, backing down a steep gravel road – G2 closes **(see illustration)**. The CAB receives voltage signals from the wheel sensors, 12 volts at pin 43 and reference voltage at pin 25. This combination tells the CAB the vehicle is decelerating in reverse on a low- or medium-friction surface, and it adjusts the solenoid duty cycle accordingly.

Traction control

Traction control is used with some front-wheel drive Chrysler and GM vehicles, as well as some rear-wheel drive Ford models.

Traction control on these models applies one or both drive wheel brakes, but does not affect engine power. If a drive wheel begins to spin forward, the signal voltage from the wheel speed sensor will increase relative to the other sensors. The CAB monitors the wheel sensor signals and activates the traction control system when this occurs.

When a spinning front wheel is detected, the CAB runs the pump, which pulls fluid from the master cylinder and uses it to apply the brake at the spinning wheel(s). To keep from applying the rear brake that's in the same hydraulic circuit as the front brake, the CAB closes the circuit's isolation valve to cut off the hydraulic pressure to the rear brake. The CAB allows hydraulic pressure generated by the pump to pass through the open inlet valve to the brake caliper.

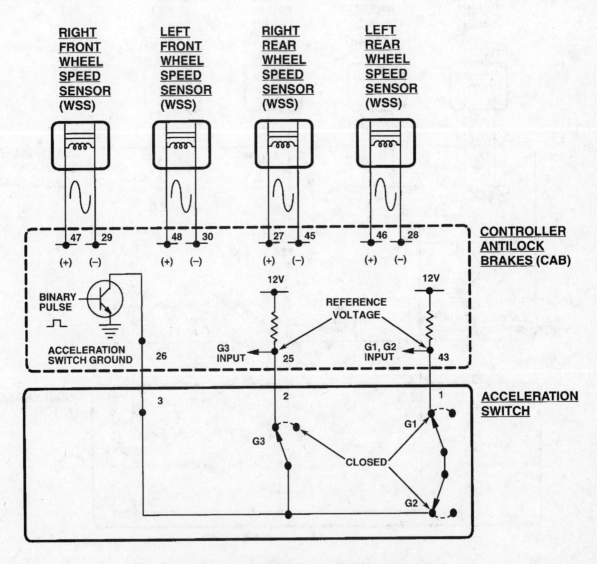

8.24 On a low-friction surface, all three switches are closed

The outlet valve is closed, so pressure can build and operate the brake. When the CAB detects that the wheel has slowed sufficiently, is closes the inlet valve, so brake pressure is held steady. Finally, when the CAB concludes that the brake can be released, it opens the outlet solenoid while keeping the inlet closed.

If the driver presses the brake pedal at any time while the traction control system is in operation, the signal from the brake pedal switch causes the CAB to deactivate the system.

The master cylinder is specially designed for use with traction control. It incorporates center valves, which open to allow brake fluid to be pulled through them while the traction control system is operating. This prevents damage to the piston seals by eliminating the need for compensating ports between the master cylinder reservoir and master cylinder bore. The rapid back-and-forth movement of the master cylinder pistons during traction control operation would cause the seals on the pistons to wear if they rubbed across compensating port openings. By eliminating the compensating ports, this cause of excessive seal wear is eliminated.

System service
Diagnosis

Diagnosing the Teves Mark IV system in Chrysler, Ford and GM vehicles requires a scan tool. Refer to the tool manufacturer's instructions.

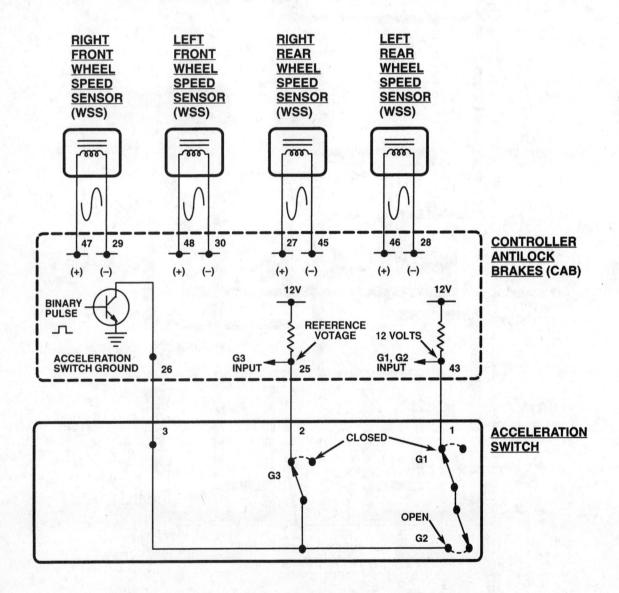

8.25 On hard braking in reverse, switch 2 is open, while 1 and 3 are closed

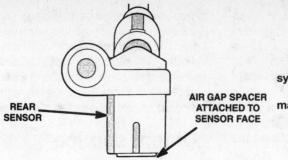

8.26 New rear wheel speed sensors for Teves Mark IV systems come with a spacer that sets the air gap; the spacer material is meant to rub off when the vehicle is driven

REAR SENSOR

AIR GAP SPACER ATTACHED TO SENSOR FACE

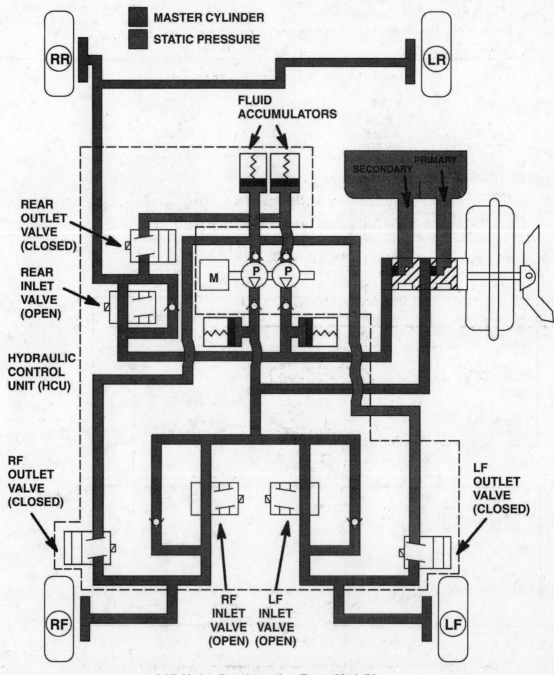

MASTER CYLINDER

STATIC PRESSURE

RR

LR

FLUID ACCUMULATORS

PRIMARY

SECONDARY

REAR OUTLET VALVE (CLOSED)

REAR INLET VALVE (OPEN)

M P P

HYDRAULIC CONTROL UNIT (HCU)

RF OUTLET VALVE (CLOSED)

LF OUTLET VALVE (CLOSED)

RF

LF

RF INLET VALVE (OPEN)

LF INLET VALVE (OPEN)

8.27 Hydraulic schematic – Teves Mark IVg

Bleeding

Warning 1: *Wear eye protection when bleeding the brake system. If the fluid comes in contact with your eyes, immediately rinse them with water and seek medical attention.*

Warning 2: *Never use old brake fluid. It contains moisture which can boil, rendering the brake system inoperative.*

Warning 3: *If, after bleeding the system you do not have a firm brake pedal, or if the ABS light on the instrument panel does not go off, or if you have any doubts whatsoever about the effectiveness of the brake system, have it towed to a dealer service department or other repair shop equipped with the necessary tools for bleeding the hydraulic modulator.*

Caution: *Brake fluid will damage paint. Cover all painted surfaces and be careful not to spill fluid during this procedure.*

Bleeding the brake lines is conventional. Bleeding the hydraulic control unit system requires a scan tool, should air manage to find its way into it. Refer to the scan tool manufacturer's instructions.

Component replacement

Refer to illustration 8.26

The sensor air gaps can be checked with a feeler gauge **(see illustration 8.10)**. **Caution:** *Use a non-magnetic (brass or plastic) feeler gauge.* Typical sensor air gaps range from 0.016 to 0.051-inch for a front wheel sensor, 0.037 to 0.057-inch for a rear sensor on a disc brake model, and 0.036 to 0.050-inch for a rear sensor on a drum brake model. The front sensor gaps are not adjustable. If they're not within the specified range, check for worn wheel bearings or bent steering knuckles. The rear sensor gaps can be adjusted, but this should only be necessary if you're reinstalling an original sensor. New sensors have a built-in spacer on the sensor face that sets the gap correctly when the sensor is pushed against the tone wheel **(see illustration)**. The rotating tone wheel then peels the spacer material off while the vehicle is in motion, leaving the gap.

The hydraulic control unit, including the pump, is replaced as an assembly.

The electronic control unit is replaced as an assembly.

Teves Mark IVg

Refer to illustration 8.27

The Mark IVg is an improved version of the Mark IV and was used in 1995 and 1996 Jeep models. It was replaced by the Mark 20 system for 1997, except in the 1997 Wrangler, which continued to use the Mark IVg.

Major changes are deletion of the pedal travel sensor and the addition of four accumulators to the hydraulic system **(see illustration)**. Two of the accumulators store fluid while the pump is running. One, with a 6 cc capacity, is for the front brakes; the other, with a 3 cc capacity, is for the rear brakes. The pump forces brake fluid into these accumulators during the decay cycle, then the fluid is returned to the brake lines during the build cycle. A third accumulator, with a capacity of 1 cc, acts as a lip seal saver; a fourth, with a capacity of 0.5 cc, reduces pump noise.

The Mark IVg pump runs continuously while the ABS is in operation, and shuts off two to three seconds after the ABS system shuts down.

For 1996, the Mark IVg includes a monitor for the pump relay. The pump's rotation sensor sends a signal to the CAB as the pump shuts off. If the signal lasts less than 400 milliseconds or longer than 3.3 seconds, the CAB assumes there is a problem with the pump and sets a diagnostic code. Another change for 1996 is that the acceleration switch is welded to its mounting bracket to make sure it is installed right side up.

Teves Mark 20

Refer to illustration 8.28

Teves Mark 20 is used in a number of 1997 and later Chrysler Corporation front wheel drive vehicles, including 1997 and 1998 mini-vans and the 1998 Cirrus, Stratus, Breeze, Sebring convertible and Neon.

The Teves Mark 20 system is very similar to the Teves Mark IVg, but the CAB and HCU are combined into a single assembly called the Integrated Control Unit (ICU). The ICU contains the solenoids, the pump and its motor, and the Controller, Anti-lock Brake (CAB). The appearance of this unit can be used to identify the system **(see illustration)**.

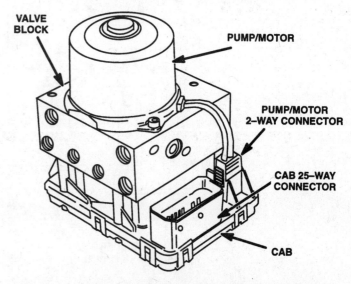

8.28 Here's the integrated control unit used on Teves Mark 20 systems (Jeep Grand Cherokee shown)

Some versions of the Mark 20 system have four hydraulic channels. Some include the Low-speed Traction Control System (LTCS).

Hydraulic system operation

Refer to illustrations 8.29 and 8.30

Two different hydraulic circuits are used, depending on the type of vehicle. Those with a relatively even front-rear weight distribution are split between front and rear of the vehicle, with three ABS channels **(see illustration)**. Those with a high percentage of the weight in the front, such as minivans and front wheel drive sedans, use a diagonally split circuit (left front and right rear in one half; right front and left rear in the other half), with four channels **(see illustration)**.

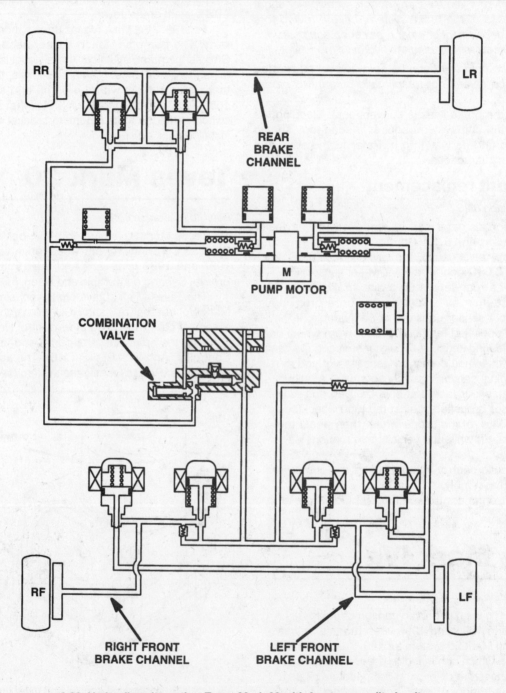

8.29 Hydraulic schematic – Teves Mark 20 with front-rear split circuits

With both systems, the hold, decay and build cycles are the same as for the Teves Mark IV, described above.

Electrical system operation

The CAB performs the same self-diagnostic checks on startup and at low speed as the Teves Mark IV. However, the low-speed test occurs at 12 mph, unless the driver presses the brake pedal before the vehicle reaches that speed. In this case, the low-speed test occurs at 25 mph.

Traction control

Refer to illustrations 8.31 and 8.32

Traction control on these models applies one or both front brakes, but does not affect engine power. If a front (drive) wheel begins to spin forward, the signal voltage from the wheel speed sensor will increase relative to the other sensors. The CAB monitors the wheel sensor signals and activates the traction control system when this occurs.

When a spinning front wheel is detected, the CAB runs

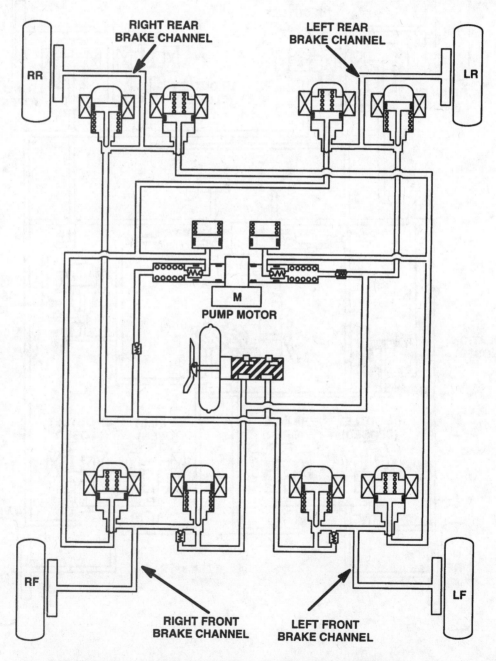

8.30 Hydraulic schematic – Teves Mark 20 with diagonal split circuits

the pump, which pulls fluid from the master cylinder and uses it to apply the brake at the spinning wheel(s). To keep from applying the rear brake that's in the same hydraulic circuit as the front brake, the CAB closes the circuit's isolation valve to cut off the hydraulic pressure to the rear brake **(see illustration)**. The CAB allows hydraulic pressure generated by the pump to pass through the open inlet valve to

the brake caliper. The outlet valve is closed, so pressure can build an operate the brake. When the CAB detects that the wheel has slowed sufficiently, is closes the inlet valve, so brake pressure is held steady. Finally, when the CAB concludes that the brake can be released, it opens the outlet solenoid while keeping the inlet closed.

If the driver presses the brake pedal at any time while

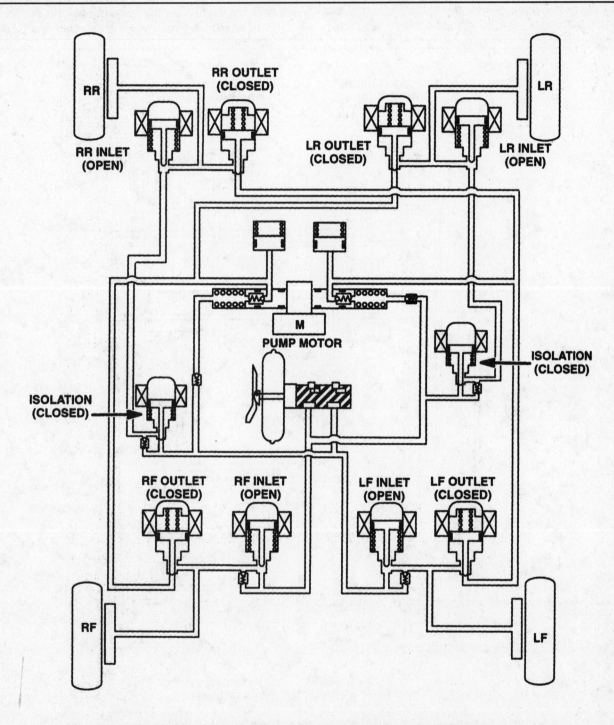

8.31 Teves Mark 20 traction control hydraulic schematic – build cycle at left front wheel shown

the traction control system is in operation, the signal from the brake pedal switch causes the CAB to deactivate the system.

The master cylinder is specially designed for use with traction control. It incorporates center valves, which open to allow brake fluid to be pulled through them while the traction control system is operating **(see illustration)**. This prevents damage to the piston seals by eliminating the need for compensating ports between the master cylinder reservoir and master cylinder bore. The rapid back-and-forth movement of the master cylinder pistons during trac-tion control operation would cause the seals on the pistons to wear if they rubbed across compensating port openings. By eliminating the compensating ports, this cause of excessive seal wear is eliminated.

System service

This is the same as for the Teves Mark IV system, with two exceptions. The wheel speed sensors are not adjustable. The CAB, pump/motor, and ICU can be replaced separately.

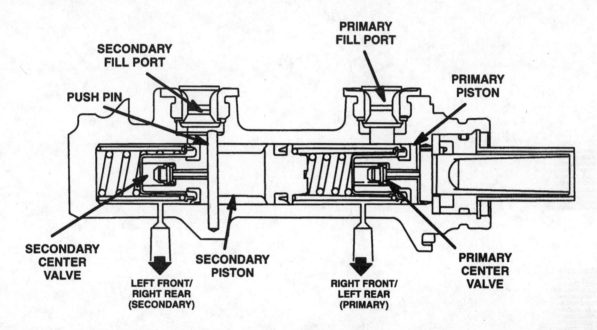

8.32 The master cylinder for Teves Mark 20 traction control systems has dual center valves, eliminating the need for compensating ports

Notes

Chapter 9
Toyota systems

Toyota uses Nippondenso and Bosch systems in many of its vehicles, but it also has some unique systems and features. These include a rear-wheel only anti-lock brake system that uses the power steering pump to boost hydraulic pressure during an ABS stop.

Rear-wheel ABS

This system is used in 1990 through 1995 Toyota pickup trucks, 1990 through 1993 4Runners and 1993 and 1994 T100 pickups.

A disadvantage of most rear-wheel ABS systems is that they have no pump or other source of hydraulic pressure other than the driver's foot on the pedal. This means that during a long ABS stop, when brake pressure is released multiple times, the pedal will drop significantly. Some systems try to compensate for this by using the ECU software to limit the number of times pressure can be released during any one stop. The Toyota system supplies the needed hydraulic pressure by using power steering pump pressure to supply hydraulic boost.

System components

Refer to illustration 9.1

System components are an electronic control unit, one speed sensor, a deceleration sensor, a hydraulic actuator, relay, ABS warning lamp and associated wiring **(see illustration)**. The hydraulic actuator contains one solenoid, a

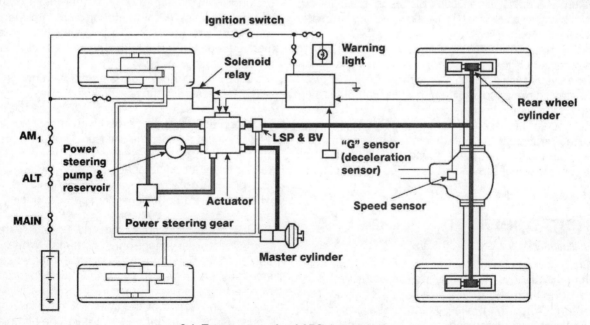

9.1 Toyota rear-wheel ABS components

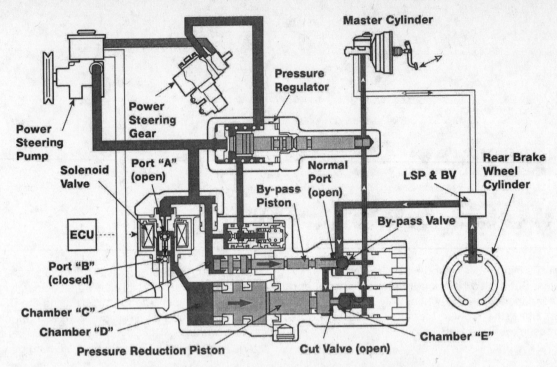

9.2 Toyota rear-wheel ABS in normal braking mode

pressure regulator valve, a relief valve, a bypass piston, pressure reduction piston, a bypass valve and a cut valve.

The pressure regulator valve applies power steering pressure to the rear brake during an ABS stop.

The solenoid is used by the ECU to control the amount of power steering pressure applied to the pressure reduction piston. The pressure reduction piston operates the cut valve and bypass valve, which route the brake fluid from the master cylinder to the rear brakes.

The bypass piston is a fail-safe device in case power steering pressure is lost. If this happens, the bypass piston opens the bypass valve, which allows master cylinder pressure to flow directly to the rear brakes without being affected by the hydraulic actuator.

The deceleration sensor communicates the rate of vehicle deceleration to the ECU. It can use this information, together with the input from the speed sensor, to calculate the rate of rear wheel slip and adjust its operation accordingly.

System operation

Refer to illustrations 9.2, 9.3, 9.4, 9.5 and 9.6

During normal braking, power steering pressure operates the cut valve and the bypass valve, holding the cut valve and the normal port in the bypass valve open **(see illustration)**. When the brake pedal is pressed, hydraulic pressure flows through the normal port of the bypass valve

to the rear brakes.

The ECU monitors the signal from the rear wheel speed sensor continuously. If it drops too quickly, indicating that rear wheel lockup is about to occur, it initiates anti-lock braking.

During the first part of an ABS stop, the ECU holds braking pressure steady. Since there isn't a specifically designed pressure hold function built into the system, it rapidly pulses between the pressure release and build modes **(see illustration)**. This has the effect of holding the pressure steady.

If holding the pressure steady isn't enough, the ECU reduces pressure at the rear brakes. It does this by sending current to the solenoid, causing it to close the upper port and open the lower port **(see illustration)**. Power steering fluid pressure against the pressure reduction piston is cut off, and the piston moves away from the cut valve. The cut valve closes, leaving a space between the pressure reduction piston and the cut valve. Brake fluid from the rear wheel cylinders flows into this space, reducing hydraulic pressure at the rear brakes.

It's at the next stage that the Toyota system differs from most rear-wheel-only systems. When the ECU decides that braking pressure at the rear wheels can be increased, it is able to more than just open up the rear brakes to more pedal pressure from the driver. The ECU changes the timing of the solenoid, causing it to stay off longer during its on/off pulses. During the off time, the inlet

Part Name	Operation	
	Pressure Increase	Pressure Reduction
Solenoid Valve	Port "A" Open	Port "A" Close
	Port "B" Close	Port "B" Open
Cut Valve	Close	←
By-pass Valve	Normal Port Open	←

9.3 Toyota rear-wheel ABS in pressure hold mode

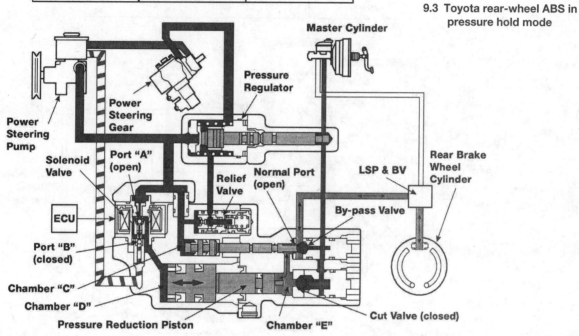

Part Name	Operation
Solenoid Valve	Port "A" Close
	Port "B" Open
Cut Valve	Close
By-pass Valve	Normal Port Open

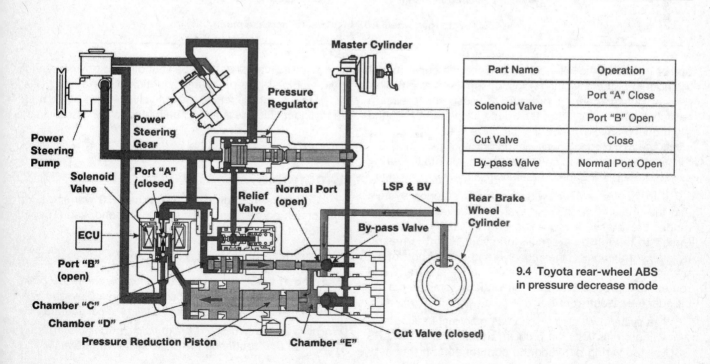

9.4 Toyota rear-wheel ABS in pressure decrease mode

Part Name	Operation	
	Pressure Increase	Pressure Reduction
Solenoid Valve	Port "A" Open	Port "A" Close
	Port "B" Close	Port "B" Open
Cut Valve	Close	←
By-pass Valve	Normal Port Open	←

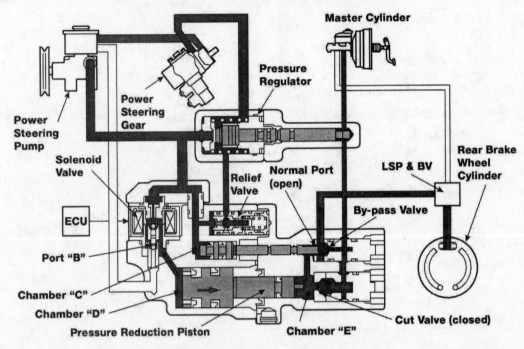

9.5 Toyota rear-wheel ABS in pressure increase mode

port at the top of the solenoid is open and the outlet port at the bottom of the solenoid is closed (see illustration). This causes power steering pressure to push the pressure reduction piston back into the space it opened up during the reduction cycle. Since the cut valve is still closed, the shrinkage of the space between the pressure reduction piston and the cut valve forces brake fluid back into the wheel cylinders, increasing the pressure within them.

If there is a problem with the power steering system and the pressure drops, the system goes into a fail-safe mode; the pressure reduction and bypass pistons are forced to the left by hydraulic pressure from the master cylinder. At this point, the cut valve and normal port of the bypass valve close, which opens the bypass port and routes fluid pressure to the rear brakes from the master cylinder (see illustration).

The system will also function as a normal braking system without rear ABS if a problem develops with the ABS ECU or the wiring between the components. If this hap-

pens, the solenoid relay will be shut off, and power steering fluid will push the pressure reduction piston and bypass valve to the right, opening the cut valve. At this point, master cylinder fluid pressure will be routed to the rear brakes.

System service

Diagnosis

Codes can be retrieved using the ABS warning lamp and check connector. Refer to the Nippondenso (Toyota) Section of Chapter 7 for details.

Bleeding

Warning 1: *Wear eye protection when bleeding the brake system. If the fluid comes in contact with your eyes, immediately rinse them with water and seek medical attention.*

Warning 2: *Never use old brake fluid. It contains moisture which can boil, rendering the brake system inoperative.*

Part Name	Operation
Cut Valve	Close
By-pass Valve	By-pass Port Open

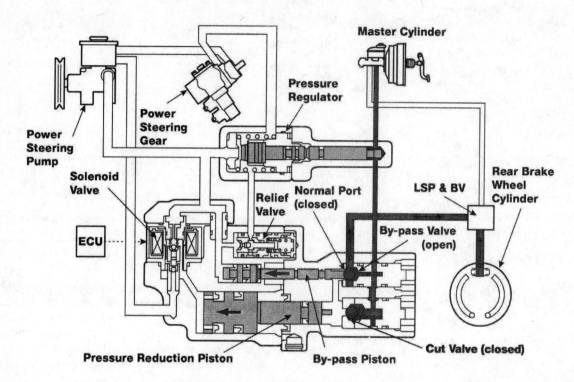

9.6 Toyota rear-wheel ABS in fail-safe mode

Warning 3: *If, after bleeding the system you do not have a firm brake pedal, or if the ABS light on the instrument panel does not go off, or if you have any doubts whatsoever about the effectiveness of the brake system, don't drive the vehicle. Have it towed to a dealer service department or other repair shop equipped with the necessary tool for bleeding the hydraulic actuator.*

Caution: *Brake fluid will damage paint. Cover all painted surfaces and be careful not to spill fluid during this procedure.*

This system can be bled in the conventional manner unless a brake line has been disconnected from the actuator or if a power steering line has been disconnected. If this has happened, bleeding this system involves first bleeding the power steering system, then bleeding the brakes in the conventional way, first with the engine running and then with the engine off. Following these steps, the power steering system should be bled again, this time using the Toyota actuator checker or equivalent test equipment. Refer to the tool manufacturer's instructions.

Component replacement

The actuator and electronic control unit are replaced as assemblies. The speed sensor and deceleration sensor can be replaced separately.

Toyota four-wheel ABS

In addition to the Nippondenso and Bosch systems used in a number of Toyota vehicles through 1996, Toyota also uses a four-sensor, three channel system. It was first used in 1993 in the Corolla, then was gradually added to other models until by 1997 it was being used in all Toyota vehicles except the Land Cruiser.

System components

Refer to illustration 9.7

The main components are the electronic control unit and the hydraulic actuator.

The system contains two solenoids per channel, one inlet and one outlet (**see illustration**). There are either three or four channels, but on models with four channels the two rear channels are controlled simultaneously (except for the Supra, which has four independently controlled channels). The actuator also contains check valves, pumps and reservoirs (one of each per hydraulic circuit).

System operation

The ECU monitors signals from the wheel speed sensors. When one or more signals drops too quickly, indicating that a wheel is about to lock up, the ECU initiates anti-lock braking.

Normal braking

Refer to illustration 9.8

During normal braking, the inlet solenoids are open and the outlet solenoids are closed (**see illustration**). This allows hydraulic pressure from the master cylinder to flow to the wheel brakes.

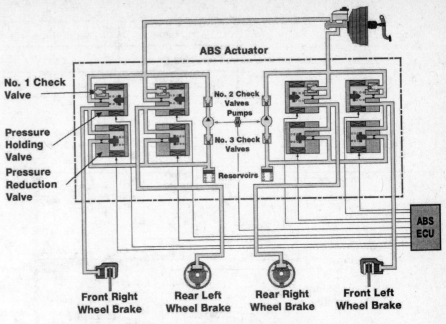

9.7 Hydraulic schematic – Toyota ABS with two-position solenoids

Anti-lock braking

Anti-lock braking begins with the pressure holding phase. The inlet solenoid for the affected wheel is closed by the ECU, which cuts off brake pressure to the wheel.

If this isn't enough, the ECU opens the outlet solenoid, allowing brake pressure to flow into the circuit's reservoir. The pump starts to run, returning released brake fluid to the

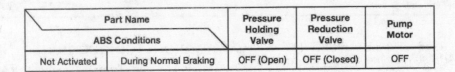

Part Name / ABS Conditions		Pressure Holding Valve	Pressure Reduction Valve	Pump Motor
Not Activated	During Normal Braking	OFF (Open)	OFF (Closed)	OFF

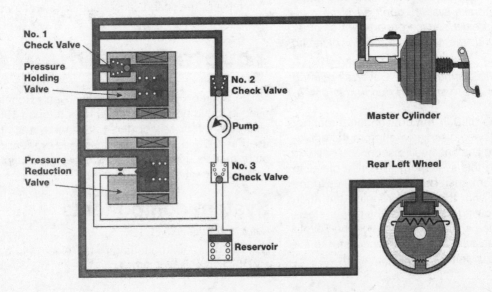

9.8 Two-position solenoid ABS in normal braking mode

master cylinder. This will be felt as pedal pulsations by the driver.

When the ECU decides that brake pressure can increase again, it opens the inlet solenoid and closes the outlet solenoid. This allows pedal pressure to operate the brake once again.

System service

Diagnosis

Trouble codes can be retrieved using the ABS warning lamp and check connector. Refer to the Nippondenso (Toyota) Section of Chapter 7 for details.

Bleeding

Warning 1: *Wear eye protection when bleeding the brake system. If the fluid comes in contact with your eyes, immediately rinse them with water and seek medical attention.*

Warning 2: *Never use old brake fluid. It contains moisture which can boil, rendering the brake system inoperative.*

Warning 3: *If, after bleeding the system you do not have a firm brake pedal, or if the ABS light on the instrument panel does not go off, or if you have any doubts whatsoever about the effectiveness of the brake system, don't drive the vehicle. Have it towed to a dealer service department or other repair shop for diagnosis.*

Caution: *Brake fluid will damage paint. Cover all painted surfaces and be careful not to spill fluid during this procedure.*

In general, bleeding of this system is the same as for non-ABS vehicles. However, due to the large number of vehicles equipped with this system, consult a vehicle-specific service manual for bleeding procedures for the main brake system and the ABS.

Component replacement

Wheel speed sensor replacement is a bolt-in job. Sensor rings are replaced together with the component they're mounted on.

The electronic control unit and hydraulic actuator are replaced as assemblies.

Traction control systems

Toyota uses two different traction control systems, one on the Supra and one on the Camry/Avalon. The two systems are based on different anti-lock brake systems and use different methods to reduce engine power during traction control system operation.

Supra traction control (TRAC)

This system uses a combination of ignition timing retard, throttle control and braking on 1993 through 1995 models, and ignition timing and throttle control only on 1996 models. It uses a sub-throttle valve, mounted ahead of the normal throttle valve in the intake passage, to regulate the throttle. A separate pump supplies braking pressure for the rear (drive) wheels during TCS operation. The system controls the rear wheels independently. A SNOW switch was added in 1996. This allows the driver to select reduced engine torque in situations where wheelspin is likely to occur.

System components

Refer to illustration 9.9

The system includes the engine management computer. On 1993 through 1995 models, there are separate electronic control units for the ABS and traction control systems. These ECUs were combined into one unit for 1996. Other components are a speed sensor at each wheel, traction control pump, separate throttle position sensors for the main and sub-throttles, pump and solenoid relays, an electric motor for the sub-throttle valve, a TRAC warning lamp, TRAC and TRAC OFF indicator lamps and a TRAC on/off switch **(see illustration)**.

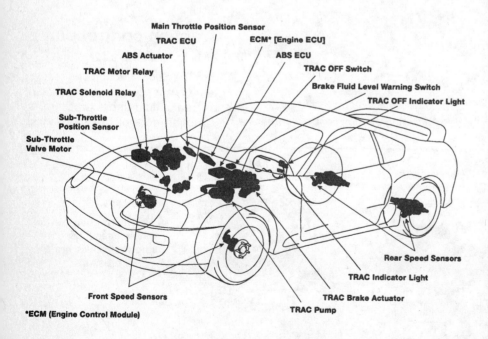

Main Throttle Position Sensor
TRAC ECU
ABS Actuator
TRAC Motor Relay
TRAC Solenoid Relay
Sub-Throttle Position Sensor
Sub-Throttle Valve Motor
ECM* [Engine ECU]
ABS ECU
TRAC OFF Switch
Brake Fluid Level Warning Switch
TRAC OFF Indicator Light
Rear Speed Sensors
TRAC Indicator Light
Front Speed Sensors
TRAC Brake Actuator
TRAC Pump
*ECM (Engine Control Module)

9.9 Supra traction control components

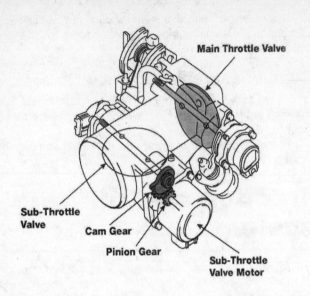

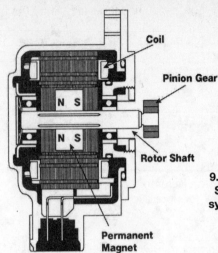

9.10 The sub-throttle in Supra traction control systems is controlled by an electric motor

Sub-Throttle Valve Motor

Sub-throttle

Refer to illustrations 9.10 and 9.11

The sub-throttle is used to restrict throttle air intake through the throttle opening during traction control operation **(see illustration)**. It employs a throttle valve similar to the main throttle valve, but mounted ahead of the main throttle valve in the throttle body. The valve is opened and closed by a stepper motor, which turns a pinion gear on the end of its shaft. The pinion gear moves a cam gear on the valve's pivot shaft, which causes the valve to open and close **(see illustration)**. The sub-throttle has a throttle position sensor, just like the one used for the main throttle, that signals the position of the throttle valve to the engine ECU, which in turn signals the traction control ECU.

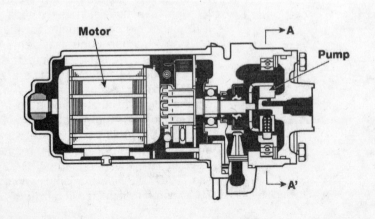

9.11 The sub-throttle is normally open, but closes during traction control operation

Traction control pump

Refer to illustration 9.12

The Supra traction control system uses a separate pump to supply brake fluid under pressure for traction control braking. Unlike

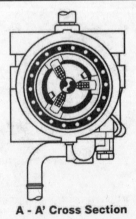

9.12 The traction control system uses a separate pump to produce braking pressure

A - A' Cross Section

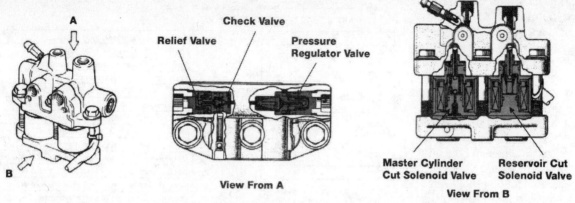

9.13 Here's the hydraulic actuator used with Supra traction control systems

the piston pump used in the ABS, the traction control pump is a radial type **(see illustration)**.

Traction control brake actuator

Refer to illustration 9.13

The actuator contains two solenoids and three spring-loaded valves **(see illustration)**. The traction control ECU controls the solenoids electrically to modulate the flow of brake pressure to the rear brakes during traction control operation. The check valve prevents brake pressure from flowing out of the calipers during traction control operation. The pressure regulator valve controls the amount of pump pressure. The relief valve limits maximum pressure in the event of a system failure.

System operation

The system turns on whenever the ignition is turned on, and then is ready to initiate traction control operation as needed. The TRAC switch allows the system to be switched off by the driver. The TRAC OFF warning lamp will illuminate when this occurs.

On startup, the system conducts a self-test, operating the traction control pump and solenoids briefly. With the shift lever in neutral or Park and the main throttle valve completely closed, it briefly moves the sub-throttle valve to the fully closed position.

Braking

Refer to illustration 9.14

Braking is used as a traction control method on 1993 through 1995 models only. During normal driving, brake fluid from the master cylinder flows through the ABS solenoids, which are open, and the master cylinder cut solenoid, which is also open **(see illustration)**.

When the ECU decides that a drive wheel is spinning, it operates the traction control pump. To route the pump's

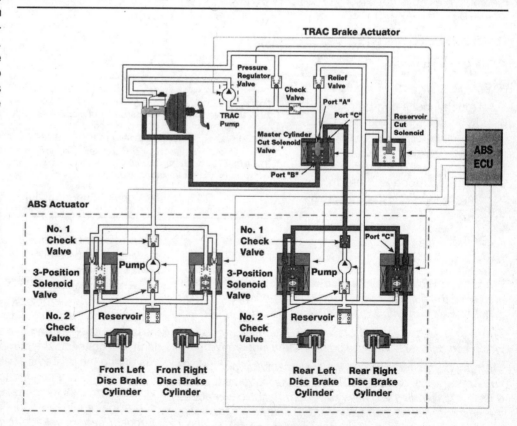

9.14 Hydraulic schematic – Supra traction control system

pressure to the brake, it closes Port B in the master cylinder cut solenoid. Ports A and C are open, which allows pump pressure to flow to the brake. The pressure regulator valve in the actuator prevents the pump from producing excessive pressure. The amount of pressure actually applied to the brake is controlled by the ABS solenoid, which is cycled between its pressure increase, pressure hold and pressure release modes.

The reservoir cut sole-noid valve in the actuator is open, allowing the return of brake fluid to the master cylinder.

Engine controls

The traction control system reduces engine torque during wheelspin by two methods; it partially closes the sub-throttle valve, restricting airflow into the engine, and it retards ignition timing. On 1996 and later models, engine controls are the only traction control methods; braking is not used.

System service

Diagnosis

Refer to illustrations 9.15 and 9.16

Trouble codes can be retrieved using the ABS warning lamp and check connector. Refer to the Nippondenso (Toyota) Section of Chapter 7 for details. To interpret traction control trouble codes, refer to the accompanying table (see illustrations).

Code No.	Indicator Lights			Code No. at TRAC ECU*2	Diagnosis
	ABS	TRAC	TRAC OFF		
11*1	O		O	43	Open circuit in solenoid relay circuit.
12*1	O	–	O		Short circuit in solenoid relay circuit.
13*1	O	–	O		Open circuit in pump motor relay circuit.
14*1	O	–	O		Short circuit in pump motor relay circuit.
15	O	O	O		Open circuit in TRAC solenoid relay circuit.
16	O	O	–		Short circuit in TRAC solenoid relay circuit.
17	–	O	O		Open circuit in TRAC motor relay circuit.
18	–	O	O		Short circuit in TRAC motor relay circuit.
21*1	O	–	O		Open or short circuit in 3-position solenoid of front right wheel.
22*1	O	–	O		Open or short circuit in 3-position solenoid of front left wheel.
23*1	O	–	O		Open or short circuit in 3-position solenoid of rear right wheel.
24*1	O	–	O		Open or short circuit in 3-position solenoid of rear left wheel.
25	O	O	O		Open or short circuit in master cylinder cut solenoid valve circuit of TRAC brake actuator.
27	O	O	O		Open or short circuit in reservoir cut solenoid valve circuit of TRAC brake actuator.
31*1	O	O*3	O	31, 43	Front right wheel speed sensor signal malfunction.
32*1	O	O*3	O	32, 43	Front left wheel speed sensor signal malfunction.
33*1	O	O*3	O	33, 43	Rear right wheel speed sensor signal malfunction.
34*1	O	O*3	O	34, 43	Rear left wheel speed sensor signal malfunction.
35*1	O	–	O	43	Open circuit in front left and rear right speed sensors.
36*1	O	–	O		Open circuit in front right and rear left speed sensors.
41*1	O	O*3	O	41, 43	Low battery voltage (9.5 V or lower) or abnormally high battery voltage (17 V or higher).
44*1	O	–		–	Lateral acceleration sensor signal malfunction.
51*1	O		O		Pump motor locked or open circuit.
55	–	O	O		Fluid level of brake master cylinder reservoir dropped causing master cylinder reservoir level warning switch to go on.
58	–	O	O		Open circuit in TRAC motor.
61	–	O	O	43	Open or short circuit in circuit which inputs TRAC system operation to ABS ECU.
62*4	–	O	O		Malfunction in ABS ECU (Involving vehicle speed signal input inside ABS ECU).
Always ON*1	O	O	O		Malfunction in ABS ECU.

O Diagnostic trouble code indicated
– Not applicable

*1 Both the code number and description of diagnosis are identical to those of the ABS ECU without the TRAC system (2JZ-GE engine model).
*2 See illustration 9.9 for the location of the TRAC ECU.
*3 The indicator light flashes only if the same diagnosis is also detected by the TRAC ECU.
*4 The ABS ECU deletes the stored code No.62 when it detects the malfunctions numbered from No.31 to No.36 (wheel speed sensor signal malfunction).

9.15 Trouble codes – Supra traction control system (1 of 2)

Bleeding

Refer to illustration 9.17

Warning 1: *Wear eye protection when bleeding the brake system. If the fluid comes in contact with your eyes, immediately rinse them with water and seek medical attention.*

Warning 2: *Never use old brake fluid. It contains moisture which can boil, rendering the brake system inoperative.*

Warning 3: *If, after bleeding the system you do not have a firm brake pedal, or if the ABS light on the instrument panel does not go off, or if you have any doubts whatsoever about the effectiveness of the brake system, don't drive the vehicle. Have it towed to a dealer service department or other repair shop for diagnosis.*

Caution: *Brake fluid will damage paint. Cover all painted surfaces and be careful not to spill fluid during this procedure.*

The traction control system must be bled whenever the master cylinder and/or power brake booster is removed. Bleeding the traction control actuator requires a wiring harness adapter (Toyota special tool 09990-00330 or equivalent) that connects the pump directly to the battery so it can run during the procedure (see illustration). If this adapter is not available, you can fabricate your own using the proper type of terminals to connect the motor, two lengths of wire, and alligator clips to connect to power and ground. **Note:** *Connect battery voltage to the terminal on the motor connector that corresponds to the Blue/Yellow wire in the har-*

Code No.	Indicator Lights			Code No. at ABS ECU[1]	Diagnosis
	ABS	TRAC	TRAC OFF		
24	–	O	–	–	Open or short circuit in step motor circuit of sub-throttle actuator.
25	–	O	–	–	Step motor does not move to a position decided by TRAC ECU.
26	–	O	–	–	Leak at sub-throttle position sensor or stuck sub-throttle valve.
31	O[2]	O	O[2]	31	Front right wheel speed sensor signal malfunction.
32	O[2]	O	O[2]	32	Front left wheel speed sensor signal malfunction.
33	O[2]	O	O[2]	33	Rear right wheel speed sensor signal malfunction.
34	O[2]	O	O[2]	34	Rear left wheel speed sensor signal malfunction.
41	–	O	–	–	Low battery voltage (9.5 V or lower) or abnormally high battery voltage (17 V or higher).
43	O	O	O	–	Malfunction in ABS ECU.
44	–	O	–	–	Engine speed signal (NE) is not input from the ECM[3] [Engine ECU] during TRAC control.
45	–	O	–	–	Short circuit in IDL signal circuit of the main throttle position sensor.
46	–	–	–	–	Open or short circuit in VTA1 signal circuit of the main throttle position sensor.
47	–	O	–	–	Open or short circuit in IDL₂ signal circuit of the sub-throttle position sensor.
48	–	O	–	–	Open or short circuit in VTA2 signal circuit of the sub-throttle position sensor.
51	–	–	O	–	Malfunction in engine control system causes malfunction indicator lamp [CHECK ENGINE warning lamp] to go on.
53	–	O	–	–	Malfunction in communication circuit to ECM[3] [Engine ECU].
61	–	O	–	–	Malfunction in communication circuit to ABS ECU.
Always ON	–	O	O	–	Malfunction in TRAC ECU.

9.16 Trouble codes – Supra traction control system (2 of 2)

O Diagnostic trouble code indicated
– Not applicable

[1] See illustration 9.9 for the location of the TRAC ECU.

[2] The indicator light flashes only if the same diagnosis is also detected by the ABS ECU.

[3] ECM (Engine Control Module)

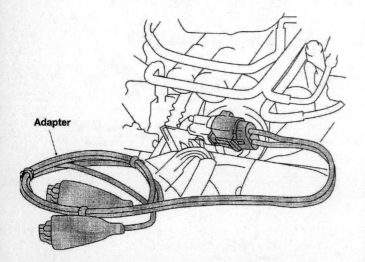

Adapter

9.17 A special adapter is required to activate the traction control pump while bleeding the system

ness, and connect a ground lead to the terminal that corresponds to the White/Black wire in the harness.

1 Disconnect the electrical connector from the traction control pump and connect the harness adapter in its place.

2 Connect a clear plastic tube to the bleed valve on the traction control actuator **(see illustration 9.13)**. Place the other end of the tube in a container, then open the bleed valve.

3 Start the engine and let it idle.

4 Connect the harness adapter to the vehicle's battery for 60 seconds. This will cause the pump to run and expel fluid from the tube. After 60 seconds, close the bleed valve, let the pump run for another 30 seconds, then disconnect the harness adapter from the battery negative terminal to shut off the pump.

5 Shut off the engine, disconnect the harness adapter and reconnect the pump's electrical connector.

6 Check the brake fluid level and top up as needed.

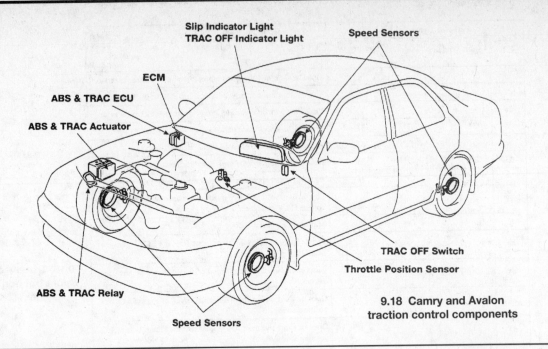

Slip Indicator Light
TRAC OFF Indicator Light

Speed Sensors

ECM

ABS & TRAC ECU

ABS & TRAC Actuator

TRAC OFF Switch

Throttle Position Sensor

ABS & TRAC Relay

Speed Sensors

9.18 Camry and Avalon traction control components

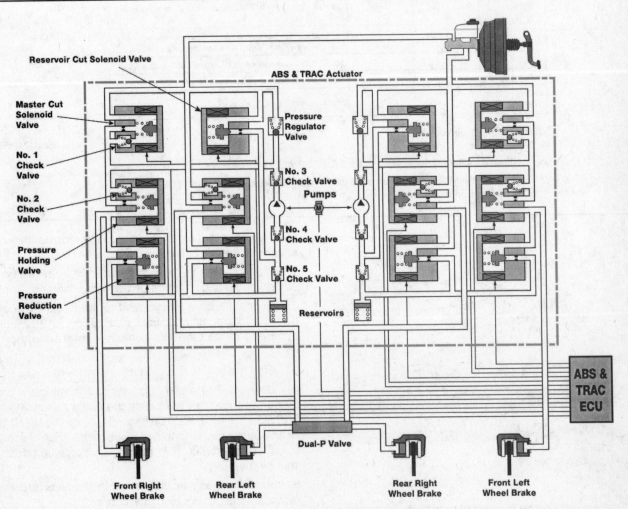

Reservoir Cut Solenoid Valve

ABS & TRAC Actuator

Master Cut
Solenoid
Valve

Pressure
Regulator
Valve

No. 1
Check
Valve

No. 3
Check Valve

Pumps

No. 2
Check
Valve

No. 4
Check Valve

Pressure
Holding
Valve

No. 5
Check Valve

Pressure
Reduction
Valve

Reservoirs

ABS &
TRAC
ECU

Dual-P Valve

Front Right
Wheel Brake

Rear Left
Wheel Brake

Rear Right
Wheel Brake

Front Left
Wheel Brake

9.19 Hydraulic schematic – Camry and Avalon ABS/traction control

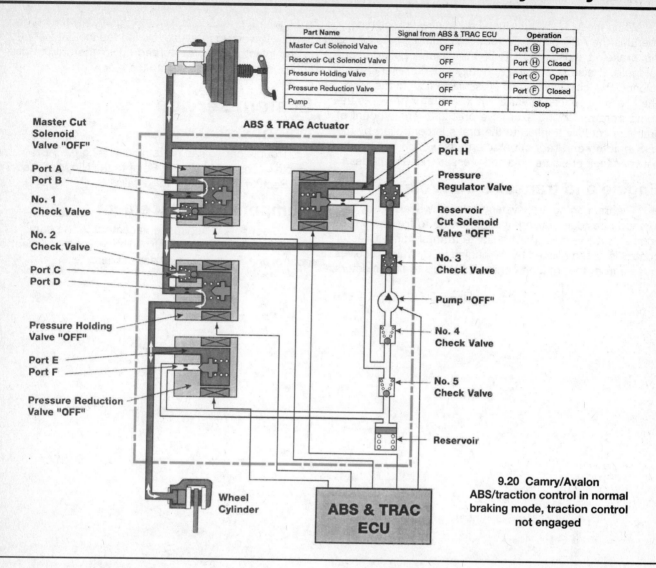

Part Name	Signal from ABS & TRAC ECU	Operation	
Master Cut Solenoid Valve	OFF	Port Ⓑ	Open
Resorvoir Cut Solenoid Valve	OFF	Port Ⓗ	Closed
Pressure Holding Valve	OFF	Port Ⓒ	Open
Pressure Reduction Valve	OFF	Port Ⓕ	Closed
Pump	OFF	Stop	

9.20 Camry/Avalon ABS/traction control in normal braking mode, traction control not engaged

Camry traction control

Traction control is optional on the 1997 and later Camry and Avalon. It's based on the Toyota ABS system described earlier in this chapter, which uses a pair of two-position solenoids per hydraulic channel.

This system uses a combination of transmission shift prevention, fuel injector cutoff and braking. The ABS pump supplies braking pressure for the front (drive) wheels during TCS operation. The system controls the front wheels independently.

System components

Refer to illustrations 9.18 and 9.19

The system uses a combined electronic control unit for the both the ABS and traction control. It also includes the powertrain control module (PCM). Other components are a speed sensor at each wheel, pump and solenoid relays, an electric motor for the sub-throttle valve, a TRAC warning lamp, TRAC and TRAC OFF indicator lamps and a TRAC on/off switch **(see illustration)**.

The combined ABS/TCS actuator contains four solenoids in addition to the eight solenoids used for anti-lock braking. Two are master cylinder cutoff solenoids, and two are reservoir cut solenoids. It also contains a pressure regulator valve that controls the amount of pump pressure **(see illustration)**.

The system turns on whenever the ignition is turned on, and then is ready to initiate traction control operation as needed. The TRAC switch allows the system to be switched off by the driver. The TRAC OFF warning lamp will illuminate when this occurs.

Braking

Refer to illustration 9.20

During normal driving, brake fluid from the master cylinder flows through the ABS solenoids, which are open, and the master cylinder cut solenoid, which is also open **(see illustration)**.

When the ECU decides that a drive wheel is spinning, it operates the ABS pump. To route the pump's pressure to the brake, it closes Port B in the master cylinder cut solenoid. It also opens the normally-closed reservoir cut solenoid, which allows pump pressure to flow to the brake. The pressure regulator valve in the actuator prevents the pump from producing excessive pressure. The amount of pressure actually applied to the brake is controlled by the ABS holding and reduction solenoids, which are cycled between their pressure hold and pressure release modes.

Engine and transaxle controls

The traction control system reduces wheelspin by two methods besides braking; it shuts off up to five fuel injectors, and it prevents the transaxle from shifting. Injector control is accomplished by the engine ECU, which receives signals from the traction control ECU. Up to five injectors are shut off to reduce power, then gradually turned back on to allow power to increase. During the increase stage, one of the injectors may be turned off temporarily to prevent engine speed from increasing too much.

System service
Diagnosis

Trouble codes can be retrieved using the ABS warning lamp and check connector. Refer to the Nippondenso (Toyota) Section of Chapter 7 for details.

Component replacement

Wheel speed sensor replacement is the same as for models without traction control. The actuator and electronic control unit are replaced as assemblies.

Applications

Audi

BMW

Chrysler Corporation cars

Chrysler Corporation cars (continued)

1991 through 1993
    Dodge Caravan
    Plymouth Voyager...................................... Bendix 10

1991 and 1992 Eagle Premier .... Bendix 10

1993 and 1994
    Chrysler Concorde/300M/LHS
    Dodge Intrepid
    Eagle Vision..................................... Teves Mark IV

1993 through 1995
    Chrysler Concorde/300M/LHS
    Dodge Intrepid
    Eagle Vision..................................... Teves Mark IV with traction control

1993-1/2 through 1995 AA .... Bendix 4

1994 and 1995 AS, AP .... Bendix 4

1995 and 1996
    Chrysler Concorde/300M/LHS
    Dodge Intrepid
    Eagle Vision..................................... Teves Mark IVg

1996
    Chrysler Town and Country
    Dodge Caravan
    Plymouth Voyager............................. Teves Mark IVg

1995 through 1997
    Dodge/Plymouth Neon
    Chrysler Cirrus
    Plymouth Breeze
    Dodge Stratus.................................. Bendix ABX-4

1996 and 1997
    Chrysler Sebring convertible.......................... Bendix ABX-4

1996 and 1997
    Chrysler Concorde/300M/LHS
    Dodge Intrepid
    Eagle Vision..................................... Teves Mark IVg with traction control

1997 and 1998
    Chrysler Town and Country
    Dodge Caravan
    Plymouth Voyager............................. Teves Mark 20

1998
    Dodge/Plymouth Neon
    Chrysler Cirrus
    Plymouth Breeze
    Dodge Stratus
    Chrysler Sebring convertible
    Chrysler Concorde/300M/LHS
    Dodge Intrepid
    Eagle Vision..................................... Teves Mark 20

1998
    Chrysler Sebring convertible
    Chrysler Town and Country
    Dodge Caravan
    Plymouth Voyager
    Chrysler Concorde/300M/LHS
    Dodge Intrepid
    Eagle Vision.. Teves Mark 20 with traction control

Chrysler Corporation trucks

1989 through 1996
    Dodge Dakota
    Dodge Ram pick-up...................... Kelsey-Hayes RWAL

1990 through 1996
    Dodge Ram van .... Kelsey-Hayes RWAL

1993 through 1996
    Dodge Dakota................................. Kelsey-Hayes EBC5H

1993 through 1997
    Dodge Ram pick-up
    Dodge Ram van .... Kelsey-Hayes EBC5H

1997
    Dodge Dakota................................. Kelsey-Hayes EBC310

1998
    Dodge Dakota
    Dodge Durango
    Dodge Ram pick-up
    Dodge Ram van .... Kelsey-Hayes EBC2 or EBC325

1989 through 1991
    Jeep Cherokee............................... Bendix 9

1992 through 1994
    Jeep Cherokee............................... Teves Mark IV

1993 and 1994
    Jeep Grand Cherokee
    Jeep Wrangler................................ Teves Mark IV

1995 and 1996
    Jeep Cherokee
    Jeep Grand Cherokee
    Jeep Wrangler................................ Teves Mark IVg

1997 and 1998
    Jeep Cherokee
    Jeep Grand Cherokee................... Teves Mark 20

1997 and 1998
    Jeep Wrangler................................ Teves Mark IVg

Chrysler Corporation imports

1984 through 1989
    Dodge Conquest.. Kelsey-Hayes RWAL

1990 through 1994
    Plymouth Laser
    Eagle Talon .... Bosch of America

1991 through 1994
    Dodge Ram 50 truck....................................... Kelsey-Hayes RWAL

1991 through 1997
    Dodge Stealth
    Eagle Talon (AWD) .... Bosch (Japanese)
    Plymouth Laser

1992 through 1997
    Dodge Colt .... Bosch (Japanese)

1993 through 1996
    Dodge Colt Vista
    Colt Summit wagon .... Bosch (Japanese)

1993 through 1996
    Colt Summit .... Sumitomo

1995 through 1998
    Chrysler Sebring
    Dodge Avenger
    Eagle Talon (2WD)... Bosch of America

Ford Motor Company cars

1985 through 1989
    Continental... Teves Mark II

1985 through 1992
    Mark VII .... Teves Mark II

1987 through 1992
    Thunderbird.. Teves Mark II

1989 through 1991-1/2
    Probe.. Sumitomo (Mazda Old Generation)

1989 through 1992
    Cougar .... Teves Mark II

1990 through 1994
    Continental
    Town Car
    Sable/Taurus.. Teves Mark IV

1992 through 1994
    Crown Victoria
    Grand Marquis .... Teves Mark IV

1993 and 1994
   Thunderbird
   Mark VIII .... Teves Mark IV
   Villager .... Bosch 2U
1994
   Mustang .... Bosch 2U
1995
   Crown Victoria
   Grand Marquis
   Continental (1995-1/4)
   Town Car.. Teves Mark IV
1995 through 1997
   Contour and Mystique .... Bendix Mecatronic

Ford Motor Company trucks and vans

1987 through 1990
   Bronco II... Kelsey-Hayes RABS
1987 through 1992
   Bronco .... Kelsey-Hayes RABS
1987 through 1994
   F-series pick-up.. Kelsey-Hayes RABS
1989 through 1994
   Ranger... Kelsey-Hayes RABS
1990 through 1994
   Aerostar
   Econoline van... Kelsey-Hayes RABS
1991 and 1992
   Explorer... Kelsey-Hayes RABS
1993 and 1994
   Bronco .... Teves Mark IVg
   Explorer... Teves Mark Ivg
1995
   Windstar... Kelsey-Hayes EBC325

General Motors cars

1986 through 1989
   Chevrolet Corvette... Bosch 2S
1986 through 1990
   Buick Electra/Park Avenue
   Cadillac Deville/Fleetwood
   Oldsmobile 98 Regency................................. Teves Mark II

General Motors cars (continued)

1986 through 1991	
Pontiac 6000 STE	Teves Mark II
1987 through 1990	
Oldsmobile 88	Teves Mark II
1987 through 1992	
Cadillac Allante	Bosch 3
1988 through 1990	
Buick Reatta	
Buick Riviera	
Cadillac Eldorado/Seville	
Oldsmobile Toronado	
Pontiac Bonneville SSE..............................	Teves Mark II
1989 through 1990	
Pontiac Bonneville (except SSE)...................	Teves Mark II
1989 through 1991	
Buick Regal	
Oldsmobile Cutlass Supreme	
Pontiac Grand Prix..................................	Delco Moraine III
Pontiac 6000 STE/AWD	Teves Mark II
1990 through 1993	
Chevrolet Corvette....................................	Bosch 2S Micro
1990 through 1994	
Cadillac Fleetwood	Bosch 2U
1991	
Oldsmobile Calais I-series	Delco/Delphi ABS VI
1991 through 1993	
Oldsmobile Toronado	Bosch 2U
Cadillac Deville.......................................	Teves Mark II
1991 through 1994	
Buick Wagon	
Cadillac Eldorado	
Chevrolet Caprice	Bosch 2U
1991 through 1995	
Buick LeSabre	
Buick Park Avenue	
Oldsmobile Delta 88	
Oldsmobile 98	
Pontiac Bonneville	
Pontiac Bonneville SSE..............................	Teves Mark IV
1991 through 1996	
Chevrolet Corsica/Beretta...........................	Delco/Delphi ABS VI
1991 through 1998	
Buick Skylark	
Pontiac Grand Am.....................................	Delco/Delphi ABS VI
1992 and 1993	
Buick Riviera	Bosch 2U

1992 through 1994
    Chevrolet Corvette .... Bosch 2U ABS/ASR
    Pontiac Sunbird .... Delco/Delphi ABS VI

1992 through 1997
    Oldsmobile Cutlass Supreme
    Pontiac Grand Prix .... Delco/Delphi ABS VI

1992 through 1998
    Buick Regal
    Chevrolet Cavalier
    Chevrolet Lumina
    Oldsmobile Achieva .... Delco/Delphi ABS VI

1993
    Cadillac Allante .... Bosch 2U

1993 and 1994
    Buick Roadmaster .... Bosch 2U

1993 through 1997
    Chevrolet Camaro
    Geo Prizm
    Pontiac Firebird.................................. Delco/Delphi ABS VI

1994
    Cadillac Concours
    Chevrolet Impala SS .... Bosch 2U

1994 through 1996
    Buick Century
    Oldsmobile Cutlass Ciera .... Delco/Delphi ABS VI

1995
    Chevrolet Corvette LT1 .... Bosch 5
    Chevrolet Corvette LT5 .... Bosch 2U ABS/ASR

1995 and 1996
    Buick wagon
    Buick Roadmaster
    Cadillac Concours
    Cadillac Deville
    Cadillac Eldorado
    Cadillac Fleetwood
    Cadillac Seville
    Chevrolet Caprice
    Chevrolet Impala SS .... Bosch 5.0

1995 through 1998
    Chevrolet Monte Carlo
    Chevrolet/Geo Metro
    Pontiac Sunfire.................................. Delco/Delphi ABS VI
    Buick Riviera
    Oldsmobile Aurora .... Teves Mark IV

1996
    Chevrolet Corvette .... Bosch 5.0
    Oldsmobile 98 .... Delco/Bosch 5.0

General Motors cars
(continued)

1996 through 1998
  Buick Park Avenue
  Buick LeSabre
  Oldsmobile 88
  Pontiac Bonneville .... Delco/Bosch 5.0

1997
  Cadillac Catera... Bosch 2

1997 and 1998
  Cadillac Concours
  Cadillac Deville
  Cadillac Eldorado
  Cadillac Seville
  Chevrolet Corvette .... Delco/Bosch 5.0
  Buick Century
  Chevrolet Malibu
  Olds Cutlass... Delco/Delphi ABS VI

1998
  Cadillac Catera
  Chevrolet Camaro
  Pontiac Firebird
  Pontiac Grand Prix.. Bosch 5.3
  Oldsmobile Intrigue.. Bosch 5.3 or Delphi ABS VI
  Chevrolet Prizm.. Lucas/Sumitomo hybrid

General Motors trucks and vans

1988 through 1993
  C/K-series pick-ups .... Kelsey-Hayes RWAL

1989 through 1995
  S/T series pick-ups .... Kelsey-Hayes RWAL

1990 and 1991
  Suburban .... Kelsey-Hayes RWAL

1990 through 1992
  Chevy Astro
  Pontiac Safari
  G-series van... Kelsey-Hayes RWAL

1990 through 1998
  Chevy Astro
  Pontiac Safari .... Kelsey-Hayes EBC310

1991
  Blazer .... Kelsey-Hayes RWAL

1991 through 1995
  Geo Tracker .... Kelsey-Hayes RWAL

1991 through 1998
S/T-series truck (four-door)............................ Kelsey-Hayes EBC310

1992 through 1998
Blazer
Chevrolet Lumina
Chevrolet Venture
C/K-series pick-up trucks
G-series van
Pontiac Trans Sport
Oldsmobile Silhouette
S/T-series trucks (two-door)
Suburban .... Kelsey-Hayes EBC310

Honda/Acura

1988 through 1995
All models .... Nippondenso, Nissin or
Sumitomo

Geo, Hyundai, Isuzu, Jaguar, Mazda, Mercedes-Benz, Mitsubishi, Nissan, Porsche, Saab

Compare the components of your system (most notably the hydraulic control unit) with the system descriptions in the individual Chapters of this manual to determine the type of ABS installed in your vehicle.

Subaru

1990 through 1992
Legacy non-turbo... Bosch
Legacy Turbo .... Nippondenso 2L

1992 through 1997
SVX .... Nippondenso 2L

1992-1/2 to 1995
Legacy.. Nippondenso 2E

1993
Legacy automatic.. Nippondenso 2L

1993 through 1995
Impreza .... Nippondenso 2E

1996
Impreza
Legacy.. Nippondenso 5.3

Subaru
(continued)

1997 and 1998
  Impreza
  Legacy.. Nippondenso 5.3i
1998
  Forester.. Nippondenso 5.3i

Suzuki

Compare the components of your system (most notably the hydraulic control unit) with the system descriptions in the individual Chapters of this manual to determine the type of ABS installed in your vehicle.

Toyota cars and vans

1987 and 1988
  Supra... Nippondenso
1988 and 1989
  Celica .... Nippondenso
1988 through 1991
  Camry.. Nippondenso
  Cressida.. Nipponsenso
1989 through 1992
  Supra... Nippondenso
1990 through 1993
  Celica .... Nipponsenso
1991 through 1995
  MR2.. Nippondenso
1991 through 1996
  Previa .... Nippondenso
1992 through 1996
  Camry (non-TMM)... Nippondenso
1993 through 1996
  Corolla
  Paseo
  Tercel .... Toyota
  Land Cruiser.. Nippondenso
1994 through 1996
  Camry (TMM) .... Bosch
  Supra... Nippondenso
1995 and 1996
  Avalon .... Bosch
  Celica .... Toyota
1996
  RAV4 .... Toyota
1997-on
  All except Land Cruiser.................................... Toyota

Toyota trucks

1990 through 1993
  4Runner... Toyota rear wheel
1990 through 1995
  Pick-up.. Toyota rear wheel
1993 and 1994
  T100 .... Toyota rear wheel
1994 through 1996
  4Runner... Toyota rear wheel
1995 and 1996
  Tacoma
  T100 .... Toyota rear wheel

VW, Volvo

Compare the components of your system (most notably the hydraulic control unit) with the system descriptions in the individual Chapters of this manual to determine the type of ABS installed in your vehicle.

Notes

Glossary

A

ABS: Anti-lock Brake System.

Acceleration Slip Regulation (ASR): The Bosch term for traction control.

Accumulator: A vessel that stores hydraulic fluid under pressure.

Adapter: See *Caliper mounting bracket.*

Air-suspended power booster: A type of power booster that contains atmospheric pressure in both chambers of the booster when the brake pedal is at rest. When the pedal is applied, the front chamber is opened to manifold vacuum, causing the diaphragm of the booster to move toward the master cylinder which assists the driver in the application of the brakes.

Anchor: The stationary portion of a leading/trailing drum brake on which the heels of the brake shoes ride.

Anchor plate: See *Caliper mounting bracket.*

Anchor pin: The stationary portion of a duo-servo drum brake on which the tops of the brake shoes rest. The secondary shoe bears against the anchor pin when the brakes are applied and the vehicle is moving forward. Conversely, when the vehicle is backing up and the brakes are applied, the primary shoe bears against it.

Anti-lock brake system: A brake control system that monitors the rotational speeds of the wheels and reduces hydraulic pressure to any wheel it senses locking up.

Arcing: A process where the brake shoes are ground to the proper curvature for the drums they are to be used with. Modern brake shoes are pre-arced.

Asbestos: A fibrous mineral used in the composition of brake friction materials. Asbestos is a health hazard and the dust created by brake systems should never be inhaled or ingested.

Asbestosis: An incurable lung disease caused by the inhalation of asbestos fibers.

Assembly Line Data Link (ALDL) connector: A diagnostic connector used in General Motors vehicles.

Automatic adjusters: Brake adjusters that are actuated by the application of the parking brake or by normal brake operation, to compensate for lining wear.

B

Backing plate: The part of a drum brake to which the wheel cylinder(s) and the brake shoes are attached.

Banjo fitting: A type of hydraulic fitting, shaped like a banjo, through which a hollow bolt passes, allowing fluid transfer from a hydraulic line to a hydraulic component.

Bleeder screw: The hollow screw that is loosened to open a bleeder valve, allowing fluid and air bubbles to pass through during a bleeding procedure.

Bleeder valve: A valve on a wheel cylinder, caliper or other hydraulic component that is opened to purge the hydraulic system of air.

Bonded linings: Brake linings that are affixed to the shoe or backing plate with high-temperature adhesive and cured under pressure and heat.

Brake adjuster: A mechanism used to adjust the clearance between the brake linings and the brake drum.

Brake balance: The ratio of front-to-rear braking force.

Brake caliper: The component of a disc brake that converts hydraulic pressure into mechanical energy.

Brake disc: The component of a disc brake that rotates with the wheel and is squeezed by the brake caliper and pads, which creates friction and converts the energy of the moving vehicle into heat.

Brake drum: The component of a drum brake that rotates with the wheel and is acted upon by the expanding brake shoes, which creates friction and converts the energy of the moving vehicle into heat.

Brake dust: The dust created as the brake linings wear down in normal use. Brake dust usually contains dangerous amounts of asbestos.

Brake fade: The partial or complete loss of braking power which results when the brakes are overheated and can no longer generate friction.

Brake lathe: The machine used to resurface the friction surfaces of brake discs or drums.

Brake lines: The rigid steel and flexible rubber hoses composing the portion of the hydraulic system that transfers brake fluid from the master cylinder to the calipers and/or wheel cylinders.

Brake lining: The friction material that is either riveted or bonded to the brake backing plates or brake pads.

Brake pads: The components of a disc brake assembly that are surfaced with brake lining and clamped against the brake disc to generate friction.

Brake pressure modulator valve (BPMV): A combined assembly of the electronic control unit and hydraulic control unit, used in some GM vehicles. Also called the Electro-Hydraulic Control Unit (EHCU).

Brake shoes: The components of a drum brake assembly that are surfaced with brake lining and forced against the brake drum to generate friction.

Brake system cleaner: A type of solvent designed exclusively for cleaning brake system components. It will not destroy plastic, rubber or synthetic rubber components and it dries quickly, without leaving a residue.

Breather port: The small passage between the master cylinder fluid reservoir and the area behind the primary cups of the pistons. This port allows fluid from the reservoir to fill the area behind the primary cups of the pistons, preventing a vacuum from being formed behind the cups when the brakes are applied, which prevents air bubbles from traveling around the lips of the primary cups as the brakes are released.

Bridge bolts: High-strength bolts used to fasten together the halves of a split brake caliper.

Burnish: The process of "breaking-in" new brake pads or shoes so the linings conform to the disc or drum friction surfaces.

C

Caliper: See *Brake caliper*.

Caliper mounting bracket: The component that connects a brake caliper to the steering knuckle, hub carrier or rear axle.

Cam: An eccentric shaped device mounted on a shaft that raises and lowers the component in contact with it. Some brake adjuster designs use a cam (or cams) to set the clearance between the brake shoes and the brake drum.

Channel: The hydraulic routing used by the anti-lock brake system to control the brake pressure at each wheel. A system may have one, three or four channels.

Clevis: A U-shaped device with a pin or bolt passing through it used for attaching the master cylinder or power booster pushrod to the brake pedal. Clevises are sometimes used in other parts of the brake system, like attaching the parking brake cable to the parking brake lever at the rear brakes.

Closed system: An anti-lock brake system with some means, generally a pump, to restore hydraulic pressure that's bled off during an ABS stop.

Coefficient of friction: A numerical value indicating the amount of work required to slide one surface against another.

Combination valve: A hydraulic valve usually incorporating a pressure differential warning switch, a metering valve and a proportioning valve. Not all combination valves contain all of these control valves.

Compensating port: The small passage between the master cylinder fluid reservoir and the pressure chamber (the area in front of the primary seals of both pistons) that allows fluid to flow in or out as necessary, depending on requirements.

Condition-latched soft code: A type of trouble code that disengages the ABS and turns on the amber light only as long as the condition, or problem, exists.

Controller, Anti-lock Brake (CAB): Chrysler Corporation's term for the electronic control unit.

Component Anti-lock Brake System: A type of Anti-lock Brake System in which the hydraulic control unit is not part of the master cylinder/power booster assembly.

Cup: A type of lip seal used on hydraulic pistons.

Cycle: A type of pressure modulation during an ABS stop. Cycles include pressure hold, pressure release (decay) and pressure build.

D

Decay: A term for hydraulic pressure reduction that occurs during an ABS stop.

Deceleration switch: A device that signals the rate of vehicle deceleration to the ECU, allowing it to adjust ABS operation accordingly.

Diaphragm: A flexible partition used to separate two chambers or elements.

Digital Ratio Adapter Controller (DRAC) module: A device used on GM vehicles to convert the analog signal from the speed sensor into a digital signal that the EBCM can use.

Discard diameter: The diameter at which a worn brake drum should be replaced.

Discard thickness: The thickness at which a brake disc should be replaced.

Disc: See *Brake disc*.

Disc brake: A brake design incorporating a flat, disc-like rotor onto which brake pads containing lining material are squeezed, generating friction and converting the energy of a moving vehicle into heat.

Dished brake disc: A disc that has worn thinner at the inner part of its friction surface. This is an abnormal form of wear.

Double anchor drum brake: See *Leading/trailing* drum brake.

Drum brake: A brake design incorporating a drum with brake shoes inside that expand to contact the drum, creating friction and converting the energy of the moving vehicle into heat.

Dual circuit brake system: A brake hydraulic system composed of two separate hydraulic circuits.

Duo-servo drum brake: A type of self-energizing drum brake that has servo action in both forward and reverse.

Dust boot: A rubber diaphragm-like seal that fits over the end of a hydraulic component and around a pushrod or end of a piston, not used for sealing fluid in but keeping dust out.

E

Electro-hydraulic pump: An electrically powered hydraulic pump used to create pressure in certain portions of the brake system. Typically found in General Motors Powermaster brake boosters and in ABS hydraulic control units.

Electronic Brake Control Module (EBCM): General Motors Corporation's term for the electronic control unit.

Electronic Control Unit (ECU): The "brain" of an ABS system. The ECU reads impulses from the wheel speed sensors to determine if anti-lock braking needs to take place. If so, the ECU controls the cycling of the solenoid valves in the hydraulic control unit.

Emergency brake: Another term for parking brake.

Equalizer: A bracket or cable connector which balances tension equally on the cables to the parking brakes.

F

Filler port: See *breather port*.

Firewall: The partition between the passenger compartment and the engine compartment. Sometimes referred to as a bulkhead.

Fixed caliper: A caliper containing one or more pistons on each side of the brake disc that is bolted to the steering knuckle, hub carrier or rear axle and is incapable of movement.

Flare-nut wrench: A wrench designed for loosening hydraulic fitting tube nuts (flare-nuts) without damaging them. Flare-nut wrenches are kind of like a six-point box-end wrench with one of the flats missing, which allows the wrench to pass over the tubing but still maintain a maximum amount of contact with the nut.

Floating caliper: A caliper that rides on bushings, has one or more pistons only on one side of the caliper and moves laterally as the piston pushes on the inner brake pad, which pulls the outer pad against the brake disc.

Four-wheel ABS: An anti-lock brake system that operates on all four wheels.

Freeplay: The amount of travel before any action takes place. In a brake pedal it is the distance the pedal moves before the pistons in the master cylinder are actuated.

Friction: Surface resistance to relative motion.

G

Gear pulser: A term used by some manufacturers, including Subaru, for the tone rings.

Glazed lining: A brake lining that has been overheated and become smooth and glossy.

Grinding: The process of resurfacing a brake disc or drum on a brake lathe using a power-driven abrasive stone.

Grommet: A round rubber seal which fits into a hole or recess, intended to seal or insulate the component passing through it.

Guide pin: A caliper mounting bolt used for fastening a floating caliper to its mounting plate.

H

Hard code: A type of trouble code that causes the ECU to disengage the ABS and not re-engage it until the problem is repaired.

Hard spots: Shiny bluish/brown glazed areas on a brake drum or disc friction surface, caused by extreme heat. Hard spots can usually be removed by resurfacing.

Hat: The portion of a detachable brake disc that comes in contact with the wheel hub.

Heat checking: Small cracks on a brake disc or drum friction surface caused by heat. Heat checks can usually be removed by resurfacing.

Hold cycle: Maintaining steady hydraulic pressure during an ABS stop.

Hold-down pin, spring and retainer: The most common method of retaining a brake shoe to the backing plate. The pin passes through the backing plate and brake shoe. The spring and retainer are fastened to the pin, which holds the shoe against the backing plate.

Hold-off valve: See *Metering valve*.

Hydraulically operated power booster: A power booster that uses hydraulic pressure to assist the driver in the application of the brakes. This hydraulic pressure usually comes from the power steering pump or an electro-hydraulic pump.

Hydraulic circuit: Part of the main brake system that includes two of the four wheel brakes and operates independently of the other two wheel brakes; all vehicles have a primary and secondary hydraulic circuit.

Hydraulic control unit: The portion of an anti-lock brake system that houses the solenoid valves and electro-hydraulic pump.

Hydraulic modulator: See *Hydraulic control unit*.

Hydroplane: The action that takes place when an accumulation of water builds up in front of a tire, causing the tire to ride on a layer of water instead of on the pavement.

Hygroscopic: The tendency to attract or absorb moisture from the air.

I

Ignition-latched soft code: A type of trouble code that causes the ECU to disengage the ABS until the ignition is shut off and turned back on; if the problem has gone away, ABS will be reactivated and the warning lamp turned out when the key is turned back on.

Inboard disc brakes: Disc brakes not mounted out at the wheels, but near the differential.

Inertia: The tendency of a body at rest to remain at rest, and a body in motion to remain in motion.

Integrated system: An anti-lock brake system with the brake booster and hydraulic modulator integrated into a unit with the master cylinder.

Isolation: This occurs when the anti-lock brake system isolates one or more wheel brakes from hydraulic pressure produced by the master cylinder, allowing the ABS to take over control of braking pressure from the driver.

K

Kinetic energy: The energy of a body in motion.

Knockback: The action of a brake disc with excessive runout pushing back the brake pads when the brakes are not applied.

L

Lateral acceleration sensor: A device that signals the ECU when the vehicle is being subjected to high g-force from a turn; the signal voltage varies according to the amount of g-force.

Lateral acceleration switch: Similar to a lateral acceleration sensor, but the switch provides a simple on-off signal, rather than the variable voltage signal provided by the sensor.

Lateral runout: Side-to-side warpage of the brake disc friction surfaces.

Leading shoe: A shoe in a non-servo action drum brake assembly that is self-energized by the forward rotation of the brake drum.

Leading/trailing drum brake: A drum brake design in which both brake shoes are attached to an anchor plate, and only one of the shoes is self-energized.

Load Sensing Proportioning Valve (LSPV): A hydraulic system control valve that works like a proportioning valve, but also takes into consideration the amount of weight carried by the rear axle.

M

Manual adjuster: A type of brake adjuster that must be adjusted from time-to-time, with the use of a hand tool.

Master cylinder: The component in the hydraulic system which generates pressure for the calipers and/or wheel cylinders.

Metering valve: A hydraulic control valve placed in the circuit to the front brakes, designed to restrict pressure to the front brake calipers until the rear brake shoes overcome the tension of the retracting springs.

N

Non-integrated system: An anti-lock brake system whose major hydraulic components are separate from the master cylinder, and are installed between the master cylinder and the wheel brakes.

Non-servo drum brake: A drum brake design in which the application of one shoe has no effect on the other.

O

Open system: An anti-lock brake system in which the brake fluid released from the brakes during an ABS stop isn't returned to the brake during the ABS stop but is stored in an accumulator

Organic linings: Brake lining material using asbestos as its main ingredient.

Out-of-round: The condition of a brake drum when it has become distorted and is no longer perfectly round. In many cases an out-of-round brake drum can be salvaged by resurfacing on a brake lathe.

P

Pad wear indicators: Mechanical or electrical devices which warn the driver when the lining material on the brake pads has worn to the point that they should be replaced.

Parallelism: The relationship between one friction surface of a brake disc and the other.

Parking brake: The mechanically actuated portion of a drum brake or disc brake caliper, used to prevent the vehicle from rolling when it is parked, applied by a lever, pedal or rod.

Pascal's Law: The law of physics stating that "pressure, when applied to a confined liquid, is transmitted undiminished." Discovered by Blaise Pascal (1623 - 1662).

Power booster: A device using vacuum or hydraulic power to assist the driver in the application of the brakes.

Pulse width modulation valve: A normally-closed valve, used in some Kelsey Hayes systems on General Motors vehicles, that opens to release hydraulic pressure from the wheel brake during an ABS stop.

Pressure bleeder: A device that forces brake fluid under pressure into the master cylinder, so that by opening the bleeder screws all air will be purged from the hydraulic system.

Pressure differential warning switch: A component of the brake hydraulic system that warns the driver of a failure in one of the circuits.

Primary shoe: The shoe in a duo-servo drum brake that transfers part of its braking force to the secondary shoe.

Proportioning valve: A hydraulic control valve located in the circuit to the rear wheels which limits the amount of pressure to the rear brakes to prevent wheel lock-up during panic stops.

R

RABS: Rear-wheel Anti-lock Brake System (Ford).

Reference signal: A signal sent to the ECU, generally by the vehicle's fastest-moving wheel, which the ECU uses for comparison with the signals from decelerating wheels.

Replenishing port: See *Breather port*.

Reservoir: A container attached to the master cylinder, either directly or by hoses, that stores extra brake fluid for the hydraulic system.

Residual pressure: Pressure remaining in a hydraulic circuit after the brakes have been released.

Residual pressure check valve: A small valve, usually located in the outlet port(s) of the master cylinder, which maintains a certain amount of pressure in the hydraulic circuit(s) when the brakes are released. Used only in drum brake hydraulic circuits to keep the lips of the wheel cylinder cups sealed against the walls of the cylinder.

Resurfacing: The process of machining a brake drum or disc on a brake lathe to remove surface imperfections from the friction surface.

Riveted linings: Brake linings that are riveted to the pad backing plate or brake shoe.

Rotor: See *Brake disc*.

Runout: Side-to-side warpage of the brake disc friction surfaces.

RWAL: Rear Wheel Anti-Lock (Chrysler and General Motors).

S

Scoring: Grooves or deep scratches on a friction surface caused by metal-to-metal contact (worn-out brake pads or shoes) or debris caught between the friction material and the friction surface.

Secondary shoe: The shoe in a duo-servo drum brake assembly that is acted upon by the primary shoe. It provides more stopping power than the primary shoe (about 70-percent).

Select-low principle: The method by which the rear brake application of an ABS brake system is monitored and controlled, based on the rear wheel with the least amount of traction.

Self-energizing action: The action of a rotating brake drum that increases the application pressure of the brake shoe(s).

Semi-metallic lining: Brake lining incorporating a high-percentage of metal in its composition.

Servo-action drum brake: See *Duo-servo drum brake*.

Sliding caliper: Similar to a *floating caliper*, but instead of riding on guide pins and bushings, the caliper slides on machined "ways" and is retained by keys or spring plates.

Solenoid: An electromagnetic valve that opens or closes to regulate hydraulic pressure in an anti-lock brake system.

Solid brake disc: A brake disc that is solid metal between its friction surfaces.

Speed sensor: A device that measures the speed of a wheel or driveaxle and sends the information in the form of an analog voltage signal to the ECU.

Sub-throttle: A throttle valve, mounted ahead of the main throttle valve in the intake tract, that controls airflow into the engine during Toyota Supra traction control system operation.

Star wheel: The portion of a brake adjuster that turns the adjuster screw.

T

Throttle relaxer: A device that mechanically controls throttle position during traction control system operation.

Tire slip: The difference between the speed of the vehicle and the speed between the tire and the ground, expressed in a percentage.

Tone ring: The gear-like ring that spins its teeth through the speed sensor's magnetic field, causing generation of voltage by the sensor.

Tone wheel: See *Tone ring*.

Torque: A turning or twisting force imposed on a rotating part.

Torque plate: See *Caliper mounting bracket*.

Traction: The amount of adhesion between the tire and ground.

Traction control: A means of preventing wheelspin due to acceleration, either by braking the spinning wheel or reducing engine power.

Trailing shoe: A shoe in a drum brake assembly that is not self-energized.

Two-wheel ABS: An anti-lock brake system that only operates on the rear wheels.

U

Uni-servo drum brake: A servo-action drum brake that only has servo action when the vehicle is braked in a forward direction.

V

Vacuum: As an automotive term, vacuum is any pressure less than atmospheric pressure.

Vacuum-operated power booster: A power booster that uses engine manifold vacuum to assist the driver in the application of the brakes.

Vacuum-suspended power booster: A type of power booster that contains vacuum in both chambers of the booster when the brake pedal is at rest. When the pedal is applied, the rear chamber is vented to the atmosphere, causing the diaphragm of the booster to move toward the master cylinder, which assists the driver in the application of the brakes.

Vapor lock: The abnormal condition that occurs when brake fluid contains too much moisture and is overheated, causing the moisture in the fluid to boil. Gas bubbles are formed in the fluid, which causes a spongy brake pedal or a complete loss of hydraulic pressure.

Vented brake disc: A brake disc that has cooling passages cast or drilled between its friction surfaces.

Viscosity: The property of a fluid that resists the force tending to cause the fluid to flow.

W

Ways: Machined abutments on which a sliding brake caliper rides.

Wheel cylinder: The component in a hydraulic system that converts hydraulic pressure into mechanical force to apply the brake shoe(s).

Wheel speed sensor: The component of an anti-lock brake system that picks up the impulses of the toothed signal rotor, sending these impulses to the ABS ECU.

Index

Haynes ABS Manual

Haynes Automotive Manuals

ACURA
*12020 **Integra** '86 thru '89 **& Legend** '86 thru '90

AMC
Jeep CJ - see JEEP (50020)
14020 **Mid-size models,** Concord, Hornet, Gremlin & Spirit '70 thru '83
14025 **(Renault) Alliance & Encore** '83 thru '87

AUDI
15020 **4000** all models '80 thru '87
15025 **5000** all models '77 thru '83
15026 **5000** all models '84 thru '88

AUSTIN-HEALEY
Sprite - see MG Midget (66015)

BMW
*18020 **3/5 Series** not including diesel or all-wheel drive models '82 thru '92
*18021 **3 Series** except 325iX '92 thru '97
18025 **320i** all 4 cyl models '75 thru '83
18035 **528i & 530i** all models '75 thru '80
18050 **1500 thru 2002** except Turbo '59 thru '77

BUICK
Century (front wheel drive) - see GM (829)
*19020 **Buick, Oldsmobile & Pontiac Full-size (Front wheel drive)** all models '85 thru '98
Buick Electra, LeSabre and Park Avenue; Oldsmobile Delta 88 Royale, Ninety Eight and Regency; Pontiac Bonneville
19025 **Buick Oldsmobile & Pontiac Full-size (Rear wheel drive)**
Buick Estate '70 thru '90, Electra'70 thru '84, LeSabre '70 thru '85, Limited '74 thru '79
Oldsmobile Custom Cruiser '70 thru '90, Delta 88 '70 thru '85,Ninety-eight '70 thru '84
Pontiac Bonneville '70 thru '81, Catalina '70 thru '81, Grandville '70 thru '75, Parisienne '83 thru '86
19030 **Mid-size Regal & Century** all rear-drive models with V6, V8 and Turbo '74 thru '87
Regal - see GENERAL MOTORS (38010)
Riviera - see GENERAL MOTORS (38030)
Roadmaster - see CHEVROLET (24046)
Skyhawk - see GENERAL MOTORS (38015)
Skylark '80 thru '85 - see GM (38020)
Skylark '86 on - see GM (38025)
Somerset - see GENERAL MOTORS (38025)

CADILLAC
*21030 **Cadillac Rear Wheel Drive** all gasoline models '70 thru '93
Cimarron - see GENERAL MOTORS (38015)
Eldorado - see GENERAL MOTORS (38030)
Seville '80 thru '85 - see GM (38030)

CHEVROLET
*24010 **Astro & GMC Safari Mini-vans** '85 thru '93
24015 **Camaro V8** all models '70 thru '81
24016 **Camaro** all models '82 thru '92
Cavalier - see GENERAL MOTORS (38015)
Celebrity - see GENERAL MOTORS (38005)
24017 **Camaro & Firebird** '93 thru '97
24020 **Chevelle, Malibu & El Camino** '69 thru '87
24024 **Chevette & Pontiac T1000** '76 thru '87
Citation - see GENERAL MOTORS (38020)
*24032 **Corsica/Beretta** all models '87 thru '96
24040 **Corvette** all V8 models '68 thru '82
*24041 **Corvette** all models '84 thru '96
10305 **Chevrolet Engine Overhaul Manual**
24045 **Full-size Sedans** Caprice, Impala, Biscayne, Bel Air & Wagons '69 thru '90
24046 **Impala SS & Caprice and Buick Roadmaster** '91 thru '96
Lumina - see GENERAL MOTORS (38010)

24048 **Lumina & Monte Carlo** '95 thru '98
Lumina APV - see GM (38035)
24050 **Luv Pick-up** all 2WD & 4WD '72 thru '82
*24055 **Monte Carlo** all models '70 thru '88
Monte Carlo '95 thru '98 - see LUMINA (24048)
24059 **Nova** all V8 models '69 thru '79
*24060 **Nova and Geo Prizm** '85 thru '92
24064 **Pick-ups '67 thru '87** - Chevrolet & GMC, all V8 & in-line 6 cyl, 2WD & 4WD '67 thru '87; Suburbans, Blazers & Jimmys '67 thru '91
*24065 **Pick-ups '88 thru '98** - Chevrolet & GMC, all full-size pick-ups, '88 thru '98; Blazer & Jimmy '92 thru '94; Suburban '92 thru '98; Tahoe & Yukon '98
24070 **S-10 & S-15 Pick-ups** '82 thru '93, **Blazer & Jimmy** '83 thru '94,
*24071 **S-10 & S-15 Pick-ups** '94 thru '96 **Blazer & Jimmy** '95 thru '96
*24075 **Sprint & Geo Metro** '85 thru '94
*24080 **Vans - Chevrolet & GMC,** V8 & in-line 6 cylinder models '68 thru '96

CHRYSLER
25015 **Chrysler Cirrus, Dodge Stratus, Plymouth Breeze** '95 thru '98
25025 **Chrysler Concorde, New Yorker & LHS, Dodge** Intrepid, **Eagle** Vision, '93 thru '97
10310 **Chrysler Engine Overhaul Manual**
*25020 **Full-size Front-Wheel Drive** '88 thru '93
K-Cars - see DODGE Aries (30008)
Laser - see DODGE Daytona (30030)
*25030 **Chrysler & Plymouth Mid-size** front wheel drive '82 thru '95
Rear-wheel Drive - see Dodge (30050)

DATSUN
28005 **200SX** all models '80 thru '83
28007 **B-210** all models '73 thru '78
28009 **210** all models '79 thru '82
28012 **240Z, 260Z & 280Z** Coupe '70 thru '78
28014 **280ZX** Coupe & 2+2 '79 thru '83
300ZX - see NISSAN (72010)
28016 **310** all models '78 thru '82
28018 **510 & PL521 Pick-up** '68 thru '73
28020 **510** all models '78 thru '81
28022 **620 Series Pick-up** all models '73 thru '79
720 Series Pick-up - see NISSAN (72030)
28025 **810/Maxima** all gasoline models, '77 thru '84

DODGE
400 & 600 - see CHRYSLER (25030)
*30008 **Aries & Plymouth Reliant** '81 thru '89
30010 **Caravan & Plymouth Voyager Mini-Vans** all models '84 thru '95
*30011 **Caravan & Plymouth Voyager Mini-Vans** all models '96 thru '98
30012 **Challenger/Plymouth Saporro** '78 thru '83
30016 **Colt & Plymouth Champ** (front wheel drive) all models '78 thru '87
*30020 **Dakota Pick-ups** all models '87 thru '96
30025 **Dart, Demon, Plymouth Barracuda, Duster & Valiant** 6 cyl models '67 thru '76
*30030 **Daytona & Chrysler Laser** '84 thru '89
Intrepid - see CHRYSLER (25025)
*30034 **Neon** all models '95 thru '97
*30035 **Omni & Plymouth Horizon** '78 thru '90
*30040 **Pick-ups** all full-size models '74 thru '93
*30041 **Pick-ups** all full-size models '94 thru '96
*30045 **Ram 50/D50 Pick-ups & Raider and Plymouth Arrow Pick-ups** '79 thru '93
30050 **Dodge/Plymouth/Chrysler** rear wheel drive '71 thru '89
*30055 **Shadow & Plymouth Sundance** '87 thru '94
*30060 **Spirit & Plymouth Acclaim** '89 thru '95
*30065 **Vans - Dodge & Plymouth** '71 thru '96

EAGLE
Talon - see Mitsubishi Eclipse (68030)
Vision - see CHRYSLER (25025)

FIAT
34010 **124 Sport Coupe & Spider** '68 thru '78
34025 **X1/9** all models '74 thru '80

FORD
10355 **Ford Automatic Transmission Overhaul**
*36004 **Aerostar Mini-vans** all models '86 thru '96
*36006 **Contour & Mercury Mystique** '95 thru '98
36008 **Courier Pick-up** all models '72 thru '82
36012 **Crown Victoria & Mercury Grand Marquis** '88 thru '96
10320 **Ford Engine Overhaul Manual**
36016 **Escort/Mercury Lynx** all models '81 thru '90
*36020 **Escort/Mercury Tracer** '91 thru '96
*36024 **Explorer & Mazda Navajo** '91 thru '95
36028 **Fairmont & Mercury Zephyr** '78 thru '83
36030 **Festiva & Aspire** '88 thru '97
36032 **Fiesta** all models '77 thru '80
36036 **Ford & Mercury Full-size,** Ford LTD & Mercury Marquis ('75 '82); Ford Custom 500,Country Squire, Crown Victoria & Mercury Colony Park ('75 thru '87); Ford LTD Crown Victoria & Mercury Gran Marquis ('83 thru '87)
36040 **Granada & Mercury Monarch** '75 thru '80
36044 **Ford & Mercury Mid-size,** Ford Thunderbird & Mercury Cougar ('75 thru '82); Ford LTD & Mercury Marquis ('83 thru '86); Ford Torino,Gran Torino, Elite, Ranchero pick-up, LTD II, Mercury Montego, Comet, XR-7 & Lincoln Versailles ('75 thru '86)
36048 **Mustang V8** all models '64-1/2 thru '73
36049 **Mustang II** 4 cyl, V6 & V8 models '74 thru '78
36050 **Mustang & Mercury Capri** all models Mustang, '79 thru '93; Capri, '79 thru '86
*36051 **Mustang** all models '94 thru '97
36054 **Pick-ups & Bronco** '73 thru '79
36058 **Pick-ups & Bronco** '80 thru '96
36059 **Pick-ups, Expedition & Mercury Navigator** '97 thru '98
36062 **Pinto & Mercury Bobcat** '75 thru '80
36066 **Probe** all models '89 thru '92
36070 **Ranger/Bronco II** gasoline models '83 thru '92
*36071 **Ranger** '93 thru '97 & **Mazda Pick-ups** '94 thru '97
36074 **Taurus & Mercury Sable** '86 thru '95
*36075 **Taurus & Mercury Sable** '96 thru '98
*36078 **Tempo & Mercury Topaz** '84 thru '94
36082 **Thunderbird/Mercury Cougar** '83 thru '88
*36086 **Thunderbird/Mercury Cougar** '89 and '97
36090 **Vans** all V8 Econoline models '69 thru '91
*36094 **Vans** full size '92-'95
*36097 **Windstar Mini-van** '95-'98

GENERAL MOTORS
*10360 **GM Automatic Transmission Overhaul**
*38005 **Buick Century, Chevrolet Celebrity, Oldsmobile Cutlass Ciera & Pontiac 6000** all models '82 thru '96
*38010 **Buick Regal, Chevrolet Lumina, Oldsmobile Cutlass Supreme & Pontiac Grand Prix** front-wheel drive models '88 thru '95
*38015 **Buick Skyhawk, Cadillac Cimarron, Chevrolet Cavalier, Oldsmobile Firenza & Pontiac J-2000 & Sunbird** '82 thru '94
*38016 **Chevrolet Cavalier & Pontiac Sunfire** '95 thru '98
38020 **Buick Skylark, Chevrolet Citation, Olds Omega, Pontiac Phoenix** '80 thru '85
38025 **Buick Skylark & Somerset, Oldsmobile Achieva & Calais and Pontiac Grand Am** all models '85 thru '95
38030 **Cadillac Eldorado** '71 thru '85, **Seville** '80 thru '85, **Oldsmobile Toronado** '71 thru '85 **& Buick Riviera** '79 thru '85
*38035 **Chevrolet Lumina APV, Olds Silhouette & Pontiac Trans Sport** all models '90 thru '95
General Motors Full-size Rear-wheel Drive - see BUICK (19025)

(Continued on other side)

Haynes North America, Inc., 861 Lawrence Drive, Newbury Park, CA 91320-1514 • (805) 498-6703

Haynes Automotive Manuals (continued)

NOTE: New manuals are added to this list on a periodic basis. If you do not see a listing for your vehicle, consult your local Haynes dealer for the latest product information.

GEO

Metro - *see CHEVROLET Sprint (24075)*
Prizm - *'85 thru '92 see CHEVY (24060), '93 thru '96 see TOYOTA Corolla (92036)*
*40030 **Storm** all models '90 thru '93
Tracker - *see SUZUKI Samurai (90010)*

GMC

Safari - *see CHEVROLET ASTRO (24010)*
Vans & Pick-ups - *see CHEVROLET*

HONDA

42010 **Accord CVCC** all models '76 thru '83
42011 **Accord** all models '84 thru '89
42012 **Accord** all models '90 thru '93
42013 **Accord** all models '94 thru '95
42020 **Civic 1200** all models '73 thru '79
42021 **Civic 1300 & 1500 CVCC** '80 thru '83
42022 **Civic 1500 CVCC** all models '75 thru '79
42023 **Civic** all models '84 thru '91
*42024 **Civic & del Sol** '92 thru '95
*42040 **Prelude CVCC** all models '79 thru '89

HYUNDAI

*43015 **Excel** all models '86 thru '94

ISUZU

Hombre - *see CHEVROLET S-10 (24071)*
*47017 **Rodeo** '91 thru '97; **Amigo** '89 thru '94; **Honda Passport** '95 thru '97
*47020 **Trooper & Pick-up**, all gasoline models Pick-up, '81 thru '93; Trooper, '84 thru '91

JAGUAR

*49010 **XJ6** all 6 cyl models '68 thru '86
*49011 **XJ6** all models '88 thru '94
*49015 **XJ12 & XJS** all 12 cyl models '72 thru '85

JEEP

*50010 **Cherokee, Comanche & Wagoneer Limited** all models '84 thru '96
50020 **CJ** all models '49 thru '86
*50025 **Grand Cherokee** all models '93 thru '98
50029 **Grand Wagoneer & Pick-up** '72 thru '91 Grand Wagoneer '84 thru '91, Cherokee & Wagoneer '72 thru '83, Pick-up '72 thru '88
*50030 **Wrangler** all models '87 thru '95

LINCOLN

Navigator - *see FORD Pick-up (36059)*
59010 **Rear Wheel Drive** all models '70 thru '96

MAZDA

61010 **GLC Hatchback** (rear wheel drive) '77 thru '83
61011 **GLC** (front wheel drive) '81 thru '85
*61015 **323 & Protegé** '90 thru '97
*61016 **MX-5 Miata** '90 thru '97
*61020 **MPV** all models '89 thru '94
Navajo - *see Ford Explorer (36024)*
61030 **Pick-ups** '72 thru '93
Pick-ups '94 thru '96 - *see Ford Ranger (36071)*
61035 **RX-7** all models '79 thru '85
*61036 **RX-7** all models '86 thru '91
61040 **626** (rear wheel drive) all models '79 thru '82
*61041 **626/MX-6** (front wheel drive) '83 thru '92

MERCEDES-BENZ

63012 **123 Series Diesel** '76 thru '85
*63015 **190 Series** four-cyl gas models, '84 thru '88
63020 **230/250/280** 6 cyl sohc models '68 thru '72
63025 **280 123 Series** gasoline models '77 thru '81
63030 **350 & 450** all models '71 thru '80

MERCURY

See FORD Listing.

MG

66010 **MGB** Roadster & GT Coupe '62 thru '80
66015 **MG Midget, Austin Healey Sprite** '58 thru '80

MITSUBISHI

*68020 **Cordia, Tredia, Galant, Precis & Mirage** '83 thru '93
*68030 **Eclipse, Eagle Talon & Ply. Laser** '90 thru '94
*68040 **Pick-up** '83 thru '96 & **Montero** '83 thru '93

NISSAN

72010 **300ZX** all models including Turbo '84 thru '89
*72015 **Altima** all models '93 thru '97
*72020 **Maxima** all models '85 thru '91
*72030 **Pick-ups** '80 thru '96 **Pathfinder** '87 thru '95
72040 **Pulsar** all models '83 thru '86
*72050 **Sentra** all models '82 thru '94
*72051 **Sentra & 200SX** all models '95 thru '98
*72060 **Stanza** all models '82 thru '90

OLDSMOBILE

*73015 **Cutlass** V6 & V8 gas models '74 thru '88
For other OLDSMOBILE titles, see BUICK, CHEVROLET or GENERAL MOTORS listing.

PLYMOUTH

For PLYMOUTH titles, see DODGE listing.

PONTIAC

79008 **Fiero** all models '84 thru '88
79018 **Firebird** V8 models except Turbo '70 thru '81
79019 **Firebird** all models '82 thru '92
For other PONTIAC titles, see BUICK, CHEVROLET or GENERAL MOTORS listing.

PORSCHE

*80020 **911** except Turbo & Carrera 4 '65 thru '89
80025 **914** all 4 cyl models '69 thru '76
80030 **924** all models including Turbo '76 thru '82
*80035 **944** all models including Turbo '83 thru '89

RENAULT

Alliance & Encore - *see AMC (14020)*

SAAB

*84010 **900** all models including Turbo '79 thru '88

SATURN

87010 **Saturn** all models '91 thru '96

SUBARU

89002 **1100, 1300, 1400 & 1600** '71 thru '79
*89003 **1600 & 1800** 2WD & 4WD '80 thru '94

SUZUKI

*90010 **Samurai/Sidekick & Geo Tracker** '86 thru '96

TOYOTA

92005 **Camry** all models '83 thru '91
92006 **Camry** all models '92 thru '96
92015 **Celica Rear Wheel Drive** '71 thru '85
*92020 **Celica Front Wheel Drive** '86 thru '93
92025 **Celica Supra** all models '79 thru '92
92030 **Corolla** all models '75 thru '79
92032 **Corolla** all rear wheel drive models '80 thru '87
92035 **Corolla** all front wheel drive models '84 thru '92
*92036 **Corolla & Geo Prizm** '93 thru '97
92040 **Corolla Tercel** all models '80 thru '82
92045 **Corona** all models '74 thru '82
92050 **Cressida** all models '78 thru '82
92055 **Land Cruiser FJ40, 43, 45, 55** '68 thru '82
92056 **Land Cruiser FJ60, 62, 80, FZJ80** '80 thru '96
*92065 **MR2** all models '85 thru '87
92070 **Pick-up** all models '69 thru '78
*92075 **Pick-up** all models '79 thru '95
*92076 **Tacoma** '95 thru '98, **4Runner** '96 thru '98, **& T100** '93 thru '98
*92080 **Previa** all models '91 thru '95
92085 **Tercel** all models '87 thru '94

TRIUMPH

94007 **Spitfire** all models '62 thru '81
94010 **TR7** all models '75 thru '81

VW

96008 **Beetle & Karmann Ghia** '54 thru '79
96012 **Dasher** all gasoline models '74 thru '81
*96016 **Rabbit, Jetta, Scirocco, & Pick-up** gas models '74 thru '91 & Convertible '80 thru '92
96017 **Golf & Jetta** all models '93 thru '97
96020 **Rabbit, Jetta & Pick-up** diesel '77 thru '84
96030 **Transporter 1600** all models '68 thru '79
96035 **Transporter 1700, 1800 & 2000** '72 thru '79
96040 **Type 3 1500 & 1600** all models '63 thru '73
96045 **Vanagon** all air-cooled models '80 thru '83

VOLVO

97010 **120, 130 Series & 1800 Sports** '61 thru '73
97015 **140 Series** all models '66 thru '74
*97020 **240 Series** all models '76 thru '93
97025 **260 Series** all models '75 thru '82
*97040 **740 & 760 Series** all models '82 thru '88

TECHBOOK MANUALS

10205 **Automotive Computer Codes**
10210 **Automotive Emissions Control Manual**
10215 **Fuel Injection Manual, 1978 thru 1985**
10220 **Fuel Injection Manual, 1986 thru 1996**
10225 **Holley Carburetor Manual**
10230 **Rochester Carburetor Manual**
10240 **Weber/Zenith/Stromberg/SU Carburetors**
10305 **Chevrolet Engine Overhaul Manual**
10310 **Chrysler Engine Overhaul Manual**
10320 **Ford Engine Overhaul Manual**
10330 **GM and Ford Diesel Engine Repair Manual**
10340 **Small Engine Repair Manual**
10345 **Suspension, Steering & Driveline Manual**
10355 **Ford Automatic Transmission Overhaul**
10360 **GM Automatic Transmission Overhaul**
10405 **Automotive Body Repair & Painting**
10410 **Automotive Brake Manual**
10415 **Automotive Detaiing Manual**
10420 **Automotive Eelectrical Manual**
10425 **Automotive Heating & Air Conditioning**
10430 **Automotive Reference Manual & Dictionary**
10435 **Automotive Tools Manual**
10440 **Used Car Buying Guide**
10445 **Welding Manual**
10450 **ATV Basics**

SPANISH MANUALS

98903 **Reparación de Carrocería & Pintura**
98905 **Códigos Automotrices de la Computadora**
98910 **Frenos Automotriz**
98915 **Inyección de Combustible 1986 al 1994**
99040 **Chevrolet & GMC Camionetas** '67 al '87 Incluye Suburban, Blazer & Jimmy '67 al '91
99041 **Chevrolet & GMC Camionetas** '88 al '95 Incluye Suburban '92 al '95, Blazer & Jimmy '92 al '94, Tahoe y Yukon '95
99042 **Chevrolet & GMC Camionetas Cerradas** '68 al '95
99055 **Dodge Caravan & Plymouth Voyager** '84 al '95
99075 **Ford Camionetas y Bronco** '80 al '94
99077 **Ford Camionetas Cerradas** '69 al '91
99083 **Ford Modelos de Tamaño Grande** '75 al '87
99088 **Ford Modelos de Tamaño Mediano** '75 al '86
99091 **Ford Taurus & Mercury Sable** '86 al '95
99095 **GM Modelos de Tamaño Grande** '70 al '90
99100 **GM Modelos de Tamaño Mediano** '70 al '88
99110 **Nissan Camionetas** '80 al '96, **Pathfinder** '87 al '95
99118 **Nissan Sentra** '82 al '94
99125 **Toyota Camionetas y 4Runner** '79 al '95

---

* Listings shown with an asterisk (*) indicate model coverage as of this printing. These titles will be periodically updated to include later model years - consult your Haynes dealer for more information.

Over 100 Haynes motorcycle manuals also available

5-98

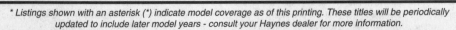

Haynes North America, Inc., 861 Lawrence Drive, Newbury Park, CA 91320-1514 • (805) 498-6703